散文自译与自评

Self-translation and Self-evaluation of Chinese Prose Writings

周领顺 （加）露丝·莳(Lus Shih) 著

苏州大学出版社

图书在版编目(CIP)数据

散文自译与自评 = Self-translation and Self-evaluation of Chinese Prose Writings：英汉对照/周领顺,(加)露丝·蒔(Lus Shih)著. —苏州：苏州大学出版社,2017.1(2021.10 重印)
ISBN 978-7-5672-2039-3

Ⅰ.①散… Ⅱ.①周… ②露… Ⅲ.①散文-英语-文学翻译-研究 Ⅳ.①H315.9

中国版本图书馆 CIP 数据核字(2017)第 012113 号

书　　名	散文自译与自评 Self-translation and Self-evaluation of Chinese Prose Writings
著　　者	周领顺　(加)露丝·蒔(Lus Shih)
责任编辑	沈　琴
出版发行	苏州大学出版社 (苏州市十梓街1号　215006)
印　　刷	江苏凤凰数码印务有限公司
开　　本	700 mm×1 000 mm　1/16
印　　张	13.5
字　　数	234 千
版　　次	2017 年 1 月第 1 版 2021 年 10 月第 3 次印刷
书　　号	ISBN 978-7-5672-2039-3
定　　价	36.00 元

苏州大学版图书若有印装错误，本社负责调换
苏州大学出版社营销部　电话：0512-65225020
苏州大学出版社网址　http://www.sudapress.com

前　言

这本《散文自译与自评》是继笔者此前编写出版的《散文英译过程》（北京：国防工业出版社，2012）一书之后又一本汉语散文英译之作。本书所收录的散文一部分来自该书，更多的是该书出版之后一个时期内的新作，新旧文章一共18篇。两书之间一个明显的不同是，《散文英译过程》一书的译者是研究生，笔者只是原文的作者和译文的评者；而在《散文自评与自译》中，笔者不仅是作者和评者，也是译者之一。本书部分散文来自《散文英译过程》一书的原文，由我们全新译出之后收录于本书，与研究生的译文相比，差异是显而易见的。

"自译"指的是译者既是实践者，也是原文的作者；"自评"指的是，译者除了是实践者之外，还是评论者。从这两点讲，市场上虽然有很多汉语散文英译的作品，但译者翻译的多是别人的散文（如张培基），鉴于译者不是作者本人，偶尔出现误译在所难免；虽然也有译者（如林语堂）翻译自己的作品，但又很少自我评价，作者、译者的心声全凭读者去揣摩，所以偶尔出现误读也在所难免。总之，即使是名家名译，也有美中不足之处。鉴于此，笔者身兼多任（作者、译者、译评者），与加拿大华人学者露丝·蒔（Lus Shih）（译者、译评者）一起，倾情推出这本小书，以弥补市场上这类作品的空缺。

散文英译是中国文化"走出去"的有效方式。本书的原文绝大多数已刊发于美国的《达拉斯新闻》（*Dallas Chinese News*），部分译文和评论刊登于《中国翻译》杂志，有的原文和译文还被多个网站转发，比如《石榴花》及其译文。为确保英译的质量，我们除了邀请美籍华人审读外，还邀请美籍学者 Fred Previc、Julia Bento 和英籍学者 Michael Flegg 等对每篇译文进行仔细修改。

在翻译实践中,文学翻译是基础;在文学翻译中,散文翻译是基础。

散文介于小说和诗歌之间,在语言的精雕细琢上兼具二者之长。在各类翻译考试中,总不乏散文翻译的身影,皆因它最能考察一个人的翻译潜能和表达才情。

做翻译理论不能脱离实践,否则便不容易揭示翻译本质的东西,毕竟翻译的经验性无处不在;做翻译实践不能脱离理论,除了将理论用于指导实践外,更重要的是从实践中归纳并升华翻译的规律,弥补既有理论的不足,继而落实于翻译的评价实践中,以提高人们的认识水平。对于融理论与实践于一体的散文翻译,《中国翻译》执行主编杨平博士给笔者的回信一语中的。她说:

一篇高质量的成果的确不易。实际上自学之友(指《中国翻译》"自学之友"栏目——笔者注)是更大的挑战:既要高水平翻译实践能力,也要高水平翻译研究能力。因此,从学术成果角度来说,一篇高质量的自学之友文章应是一篇高质量的理论与实践相结合的学术成果。

本书使用"自译与自评"作为书名的一部分,是有意提醒学习者提高双语水平和理论修养之于译好散文的重要性。学习者如果能够不断自创、自译,将会有效提高自己的双语水平;如果能够在此基础上不断自评,无疑会提高自己的理论修养,对于研究者甚至能够比较容易地找到更接地气、更加务实的研究课题。比如,笔者发表在《解放军外国语学院学报》(2016 年第 6 期)的《"作者译"与"译者译"——为"自译"重新定性》就是有关的研究内容。散文英译也是中国文化"走出去"的一部分,而笔者发表在《中国社会科学报》(2016 年 11 月 14 日)的《拓展文化"走出去"的翻译传播机制研究》就涉及有关的构想,被人民网、搜狐网、今日头条、全国哲学社会科学规划办公室、中国社会科学网、中国宗教网、中共中央编译局、中国出版等 20 多家大型网站转发。

本书有三个板块：Ⅰ. 散文翻译纵横；Ⅱ. 散文英译实践；Ⅲ. 散文英译专评。"散文翻译纵横"阐述了散文翻译的"美"与"真"、"信"与"达"、"译"与"评"，作者的"创"与"译"，以及译者的"译"与"美"等几对关系，为读者赏析英译实践充作理论的先导；"散文英译实践"选择了12篇散文的英译，每篇原文和译文之后都提供了注释，对于特别的译笔之处和翻译的过程做了点睛式的诠释；"散文英译专评"选择了6篇散文的英译，并以专题的形式结合译文进行评价，将理论与实践紧密结合，做到以理服人。或者说，第一部分重在理论引导，第二部分重在实践演示，第三部分重在理论与实践的充分融合。本书收录的18篇散文，其主题涉及动植物、自然风物、生活杂感、观光游记等内容；翻译和评价部分均由笔者和露丝·蒔共同完成。

附录部分提供两篇笔者创作的原文，供初学者试译。

本书获扬州大学出版基金资助。

周领顺

2017年1月

目 录

- **I. 散文翻译纵横** /001

    翻译的"美"与"真"
    ——以一篇英译汉为例 / 003

    翻译的"信"与"达"
    ——以一篇汉译英为例 / 011

    翻译的"译"与"评"
    ——以翻译和评价实践为例 / 021

    译者的"译"与"美"
    ——以翻译和美化实践为例 / 028

- **II. 散文英译实践** / 041

    一只麻雀/A Little Sparrow / 043/044

    我有野鸭三两只/Wild Ducks Show Up There for Me in Twos and Threes / 048/049

    竹/Bamboo / 054/055

    尝樱桃/The Cherry Feast / 060/061

    盆栽/Potted Plants / 064/065

    温情电梯/Warmth in the Elevator / 069/070

    下雪的季节/The Season of Snow / 073/074

    一轮舞阳照贾湖/Jiahu：Site of Shining Glory / 079/081

    青岛纪行/A Trip to Qingdao / 087/088

    汉墓健身之行/A Cycle Ride to the Mausoleum / 092/093

温馨时刻：文友同游达拉斯/Happy Moments:

    A Tour of Dallas with Literary Friends / 097/099

别了，得州/Farewell, Texas / 103/104

Ⅲ. 散文英译专评 / 107

石榴花/Pomegranate Flowers / 109/110

汉语散文英译中的韵味再现原则 / 115

节俭意识与道德行为/On Frugality and Morality / 122/123

逻辑性与艺术性的统一 / 128

得州云霞/Clouds and Sunsets in Texas / 134/135

汉语描写文主观描写的英译再现 / 140

姜太公钓鱼/Jiang Taigong in Fishing / 149/151

文化联想与讲好中国故事 / 156

春风十里扬州路：人在扬州/The Glamorous Yangzhou:

    My Personal Experience / 165/167

文学翻译的忠实度和文化传播的有效性 / 174

喝茶与品茶/Tea Drinking vs. Tea Sipping / 181/182

中国茶文化的翻译与传播 / 187

- 附录Ⅰ　"第二十七届韩素音青年翻译奖"竞赛汉译英
  参考译文 / 194
- 附录Ⅱ　My Life's Sentences 参考译文 / 196
- 附录Ⅲ　试译原创散文 / 199
- 参考文献 / 203
- 后记 / 207

Ⅰ·散文翻译纵横

翻译的"美"与"真"
——以一篇英译汉为例

当讨论散文翻译并从中鉴别汉英差异时,就不仅仅涉及"汉译英",也应包括"英译汉",只有通过对比,才能更清楚地看出二者的异同。这里主要通过一篇散文("My Life's Sentences",作者是 Jhumpa Lahiri)的英译汉来说明散文翻译"美"与"真"的问题,并兼及汉英之间的一些表达差异。另外,选择这样一篇英译汉,还在于契合本书"自创"的主题,因为原文的作者就是一位作家。该文记述了作者培养良好写作习惯的方法、途径,可以启发学习者养成良好的写作习惯,打下坚实的语言基础。先看这篇英语散文的原文:

My Life's Sentences

In college, I used to underline sentences that struck me, that made me look up from the page. They were not necessarily the same sentences the professors pointed out, which would turn up for further explication on an exam. I noted them for their clarity, their rhythm, their beauty and their enchantment. For surely it is a magical thing for a handful of words, artfully arranged, to stop time. To conjure a place, a person, a situation, in all its specificity and dimensions. To affect us and alter us, as profoundly as real people and things do.

I remember reading a sentence by Joyce, in the short story "Araby." It appears toward the beginning. "The cold air stung us and we played till our bodies glowed." I have never forgotten it. This seems to me as perfect as a sentence can be. It is measured, unguarded, direct and transcendent, all at once. It is full of movement, of imagery. It distills a precise mood. It radiates with meaning and yet its sensibility is discreet.

When I am experiencing a complex story or novel, the broader planes, and also details, tend to fall away. Rereading them, certain sentences are what greet me as familiars. You have visited before, they say when I recognize them. We encounter books at different times in life, often appreciating them, apprehending them, in different ways. But their language is constant. The best sentences orient us, like stars in the sky, like landmarks on a trail.

They remain the test, whether or not to read something. The most compelling narrative, expressed in sentences with which I have no chemical reaction, or an adverse one, leaves me cold. In fiction, plenty do the job of conveying information, rousing suspense, painting characters, enabling them to speak. But only certain sentences breathe and shift about, like live matter in soil. The first sentence of a book is a handshake, perhaps an embrace. Style and personality are irrelevant. They can be formal or casual. They can be tall or short or fat or thin. They can obey the rules or break them. But they need to contain a charge. A live current, which shocks and illuminates.

Knowing—and learning to read in—a foreign tongue heightens and complicates my relationship to sentences. For some time now, I have been reading predominantly in Italian. I experience these novels and stories differently. I take no sentence for granted. I am more conscious of them. I work harder to know them. I pause to look something up, I puzzle over syntax I am still assimilating. Each sentence yields a twin, translated version of itself. When the filter of a second language falls away, my connection to these sentences, though more basic, feels purer, at times more intimate, than when I read in English.

The urge to convert experience into a group of words that are in a grammatical relation to one another is the most basic, ongoing impulse of my life. It is a habit of antiphony: of call and response. Most days begin with sentences that are typed into a journal no one has ever seen. There is a freedom to this; freedom to write what I will not proceed to wrestle with. The entries are mostly quotidian, a warming up of the fingers and brain. On days when I am troubled, when I am grieved, when I am at a loss for words, the mechanics of formulating sentences, and of stockpiling them in a vault, is the only thing that centers me again.

Constructing a sentence is the equivalent of taking a Polaroid snapshot: pressing the button, and watching something emerge. To write one is to document and to develop at the same time. Not all sentences end up in novels or stories. But novels and stories consist of nothing but sentences.

Sentences are the bricks as well as the mortar, the motor as well as the fuel. They are the cells, the individual stitches. Their nature is at once solitary and social. Sentences establish tone, and set the pace. One in front of the other marks the way.

My work accrues sentence by sentence. After an initial phase of sitting patiently, not so patiently, struggling to locate them, to pin them down, they begin arriving, fully formed in my brain. I tend to hear them as I am drifting off to sleep. They are spoken to me, I'm not sure by whom. By myself, I know, though the source feels independent, recondite, especially at the start. The light will be turned on, a sentence or two will be hastily scribbled on a scrap of paper, carried upstairs to the manuscript in the morning. I hear sentences as I'm staring out of the window, or chopping vegetables, or waiting on a subway platform alone. They are pieces of a jigsaw puzzle, handed to me in no particular order, with no discernible logic. I only sense that they are part of the thing.

Over time, virtually each sentence I receive and record in this haphazard manner will be sorted, picked over, organized, changed. Most will be dispensed with. All the revision I do—and this process begins immediately, accompanying the gestation—occurs on a sentence level. It is by fussing with sentences that a character becomes clear to me, that a plot unfolds. To work on them so compulsively, perhaps prematurely, is to see the trees before the forest. And yet I am incapable of conceiving the forest any other way.

As a book or story nears completion, I grow acutely, obsessively conscious of each sentence in the text. They enter into the blood. They seem to replace it, for a while. When something is in proofs I sit in solitary confinement with them. Each is confronted, inspected, turned inside out. Each is sentenced, literally, to be part of the text, or not. Such close scrutiny can lead to blindness. At times—and these times terrify—they cease to make sense. When a book is finally out of my hands I feel bereft. It is the absence of all those sentences that had circulated through me for a period of my life. A complex root system, extracted.

Even printed, on pages that are bound, sentences remain unsettled organisms. Years later, I can always reach out to smooth a stray hair. And yet, at a certain point, I must walk away, trusting them to do their work. I am left looking over my shoulder, wondering if I might have structured one more effectively. This is why I avoid reading the books I've written. Why, when I must, I approach the book as a stranger, and pretend the sentences were written by someone else.

散文属于"美文",汉英皆然。因此,"求美"是首要的选择。许渊冲(2000)在论述"求美"和"求真"的关系时说道:

求真是低标准,求美是高标准;真是必要条件,美是充分条件……如果真与美能统一,那自然是再好没有;如果真与美有矛盾,那不是为了真而牺牲美,就是为了美而失真。如译得似的诗远不如原诗美,那牺牲美就是得不偿失;如果译得"失真"却可以和原诗比美,那倒可以说是以得补失;如果所得大于所失,那就是译诗胜过了原诗。

许渊冲教授虽然讨论的是诗歌翻译的"美"与"真",但同样适用于散文的翻译。优美的意境是借优美的语言加以表现的。或者说,"美"主要并首先表现在语言上。这里仅就散文"My Life's Sentences"的汉译,谈谈散文翻译"求美""求真"的原则问题。

一、"美"与"求美"

第一,再现原文之美。修辞是作者有意而为的,也是美文的主要表现。在翻译时,如果能给予再现,则应以再现为主。例如:

〔1〕The best sentences orient us, *like* stars in the sky, *like* landmarks on a trail.

原句用的是明喻,而且使用了两个比喻词 like,即使把第二个 like 删除而变为 like stars in the sky and landmarks on a trail,也照样能够成立。重复比喻词,即在明喻修辞格中嵌套了反复修辞。把作者的用心处尽可能翻译出来,才算是向作者尽了"忠",向读者尽了"责",故译为:

但语言是永恒的,美句就像夜空里的星星、像小道上的路标,引导我们前行。

在组织方式上,散文"形散而神不散";从美的角度讲,"形散"说明美是全方位的。如果能达到句句照应,当然最为理想,但如果因为语言差异或者翻译后不符合译语的美感特质,则不妨退而求其次,即确保一段话内或一个句子前后美所营造的整体氛围不变,保持文章整体文学性不变。例如:

〔2〕I noted them for *their* clarity, *their* rhythm, *their* beauty and *their* enchantment.

作者重复使用了代词 their，但在译语里重复使用代词，则不免有拖沓板滞之感。刘宓庆(1998)、范仲英(1997)根据汉英语言的差异，提出要在汉译文中适当减少人称代词的使用，故例[2]可译为：

我注意到，这些句子集简洁、韵味、美感和魅力于一体。

译文以简洁取胜，在一定程度上弥补了原文的修辞损失。不过，原文反复修辞之美，却在本段话另一个不相干的句子中得到了"再现"，即：

[3] To *conjure* a place, a person, a situation, in all its specificity and dimensions.

变出个地名，变出个人名，变出个情境，真实而细腻。

刘丹青(2010)研究发现，"在类型上汉语是一种动词型或者说动词优先的语言，而英语是一种名词型或者说名词优先的语言，两者分别代表了两种在词类的语法优先度上相对立的语言类型"。连淑能(1993:122)说，"汉语动词的重复或重叠，以及与此相关的句式排比或对偶，可以明显地加强汉语动态感的表现力"。

似乎可以这样归纳：所谓"再现原文之美"，实际又有狭义（如例[1]，一句话内）和广义（如例[2]，一段话内）之分。

第二，切换原文之美。比如，切换为四字结构、流水短句和新的句式等。

[4] It is *measured*, *unguarded*, *direct and transcendent*, all at once. It is full *of movement*, *of imagery*.

拿捏仔细、顺手溜出、直白质朴、卓尔不群，一股脑，这些感觉就都来了；充满动感，富于想象。

measured, unguarded, direct, transcendent 这四个词两两对应，结构平稳，与英语并列结构功能相一致的是汉语的四字结构，所以"切换"为四字结构，恰如其分。

[5] *They* can be formal or casual. *They* can be tall or short or fat or thin. *They* can obey the rules or break them. But *they* need to contain a charge. A live current, which shocks and illuminates.

可以正式，可以随意，高矮胖瘦，无所不能；或遵从规则，或打破常规，但一定要带着电，摄人魂魄，闪光发热。

把几句话并合处理后，自然"切换"为汉语的流水短句，使译文的节奏感得到了增强。

[6] *I* experience these novels and stories differently. *I* take

no sentence for granted. *I* am more conscious of them. *I* work harder to know them. *I* pause to look something up. *I* puzzle over syntax I am still assimilating.

<u>我</u>以别样的方式体验用意大利语写就的小说和故事。<u>我</u>一句也不敢瞎猜,敏感有加,为了多一份了解,<u>我</u>更加用功。<u>我</u>驻足查询,对<u>我</u>在吸收学习的句法结构也困惑不已。

原文的排列顺序被"切换"后,代词"我"被放在不同的位置,避免了全部放于句首而在译文语言里引起的单调感。

[7] Sentences are the bricks *as well as* the mortar, the motor *as well as* the fuel. They are the cells, the individual stitches.

句子<u>是</u>泥浆、砖块,<u>是</u>燃料、引擎,<u>是</u>机体的细胞,<u>是</u>衣服的针脚。

原文句子两处以 as well as 短语连接,而在紧接的两句话中,这一短语又被省略了。译文把几句话并列起来,保持了句子的长短交错,并通过重复"是"字,增强了抑扬顿挫的效果。汉语"具有音乐性强的特点"(黄伯荣、廖序东,2000:10),如果翻译后"读起来'不上口',总还是件憾事"(吕叔湘,1983:23)。

切换美的方式有很多,但总的原则是:如果原文在原语世界里有美感,但在进入译语世界后有所损失,则不妨尽力寻找另外可以被译文读者接受的方式"曲线救'美'"。

第三,超越原文之美。"译文超越原文"之语常被人诟病,原因是担心译者难以"抑止不适当的写作冲动"(钱锺书,1984:705),但"发挥译语优势"(许渊冲、奈达语)之说却能被普遍接受。汉语有着怎样的优势?季羡林(2003)给予了高度的评价:

语言的功能在于传递思想、表达感情,哪一种语言能传递、表达最简洁而又充分,最明白而又含蓄,最丰富而又不枯燥,最生动而又不油滑,它就是最好的语言。汉语就是这样一种语言。

具体而言,其一,汉语喜欢四字结构(如上文例[4])。"四音节的成语占95%以上。"(张斌,2002:257)季羡林(2003)说:"为什么汉语成语多四字?理论上的解释,我目前还做不出来。"范开泰、张亚军(2000:243)是这样回答的:"成语四个音节,两个音步,匀整对称……有节奏感。能体现汉语的民族风格,使汉语语音上的优势得到充分利用。"

其二,汉语青睐流水短句(如上文例[5])。"流水句之所以能自由自在,如行云流水,是由现代汉语语用平面的语序的灵活性和口语化这两个因素决定的。"(陈昌来,2000:254)

其三,汉语崇尚简洁凝练(如下文例[8])。"由于汉语韵律性特征明显和长期以来书面上运用汉字等原因,形成了汉语表达上力求简约的民族语言心理。"(范开泰、张亚军,2000:251)季羡林(2003)说:"表达同样的思想感情,汉文是付出的劳动量最少的语言,用的时间最短的语言,几千年来,从我们的老祖宗起就使用这种语言,我们节省出来的劳动力和时间,连用天文数字也是难以算得清楚的。"因此,在翻译时要特别注意"言以简为贵"(宋·杨时《二程粹言·心性篇》)之理的运用。例如:

[8] After an initial phase of *sitting patiently*, *not so patiently*, *struggling to locate them*, *to pin them down*, they begin arriving, fully formed in my brain.

经过第一个时期的耐心、浮躁、圈选、装订之后,句子就自然而然地涌进我的脑海里。

如果说,译者展现汉语的优势是以超越原文为目的的,那么有的译文或可说是"水到渠成""歪打正着"了。比如"Over time, virtually each sentence I receive and record in this haphazard manner will be sorted, picked over, organized, changed."一句,从美的角度讲,仍有需要改进之处。sorted,picked over,organized,changed 是并列关系,但有三处用的是单个的词,唯独 picked over 用的是短语,不够对称,而当翻译为"从长远看,我以这种随意的方式收集、记录的每个句子都要分类、挑拣、组织、改变"时,却因汉语言简意丰的特点,无形中增强了节奏感,"超越"了原文。

二、"真"与"求真"

"真"是就原文意义而言的,建立在原文"真"意基础之上的美才是真美。比如,同是一个 rich lady,新中国成立前译作"阔太太"算得体,今天译作"富婆"才恰当;汉译英的 police officer,在中国封建社会的故事里应还原为"衙役",今天默认的却是"警官"。在时代性上反映为"真",在语言表达上反映为"美"。

在理解作者畅谈创作体验的意图之后,我们就不宜再将"The cold air stung us and we played till our bodies glowed."一句作常规翻译(网上译为:"寒风刺骨,我们玩啊玩,一直玩到身上感到热烘烘的。")。原因是,句子里的 sting 和 glow 正是作者想要表达的形象化用词,不形象化译出来,就不足以表现作者意欲表达"语不惊人死不休"(杜甫语)的真意。所以,笔者才译为"寒风咬,玩兴浓,玩到身上红彤彤"这样有违常规却又无意中押了尾韵("浓"和"彤")的表达形式。

"真"还可以从别的角度进行一番讨论,比如作者写作经历与译者写作经历契合之真。原文所述的作者个人写作习惯与笔者(译者)的写作习惯相似,所以理解就比较有把握(如把 journal 理解为"日记"而非"杂志"),表达就比较到位(如把"The entries are mostly quotidian, a warming up of the fingers and brain."译为:"下笔处,多无惊人之语,是练手、练脑而已。")。钱锺书当年建议杨必翻译萨克雷的《名利场》,结果杨必一举成名,说明钱锺书不仅对萨克雷的作品内容、风格特点有深刻的了解,也对杨必的个人性格等都十分了解(吕俊、侯向群,2001)。

散文难译,难就难在"求真"基础之上再"求美",且要美得自然、美得出神入化。对于英译汉,尤其如此。汉民族的传统审美观总体上是以神驭形的,所谓"文曲星""文似看山不喜平""夺(脱)胎换骨""出神入化""空灵""神似""化境""不隔""羚羊挂角,无迹可求""超凡脱俗""传神之笔""神来之笔""神采飞扬""如椽之笔""言之无文,行而不远"之理或无"斧凿之痕"、不"味同嚼蜡"等之谓是也。

散文的语言,如诗如画。若要散文翻译得传神达意,更上层楼,就有必要夯实双语功底,加强双语修养。比如,如果把"It is the absence of all those sentences that had circulated through me for a period of my life. A complex root system, extracted."(失去的是那些曾经在我生命中往复循环的美句,<u>萎缩的是曾经维系枝繁叶茂的庞大根系</u>。)译为"失去的是那些曾经在我生命中往复循环的美句,<u>复杂的根系萎缩了</u>",其韵味则大打折扣。一是因为原文的意境再现不够充分,使上下衔接有些唐突;二是因为失却了前一译文中"句"和"系"变体韵式而产生的韵味。

翻译的"信"与"达"*
——以一篇汉译英为例

我们先看原文。

保护古村落就是保护"根性文化"

传统村落是指拥有物质形态和非物质形态文化遗产,具有较高的历史、文化、科学、艺术、社会、经济价值的村落。但近年来,随着城镇化快速推进,以传统村落为代表的传统文化正在淡化,乃至消失。对传统村落历史建筑进行保护性抢救,并对传统街巷和周边环境进行整治,可防止传统村落无人化、空心化。

古村落是历史文化遗存的特有形式之一,是地方历史经济发展水平的象征和民俗文化的集中代表。古村落文化是传统文化的重要组成部分,它直接体现出中华姓氏的血缘文化、聚族文化、伦理观念、祖宗崇拜、典章制度、堪舆风水、建筑艺术、地域特色等。

古村落是传统耕读文化和农业经济的标志,在当前城市化巨大浪潮的冲击之下,古村落不可避免地被急功近利所觊觎和包围,之所以强调保护古村落,不是为了复古,更不是为了倡导过去的宗族居住生活模式,而是为了了解和保留一种久远的文明传统,最终是为了体现现代人的一份历史文化责任感。

古村落与其说是老建筑,倒不如说是一座座承载了历史变迁的活建筑文化遗产,任凭世事变迁,斗转星移,古村落依然岿然不动,用无比顽强的生命力向人们诉说着村落的沧桑变迁,尽管曾经酷暑寒冬,风雪雨霜,但是古老的身躯依然支撑着生命的张力,和生生不息的人并肩生

---

* 本文是中国翻译协会主办的"第二十七届韩素音青年翻译奖"竞赛针对汉译英参赛译文的评析,由集体讨论,杨成虎、陈文安执笔,原刊于《中国翻译》2015年第6期。鉴于笔者(周领顺)是评审委员会成员之一,又具体在汉译英小组参与讨论,故收录于本书,以飨读者。原文题目为《得体译文的"信"与"达"辩证》,收录于本书时做了部分调整和删节。

存,从这点上说,沧桑的古村落也是一种无形的精神安慰。

在城市进入现代化的今天,对待古村落的态度也就是我们对待文化的态度,一座古村落的被改造或者消失,也许很多人没有感觉出丢了什么,但是,历史遗产少了一座古老的古村落,就少了些历史文化痕迹,就少了对历史文化的触摸感,也就很容易遗忘历史,遗忘了历史,很难谈文化延承,同时失去的还有附加在古村落上的文化魂灵。

看一个地方有没有文化底蕴,有没有文化割裂感,不仅要看辉煌灿烂的文物遗留,还可以从一座座古村落上感受出来,从古村落高大的厅堂、精致的雕饰、上等的用材,古朴浑厚、巧夺天工的建筑造型上感受出来……对于古村落,不得不改造和推倒时,同样需要三思而行。

本届汉译英比赛原文是《保护古村落就是保护"根性文化"》一文中的一部分,谈中国当代经济社会城镇化建设中古村落及其所代表的传统文化的保护问题。评审组经过对所收 825 篇译文的认真评审,现从得体译文的"信"与"达"辩证关系的角度对参赛译文情况做一综述性评析。

大多数参赛选手均认真翻译,仔细研读原文,斟酌译文的得体表达,文思较为缜密,译文语言措辞较为准确,有的还附上了注释。然而,就参赛选手对"信"与"达"辩证关系的灵活掌握和译文的得体性而言,佳作显得较少。不少参赛选手的译文局部有不错的处理,但见树不见林,译文措辞、句式选择等内部关系不甚协调,缺乏语篇意识。总体上看,普遍存在的问题主要是对原文的"信"和译文的"达"两者辩证关系处理不当,多数信而不顺,对原文亦步亦趋,不敢越雷池半步,致使译文晦涩不畅;也有一些译文顺而不信,变译失当,天马行空,任意发挥,未能顾及对原文的忠实。好的翻译需要"信"与"达"兼顾,做到两者辩证,不能偏颇一方。下面从原文标题的英译、原文文化负载词的英译和原文句式的英译调整三个方面来讨论。

一、标题的英译

一篇文章,标题首先映入读者的眼帘,简洁、准确、生动的标题一下子就能勾起读者的兴趣。标题的英译也要收到同样的效果。本届汉译英原文标题颇见特色。参赛选手以各种英译方式体现了他们的思考和处理水平。这里选出 20 个代表性实例加以评析。

直译：

[1] To Protect the Old Villages Is to Protect the Root of Culture

[2] To Preserve Old Villages Is to Preserve a Root-bound Culture

[3] Protecting Old Villages Is Protecting a "Root-based" Culture

[4] To Protect Ancient Villages Is to Preserve "Root Culture"

[5] To Protect the Ancient Villages Is to Retain the "Root Culture"

转译：

[6] Ancient Village Preservation Equals "Root Culture" Protection

[7] Protecting Ancient Villages Means Preserving the Root Culture

[8] Ancient Village Protection Epitomizes "Root Culture" Rescue

[9] Preservation of Ancient Villages as a Way to Protect Our Root Culture

[10] A Reservation of Ancient Complex as the Root of Chinese Culture

深度转译：

[11] Preserving Chinese Cultural Prototypes—Ancient Villages

[12] The Preservation of Ancient Villages—the Shelter of Our Cultural Root

[13] The Preservation of Ancient Villages—the Root of Our Culture

[14] To Preserve "Ancient Villages", to Protect the "Root of Culture"

[15] Preserving Ancient Villages, Safeguarding the Root of Culture

[16] Traditional Villages Survive, Root Cultures Thrive

[17] Protecting Ancient Villages: Saving Root Culture

[18] Ancient Villages Conservation in Action: A Move to Protect Our "Cultural Roots"

[19] Guard Our Root: Traditional Villages

[20] Traditional Villages: "Aborigines" of Chinese Culture

原文标题"保护古村落就是保护'根性文化'"是以命题句形式出现的判断结构，表达了作者的主张和文章的主旨，英译采用相应的判断句是最可取的。英语文章有类似结构的标题，如美国作家 Max Shulman 有一篇著名的短篇小说，标题就叫"Love Is a Fallacy"。另外，英语中也有"To see is to believe/Seeing is believing."等句式。因此，第一种直译是既能体现"信"，又能体现"达"的译法。第二种转译将"就是"转译成 equals, means, epitomizes, as 等动词或介词。这种译法未考虑原文的命题句及其作用,在理解与表达上虽无不可,但从文章表达的内在机制上还是稍逊一筹。第三种深度转译使用破折号、逗号和冒号等标点符号,是在考虑如何避免"就是"判断句式的英译以及两个"保护"的重复。从英文不习惯重复性表达的角度来说,这种考虑也有几分道理,但这些深度转译的实例对原文标题表达方式的理解显得有欠深刻,在英译表达上出现了过译(overtranslation)现象,达而不信。但像[16]运用了押韵的方式,具有一定的修辞效果,也不失为一个亮点。

除了句式的处理以外,标题中的词语处理也值得讨论。首先是动宾短语"保护古村落"和"保护'根性文化'"的译法,以上实例有使用动词不定式短语、动名词短语、名物化的名词短语等多种形式,最可取的是动词不定式短语,强调动作性和未来性,符合文章强调中国在现代化和城镇化建设中需要保护传统文化和古村落的题旨。其次是"根性文化"这一概念的译法,多数实例均采用(our) root culture(s) 或 the root of (Chinese 或 our) culture,少数译者使用了 root-based culture 或 root-bound culture,只有极少数译者采用 cultural roots 的译法。"根性文化"是全文的一个核心概念,必须译好。这里有两个问题需要讨论:一是究竟将 root 用作修饰成分作定语为好,还是将其视为中心语为好?二是究竟使用单数为好,还是使用复数为好? root 一词可以用作定语修饰名词中心语,语法上没有错,如 the root causes of poverty, the root conviction, 但这样使用的意思是"基本的"(basic),与"根性"的意思尚有出入;在 the root 后接 of 短语,这时 the root 的意思是"根源"(original cause),如 the root of tragedy, the root of all evil 等,或"根部"(the root part),如 the root of the tongue, the root of one's hair 等,而与 culture 搭配起来,表达的是"文化的根源"之义,而非"根性文化"。由此,选择将 root 用作中心语方为合适。采用 roots 复数形式更能表达"根性"之义,也与文化相关。根据 *Collins COBUILD Essential English Dictionary*(1989)的 roots 复数形式的解释,your roots are the place or culture that you or your family grew up in, which you have now left。这一解释正是这篇文章所要表达的意思,尤其是与文化的直接关联。经过以上比较和推敲,英译不必拘泥于原文的搭配形式,在语义的深刻理解上,使用 cultural roots 较为合适。

二、文化负载词的英译

"文化负载词"是指语言系统中最能体现语言承载的文化信息、反映人类的社会生活的词汇,反映了语言文化的系统性差异以及词汇的语别特征。文化负载词的概念自从许国璋先生提出后,翻译界对如何翻译此类特殊词语进行了大量探讨(如王银泉,2006)。本届汉译英原文涉及中国传统文化的相关内容,出现了多个文化负载词,如"无人化""空心化""中华姓氏""典章制度""堪舆风水""耕读文化""酷暑寒冬""风霜雨雪"等,给英译增添了难度。过于强调原文词语的文化特征,会致使译文不流畅,若过于简约,则又不能体现原文的含义。下面就参赛选手对原文中出现的主要文化负载词的英译情况分别予以评析。

[1] 对传统村落历史建筑进行保护性抢救,并对传统街巷和周边环境进行整治,可防止传统村落无人化、空心化。

参赛译文1:Therefore, a timely salvaging of the villages' historic buildings and a thorough improvement of the streets, alleys and surrounding areas can serve to relieve the large-scale exodus of their inhabitants and mitigate their worsening condition.

参赛译文2:Taking protective measures to preserve their historical buildings and renovate their traditional streets and lanes as well as their surrounding environment can help them avoid being depopulated and hollowing out.

参赛译文3:The preservation of historical architecture of traditional villages, ancient streets and local surroundings can help prevent the traditional villages from becoming deserted and desolated.

参赛译文4:In view of this, it is imperative that emergency measures be taken to protect traditional dwellings and rectify the surrounding environments, such that the depopulation and decentralization of old villages will be reserved.

以上参赛译文对"无人化""空心化"的理解均无误,在信息上做到了对原文的忠实,但前两种译文均欠妥当,信而不达。有的借用《圣经》的 exodus 这一说法。该词的意思是"(大批或成群的)外出,离开"或"(大批人的)移居国外",与中国目前城镇化建设中村落居民大量减少的现象差异较大。参赛译文 3 使用 deserted and desolated 这样的普通译法来表达,符合散文通俗化的语言风格,颇能达意。参赛译文 4 中 depopulation 和 decentralization 较好地体现了原文的概念,特别是"化"的概念,但这两个单词有些正式,在语体上与散文化的语言要求显得有些不协调。另外,各译文不足之处是译者使用了并列连词 and 来连接,应使用选择连词 or 为宜。

[2] 古村落文化是传统文化的重要组成部分,它直接体现出中华姓氏的血缘文化、聚族文化、伦理观念、祖宗崇拜、典章制度、堪舆风水、建筑艺术、地域特色等。

参赛译文 1:Traditional village culture, an integral part of traditional culture, manifests the consanguinity culture, clan culture, ethical values, ancestral worship, decrees and regulations, Feng Shui (an ancient Chinese philosophy in choosing sites), architectural style and regional characteristics behind Chinese surnames.

参赛译文 2:They are part and parcel of our traditional culture, and bear direct testament to the bloodline, clan traditions, ethics and beliefs, ancestral worship, codes and institutions, feng shui practices (or geomancy), architecture and arts, and geographic identities of the Chinese nation.

参赛译文 3:Being an important part of traditional culture, they directly represent the characteristics of the blood lineage culture of Chinese family names, clan culture, ethics, ancestor worship, institutions and systems, geomancy and fengshui, architecture and local features.

参赛译文 4:They form an important part of traditional culture, shedding light on China's blood-based surname culture and gregarious lifestyle, as well as its ethic values, ancestral worship, traditional institutions, feng shui, architectural style and regional features among others.

以上参赛译文对原文中出现的"典章制度""堪舆风水"等文化负载词理解均无误,但因为英文中没有完全能够体现原义的相关词语,致使译文信而难达。中国古代很早就注重"典章制度"的建设,形成了灿烂的古代文明,这与西方现代国家的文明发展过程有较大差异。从严格意义上讲,英文中没有与之对应的说法。以上译文中 decrees and regulations, codes and institutions, institutions and systems, traditional institutions基本上是从各种汉英词典中查阅出来的英文词语,每种译法均有一定的道理,但又都不甚准确。经与外籍专家反复讨论,同时参照百度百科对"典章制度"的专门解释和英译名称,参考译文确定为 rules and institutions。根据一般辞书提供的解释,"堪舆风水"中,"堪舆"与"风水"同义,英译其中一个即可,译者基本上译的是"风水"一词。因英文中已有外来词 *fengshui*(或 *feng-shui*),参赛译文大多数均采用了这一音译词(有的选手未使用斜体,或将其大写,这样做均不符合书写规范),也有使用英文 geomancy 一词的,应该说也可以,但该词难以表达中国文化特色,还是音译词更好些。

[3] 古村落是传统耕读文化和农业经济的标志……

参赛译文1:Ancient villages are a symbol of the traditional farming-reading culture and the agricultural economy…

参赛译文2:Ancient villages are the mark of traditional farming-studying culture and traditional agrarian economy…

参赛译文3:Ancient villages are symbols of Chinese traditional studying-while-farming culture (a concept of half-studying and half-farming life style of some ancient Chinese intellectuals) and agricultural economy…

参赛译文4:The ancient villages are a mark of the traditional gengdu culture and agrarian culture…(添加了尾注:A system of rural education in China in which people are engaged in both farming and studying or teaching.)

同样,参赛选手在理解"耕读文化"上均无误,但这一汉语文化特色浓郁的概念在英文中尚无类似的固定词语。以上译文既有意译,又有音译,做出了各种尝试。意译均使用了动词-ing 形式和连字符,这些都是很好的,主要问题是:是使用 reading 为好,还是 studying 为好,还是有更好的英文词可用?参赛译文3虽然意思较为清晰,但结构上显得壅塞,不够简洁,难说是理想的译法,括号的使用显得不够简洁。参赛译文4采用了音译加注(此注不甚准确),但也不失为一种译法。经反复商量,参考译文采用了 the scholar-farmer lifestyle,这样做有两个好处:一是避免了 reading 与 studying 两者谁好的纠缠;二是避免了音译给读者产生的陌生感,因为英文中尚无这样的音译词。另外,使用 lifestyle 将"文化"一词的词意进行具体化处理,可以避免译文中 culture 一词的重复。

[4] 尽管曾经酷暑寒冬,风雪雨霜,但是古老的身躯依然支撑着生命的张力,和生生不息的人并肩生存……

参赛译文1：Defying harsh weather and filled with vitality, they have existed to this day as constant companions to the dauntless Chinese people...

参赛译文2：They have endured extreme temperatures and stood amidst the storm and tempest, but their ageing bodies are still imbued with youthful vigor, surviving generation after generation...

参赛译文3：They have survived countless scorching summers and freezing winters, sheltering generations of people despite their growing decrepitude...

参赛译文4：Winter or summer, rain or shine, it's the ancient buildings that sustain life, standing side by side with the villagers, generation after generation...

以上参赛译文对"酷暑寒冬""风霜雨雪"做了各种英译处理,有简单的(如译文1),有复杂的(如译文3),也有较适中的(如译文4),这些译文均力图表达原文中这两个习语的意思。从英语文章表达习惯来看,参赛译文多数信而不达,偏向了原文,致使译文不流畅。参考译文在"信"与"达"之间反复掂量,确定为 Weathering countless blistering summers and bitter winters and punishing storms and blizzards, they remain an inextinguishable source of vitality...

此外,原文中还有一些词语虽然不是文化负载词,但要译好,还须考虑语义的协调和上下文和谐。

三、原文句式的英译调整

句式特征实际是思维特征的反映,翻译中句式的转换是至为重要的。译者以句子为单位进行操作,原文一个句子,译文可以处理成一个句子,也可以处理成几个句子,究竟如何处理,要遵循译文整体表达的需要(许钧、穆雷,2009：266)。句式调整和句法结构的选择要出于文章主旨的表达需要,也要使上下文和谐地衔接。英汉语之间的类型学差异主要表现在这两门语言的句法结构上,表面上相同的结构在不同语言中的功能可能会有根本的不同。如英语中没有主语的句子主要是祈使句,而汉语中没有主语的句子还可以是陈述句。在句式英译的处理上要做到"信"与"达"的辩证关系要比词语英译更难,因为前者是思维模式上异同的辩证关系,而后者是概念模式的辩证关系。选用各种合适的英语句法结构实际是要求译者对英语思维模式、英文章法及行文习惯有深刻的理解和灵巧的运用。一般译者往往被原文句式牵着鼻子走,难以自如地使用译入语的句法结构。本届汉译英原文句式多数都是典型的汉语流水句,不少地方重复使用某些结构或词语,而英译可以使用主从句,一般情况下不重复使用相同的结构或词语。另外,英译这篇散文还要在句式表达上注重流畅性以及句子之间的衔接性。

[5] 但是,历史遗产少了一座古老的古村落,就少了些历史文化痕迹,就少了对历史文化的触摸感,也就很容易遗忘历史,遗忘了历史,很难谈文化延承,同时失去的还有附加在古村落上的文化魂灵。

参赛译文1:A lack of it, however, means a loss of the existence of the historical culture. Then this will make a touch of the historical culture difficult, as a result of which, the history may be passed into oblivion. If so, there will hardly be cultural continuation to speak of. Meanwhile, the soul of the historical culture that it bears will also vanish.

参赛译文2:… but to historical legacy, losing one traditional village means not only losing the cultural spirits attached to it, but also losing some traces of history and culture and the sense of touch on them, without which history could be easily forgotten and culture succession would become difficult as history has faded into oblivion.

参赛译文3:However, in terms of historic heritage, the loss of one ancient village means loss of cultural and historical vestige and loss of a literal way of touching the history and culture, which would lead to oblivion of our history. If history is forgotten, cultural inheritance will be in vain, and the soul of culture embodied in the villages would be gone.

原文这一较长的流水句表达的是原作者连续不断的思绪和前后因果关系的承接,而英文没有这样的流水式表达,因此英译时一定要将这一长句拆分成符合英文表达习惯的句法结构。以上几种译文在英语句法结构的选择上均有一定的思考,不约而同地使用了由定语从句(由which 引导)以及状语从句(由 if 引导)构成的主从句,主句中的谓语均使用了动词 mean,但处理方式又各自不同,参赛译文 1 和 3 分别使用了两个和三个独立句,而参赛译文 2 只用一个独立句。英译中,句式的调整不但要符合英语句法表达的习惯,而且也要表意清晰。由此,本句的参考译文减少定语从句的结构,力图增强句式的流畅感:But losing one such village would mean erasing a cultural footprint from the landscape of history, and disengaging us from an intimate feel of what has been passed along by history. A distinct danger would thus emerge that we may be further distancing ourselves from our own past. And any loss of our cultural attachment to an ancient village would create one more obstacle to the continuation of our cultural traditions. 参考译文使用了三个独立句,但句子结构和内部词语之间的衔接性强,表意顺畅。

我们真诚地希望,在今后的韩素音青年翻译奖竞赛中,参赛选手能够注意到本届译文存在的有关问题,要在原文主旨和语义的深层次上进行英译,尽量不要在语言表层词语上英译;对重要概念的英译,要查阅权威英文词典对词条语义的解释和习惯的搭配;要尽量脱离原文句法结构的束缚,使用英语句法特征进行思想表述,做到既信且达。

翻译的"译"与"评"
——以翻译和评价实践为例

翻译水平指的是翻译实践水平,至于高低之谓,一定是认识上的。绕来绕去,终究还要回归到翻译的一个古老话题,即翻译之本与翻译之为的主题之上,而翻译之本与翻译之为又必须通过翻译实践而演绎。

关于翻译的"译"与"评",笔者根据自己的实践和体验,简略回答以下有关翻译之本和翻译之为的问题。

一、怎么译、怎么评?
——当理想遭遇现实

翻译之本是要顾念翻译作为翻译的根本,确保译文和原文如影随形;翻译之为是要看翻译的实际作为,译者为了特殊的目的,僭越原文也在所不惜。前者体现于翻译的道德层面,后者体现于翻译的现实层面。道德约束而欲达到的是一种理想状态。

在道德层面上,讨论的是"该不该""该怎么样"的问题;在现实层面上,讨论的是"会不会""会怎么样"的问题。比如,在道德层面上,翻译应该忠实于原文的意义,但在现实层面上,译者受各种因素的影响,会出现"会不会""会怎么样"的问题。就像在生活中,一个行路人"应该"遵守交通规则,但也"会"为了图方便而出现抄近道、横穿马路的现象。

该怎么译呢?求真为本。会怎么译呢?务实为用。毕竟翻译活动是有目的性的。该怎么评呢?以"忠实"为本;全面考证意味着客观;理论分析意味着科学。会怎么评呢?常以己律人,即以自己之"履"套别人之"足",以"译文"产生的翻译外效果审视翻译内的问题等。

就翻译作为一项社会活动而言,仅做语言内的评价,应对的只是译文和原文的关系,所求的只是译文对应原文之真。同时做语言外评价,是动态评价,译评者不仅应对译文和原文的关系,也应对译文和社会需求的关系,译者犹如走入社会的市场调查者,调查的是译文的务实效果。比如,对于《红楼梦》译本,多数译者做的是语言内评价,只关注译者对原文的关系,理解正确、到位的就是好的译者和译本,因此,杨宪益夫妇是好译者,他们的译本是好译本,而霍克斯针对的是市场需求,所以与前者是有差异的。用此标准评价前者,用彼标准评价后者,自然都是不全面的,与译者的定位背道而驰。

翻译就是以原文为本、以译文为用的平衡之学。翻译是译语再现原语意义程度不等之物或之为(周领顺,2014a:4)。或者说,翻译是含有"翻译"含量多寡的那种东西或作为,不再现原文意义的所谓"翻译"不是翻译,而是破坏翻译生态平衡的行为。

二、准不准、好不好?
——翻译从"方法"进,鉴赏却不从此出

传统上人们认为,会查词典,就会翻译。实际情况却不是这样。这里有两个层次:一个叫"准不准",一个叫"好不好"。

在外语学习的过程中,一般所谓的翻译,只是教学和学习的手段。例如,I came to the class so late that I was scolded by my teacher. 这一句可有不同的译文。

译文1:我上课是如此地晚以至于受到老师的批评。

译文2:我上课晚了,老师批评了我。

译文1是练习词组 so ... that 时使用的,所以该词组不翻译出来,反而不好,但在交际场合里,翻译出来则显得呆板、教条,因为有违背于我们的阅读接受习惯。

翻译教材上一般都要罗列翻译方法。但是,前人的翻译方法只表明翻译实施的合法性和可操作性。翻译方法是逻辑思维的结晶,而翻译的过程则是形象思维的过程。形象思维的过程是"跟着感觉走"的过程。译者释放的译文,一定是综合考虑了各种因素(目的因素、读者对象、赞助人的要求、社会的接受度等)的结果,因此任何方法都不可能事先预定,更不能死记硬背和机械套用,那样不仅不能提高翻译的速度,也难以提高翻译的质量和人们对于译文之"好"的认可。"跟着感觉走"的实质是"在心理上跟着原文意义和社会需求走",是对于周围一切因素在心理上的把握。

滑稽的是,在鉴赏翻译时,绝不会因为译者使用了哪种翻译方法或者凭其使用翻译方法的多寡评判翻译的好坏。鲁迅《秋夜》里的"我家门前有两棵树,一棵是枣树,另一棵也是枣树"一句,如果译者采用翻译上的"合并法",将其变为"我家门前有两棵枣树",鲁迅能高兴吗?鉴

赏者能认可吗？

翻译要因情因景而定，不可生搬硬套。如果事先就给自己贴上了"直译""意译"的标签，便会产生死板的译文，起码会束缚自己的手脚。比如 I love you. 一句，即使标榜自己是喜欢意译方法的人，你有必要绞尽脑汁，故意避开常见的直译文"我爱你"而想象出一个意译文吗？对于 it is said that... 结构，即使标榜自己是喜欢直译方法的人，是不是一定要翻译成不伦不类的"它被说"呢？事实上，是不是一定要明确什么样的方法，并不是问题的关键。关键是不管采取什么样的方法，目的无非是要译文"出彩"。只有出彩的译文，才可能打动人；只有出彩的译文，应试时才可能打动阅卷人，才可能得到较理想的成绩。

三、翻译上的"度"由谁来把握？
——译者和评者各有分工

翻译界最头疼的问题之一就是翻译上的"度"。比如，刘英凯（2002）说："每读到这个'度'字，我就不免有个疑问：这个'度'如何界定？由谁来界定？'度'的界定有没有可操作性、程序性和可传授性？如果这些都没有，那么，它的可检验性何在？这岂不是又坠入'神而明之，存乎其人'这类的空泛玄虚的不可知论的泥潭里去了吗！"不知不觉间，研究者感到头疼的"度"却是因为越界而帮译者去把握造成的，"井水"犯了"河水"。译评者作为理论家和研究者，其对于实践家译者的规定，往往难以得到满意的回应，道理同文学评论家和作家之间的关系一样。"度"是有层次性的，分角度看，这一问题并不难回答。

把握翻译上"度"的有两类人：第一类是直接影响翻译的译者，第二类是评价翻译质量的译评者。对于译者而言，翻译上的"度"是心理上的、认知上的；对于译评者而言，翻译上的"度"是物质上的、客观上的。而译评者角度上的"度"还可以再细分为译评者规定译者译前执行的"度"和译者译后译评者可以描写的"度"。

说译者角度上的"度"是心理上的、认知上的，是因为任何译文都是译者权衡各种要素的结果，译者一旦将译文正式公示出来，他便是基本上认可了译文的平衡性，维持了心理上可以接受的平衡度，至于译者具体的心理过程或潜或显，有待研究者破解。虽然有外界的干预，但无论谁干预译者的行为，最终都要经过译者认可这一关。

说译评者角度上的"度"是物质上的、客观上的，是因为译者的译文是不是逾越了"翻译"的范畴，即译者是不是改变了原文的意义，是决定翻译是不是"翻译"的性质问题。翻译是语码的转换和意义的再现,但再现的一定是原文的意义,此所谓"翻译即译意"之理。

不管是对于译者还是译评者,"度"表现在多个方面,比如归化和异化的度、直译和意译的度、翻译和再创作的度等。谈"度"就是谈平衡。许钧(2002:87)说:"翻译是一种'平衡'的艺术,好的翻译家就像是'踩钢丝'的行家,善于保持平衡,而不轻易偏向一方,失去重心。"

四、翻译有着怎样的状态?
——本真竟是"混血儿"

最典型的莫过于"自译"。有的自译者兼具作者的特征,因为同时面对两个版本的读者,所以为适应各自读者的需求,就会表现出更大的自由。因为自由,所以"译文"既可被认为是创作,又因为有既存的文字基础而被认为是翻译。但如果说"自译"太过典型,不妨看看人们常说的"翻译"和"创作"的关系吧。

"翻译"就是翻译,"创作"就是创作,本来是泾渭分明的。如果把"翻译"叫"创作",把"创作"叫"翻译",肯定是要乱套的。试想,现实中人们在参评作家系列职称的作品中看到了翻译的影子,在参评翻译系列的作品中看到了译者过多创造的痕迹,或许作家或译者会被当作"剽窃者"而受人诟病,但偏偏就有"翻译是再创作""翻译是二度创作""翻译是对原文的改写"等诸多处于中间状态的说法,表现了翻译属于"混血儿"的本真状态。

鉴别"翻译"和"创造"的根本在于:超出了原文不存在的意义不是翻译,略去了原文中存在的意义不是翻译,改变了原文本来意义的也不是翻译。归根结底,不是原文意义的所谓翻译都不是翻译,所以除了"翻译"之名外,还有"译写"等。笔者发表过一篇叫《尝樱桃》的短文,其中有这样一句:

老家有个小院,院子里有树,层层叠翠,唯有那两棵樱桃树,满身裹着霞帔。

In this courtyard grow verdant plants, among which are two cherry trees bearing red fruit just like two beautiful Chinese brides in red capes.
(周领顺,2012:50–51)

其中的"霞帔"处理为 two beautiful Chinese brides in red capes。"霞帔"以其艳丽如彩霞,故名。研究生选择性地将其阐释为"美丽的中国新娘穿着的披肩服饰",引人之处在于选择了 brides,考虑到读者为说英语者,所以添加了 Chinese。这是读者认可的好译文,但明显夹杂着创作的成分,起码说把原文的暗喻处理为明喻了。

再拿翻译技巧上的"直译"和"意译"标签为例。有文章经常举这样一则格言:

Don't lock the stable door after the horse has been stolen.

直译文:不要等马被盗后,才去锁厩门。

意译文:不要贼走关门。

然后设问:是直译好还是意译好? 而给出的答案一般又显示意译优于直译。意译文与直译文相比,得失共存。"得":简洁;四字结构("贼走关门")有节奏感。"失":有歧义;失掉了原文的形象("马""厩门"等)。意译文并不是真正的意译,而是"非直译"或"非意译",是中间状态。所以,巴金(1951)认为,"翻译的方法其实只有一种,并没有'直译'和'意译'的分别。好的翻译应该都是'直译',也都是'意译'"。

较理想的做法是,直译兼顾意译,保留原文的形象,译出作者的深意,保留或增加简洁、上口等美感元素,尽量避免可能产生的歧义。方法上直译、意译参半:意译时不完全舍弃原文形象,直译时又不在形式上亦步亦趋,做到言简意赅,符合格言警句等的特点。笔者尝试将上文这一句英语格言处理为"莫待马儿盗,方知锁厩门"。甚至也可仿照汉语成语"亡羊补牢,犹未为晚",将其改造为"亡马锁门,悔之晚矣"。"悔之晚矣"是对原文深层意义的再现,是对前半句意义可能不够明晰之处的有效补充,是意译部分。在"求真—务实"译者行为连续统评价模式(周领顺,2014a:87-92)上,译者对原文的求真一般是选择性的,比如该格言中对于原文形象的求真,而务实是多方面的,但总体上是交际效果之实。原意译文所求之真,只是原文的内容,但表述不是十分明晰。

翻译方法的"杂糅"正说明译者的审时度势。在实践上,不管是以求真为主兼顾务实的译文,还是以务实为主兼顾求真的译文,译者综合各种因素考虑后释放出来的译文便是自以为平衡的译文,至于事实上是否如此,需要译评者的考查和检验,需要译评者给予描写和解释。

五、理论家是纸上谈兵吗?
——是骡子是马牵出来遛遛

理论家的作用在于借理论的工具提高认识,寻找语言和翻译的规律等,自己不一定要亲自翻译。他们开展的翻译批评实践也是实践。正如裁判自己不一定要把球打得最好,声乐教育家自己不一定要把歌唱得很有名,文学评论家自己不一定要创作小说,军事理论家自己不一定要会打枪或者一定要百发百中一样。不过,对于以实践为主的译者而言,最好兼具理论家的眼光。这样不仅能评价别人,也能使自己的译文做到有理有据,并能悟出其中的道理。"是骡子是马牵出来遛遛",在实践者的眼里,最有说服力,而学生上翻译课的最大挑战就在这里。下面笔者以自身为例,试举几例。

培根的散文"Of Beauty"有多种译文,原文的首行为:"Virtue is like a rich stone, best plain set; and surely virtue is best in a body that is comely, though not of delicate features; and that hath rather dignity of presence than beauty of aspect."笔者将其译为:"德之如玉,素净为上;德之于人,气质为上。乖巧或可不足,然轩昂之气,实非貌美所能比。"笔者以匿名的形式将自己的这个译文和其他几个译文同时呈现给全班学生,结果是,学生对笔者译文的接受度竟明显高于其中的一些译文。

下面这段文字:"Mary Louise is not as naive as she acts. Actually, she's been dating boys since she was in the seventh grade. When she was in the eighth grade, she went to a high school dance with a junior. She loves to flirt in a quiet, shy way, and she knows how to blink those big, dark eyes to attract attention. She's the kind of girl that can steal a boyfriend before you realize what's happened."笔者将其译为:"马莉·路易貌似单纯,实则不然:初一学约会,初二邀人舞。最喜卖弄风骚,悄然而羞涩;深谙传情之道,顾盼而生姿。生性若此,俘获男友于未知。"并将其展示给学生,也得到了他们的喝彩。由此笔者悟出:中国读者具有深深的"恋古情结"。

又如,林语堂作品中的这几句:"Life, then, is really a dream, and we human beings are like travelers floating down the eternal river of time, embarking at a certain point and disembarking again at another point in order to make room for others waiting below the river to come aboard."笔者的译文是:"人生就是一场梦,而人若行旅,漂泊于亘古的时间长河:上船终有下船时,河边还有后来客。"译文显得端庄得体,契合原文的主题和风格。而公开出版的原译文"人生真是一场梦,人类活像一个旅客,乘在船上,沿着永恒的时间之河驶去。在某一地方上船,在另一个地方上岸,好让其他河边等候上船的旅客。"则遭到了学生的质疑。这是因为原译存在不少的问题。比如,"人类"和"一个"搭配在逻辑上有问题,"人类"是集合名词,"集合名词前头不能加个体量词……这类名词前头只能用表示群体的量词(集合量词或不定量词)"(朱德熙,1982:

41－42）；"驶去"和"好让"的目的性太强,似去迎接其他旅客;"某一地方"与"另一个地方"不对称;"上船""上岸"不言而喻,汉语言简意赅,不一定要表现出出发地和终点等。此外,原译还存在语法问题,比如,"好让其他在河边等候上船的旅客"语法不通,句子是不完整的,应改为"好让其他在河边等候上船的旅客上船"。更重要的是,原译没能很好地再现原文的文风。何以见得？最有力的证据是寻找作者类似风格的文字。

原译少了古色古香的味道,不合林语堂之风。而且,原文是人生感悟,不宜翻译得太直白。由此笔者也悟出,中国读者对于警句寄予了言简意赅的期许。尽管翻译界有过语言上异化、归化的争论,但对于像林语堂这样的华裔英语作者的作品,又毫无疑问地期待着用地道的译文还原地道的原文,即用地道的汉语还原该华裔作者地道的汉语文风。此时,语言上的归化成了必选的答案。道理很简单,作者是华裔,写的是中国事,也就无所谓"异国情调"。从向作者靠拢的角度,应归入异化,而从向作者母语背景的角度靠拢,却应归入归化。

诸如此类,把道理悟出后,自然会对未来的实践有所启迪。杨自俭(2003)认为,"从事翻译理论研究最好有较多的翻译实践(最好各种文体的汉外互译都做过),这很实际,也易于把经验升华为理论,当然也易于用理论指导实践……从事理论研究多的人没工夫做翻译实践,或做翻译实践不多,也不是错误,但也是一个不足"。2003年,笔者在《上海科技翻译》发起的那场"翻译理论和实践关系"大讨论就见证了笔者不愿做"空头理论家"的志趣。

多一点理论,译者就能更容易使自己的实践在翻译学允许的范围内行事;多一点理论,实践时就会多一分理性,毕竟评判实践的专家是理性的;多一点理论,遇到个性文化信息需要处理时,就会减少一份茫然。看待翻译的好坏,存在着观念上的更新问题。翻译研究者需要更新的是译评者"怎么评"的观念,这是译评者怎样看待文本上"原文求真"和"译文求用"之间,以及译者在"求真为本"和"务实为上""务实为用"之间为保持理想平衡而在事实上把握的问题。总之,兼顾理论而实践,是提高翻译实践技能和理性认识翻译实践之实的一条坚实之路。唯此,翻译之本和翻译之为才能得到良性的演绎。

译者的"译"与"美"
——以翻译和美化实践为例

按照一般的定义,散文指诗歌、戏剧、小说之外的文学作品。散文最显著的文体特征在于"形散而神不散"。"形"是散文的外在形式,主要指它取材广泛,表现手法又灵活多样;"神"则是它的内在意蕴,主要指主题、思想、情感、意境等。朱延庆将散文的主题比作灵魂,将结构比作骨架,将语言比作血肉,而诗意则是神气(王治江,2003:39)。对于成功的散文作品来说,这些要素都是至关重要的,但语言这个因素或许尤其重要,因为其他内在的东西往往借助语言这个载体来体现,假如语言苍白无力、平淡无味,则"皮之不存,毛将焉附"。除了传递思想外,散文在语言文字上具有音乐般的音韵节奏美感,具有独特的审美价值,能给读者带来美的阅读享受。"散文要吸引读者,除了感人的情、化人的理之外,还必须有富于艺术感染力的语言。"(党争胜,2008:26)

作为文学作品,散文的文学性在于它的美学意义。散文是美的,美在语言。从表现形式的角度看,比喻、拟人、夸张等修辞手段,以及想象、对比、象征等写作手法的运用增强了文章的艺术感染力;从音韵节奏的角度来看,和谐的韵律、长短交错或平行对称的句子分布、表达性或修辞性的重复等调节手段使得文章富于音乐般的韵律节奏美感。可以说,散文的魅力很大程度上在于优美的语言,能给读者带来美的享受。

由此可见,散文的翻译最终或许就是落实到如何体现原文的语言美这个最基本的方面。要翻译好散文,一般是比较难的,会牵涉很多因素,有原文的理解、译文的表达、翻译策略的把握、两种语言之间异同的了解、背景知识的储备等一系列问题。此外,译者还要具备一定的美学鉴赏能力和表达能力。译者既要传情达意,又要考虑美感,不能顾此失彼,难度自然比较高。对此,我们有切实的体会,绞尽脑汁,不断地推敲,来回交换意见,是经常的事,"译无止境"用于描述散文的翻译过程再恰当不过。

我们从2014年的6月开始翻译书中收录的散文,到书的最终完成,一共花了两年多的时间。在这个过程中,我们反复商讨,修改译文,尽可能地完善细节。虽然本书收录的篇目不多，但是我们在翻译过程中倒也积累了不少的思考和体会，对于具有一定共性的方面，我们觉得有必要进行一番整理和归纳，作为我们翻译实践的一个总结。

本书收录的散文内容涉及人、景、物、动物、事等与作者生活有关的不同方面，随着主题和内容的变化，描写、叙述、抒情、说明、议论等不同的表达方式，华丽、典雅、平实、诙谐、辛辣等不同的语言风格，也交织渗透，切换变化。比喻、拟人、夸张、设问、排比等多种修辞格的使用，让文章更加形象、生动，提高了文章的表现力和可读性。

原文的主题、内容、语言风格、意境等都是通过语言形式来体现的，包括用词、句式的安排、音韵节奏的调节、修辞格的使用等手段。这些外在手段的使用随主题或内容的不同而异。例如，《汉墓健身之行》《节俭意识与道德行为》等以表达思想为主，语言风格端庄、古雅；《我有野鸭三两只》《温馨时刻：文友同游达拉斯》等以叙述经历为主，词语、句法结构等朴实、亲切，很少使用古色古香的表达方式；而《下雪的季节》《得州云霞》等则以描写景物为主，用词平易，但大量使用比喻、排比、拟人、夸张等修辞手法，营造了华丽、壮观的气氛。

在翻译的过程中，我们自始至终力图把握好一个总体原则，即在内容上尽量贴近原文，在此基础上，以符合译语表达习惯的方式，译出原文的语言风格和美学因素。"翻译必须做到既准确而又通顺。准确，说的是译文内容与原文一致；通顺，说的是译文符合译入语的语言规律，不但是同，而且很自然。"（金堤，1989：117）。在贴近原文和符合译语之间存在矛盾时，我们偏向于遵从译语的表达习惯，以便让译语读者获得类似于原语读者的阅读感受。

译出原文的内容主要指传递语义，包括表达出原文的主题、思想、文化信息、隐含的信息、色彩等，这是翻译的重要方面，必须做到准确、充分，否则就是译者没有尽到全责。尽管作者也是译者之一，但并没有任意提高译者的自由度，无端增加创作的成分，而是在尊重原文和顾全译文之间，力争把握好一个比较理想的平衡度。

语言风格和美学因素是体现散文文学属性的重要方面，我们在翻译时致力于最大限度地加以再现，这是本文题目中所说的"美"的意思，即"美化"。从形式的角度可以把握的、体现原文文学性的成分有词语、句法结构、修辞手段、音韵节奏的调节手段等。此外，本书的多篇原文中都引用了古诗/古体诗（句），这些古诗/古体诗（句）大大地提升了原文的文学性，因此，这一内容的翻译我们在此也一并加以讨论。

一、词语的选择

首先,词语是构词成句最基本的单位,也是构成散文语言风格最重要的部分之一。在文体类别上,散文属于文学作品,作者往往会采用大量文学色彩浓厚的词语。在本书收录的散文里面,有不少篇目在用词方面体现出华丽、典雅的风格,在译文中我们也应相应地使用文学色彩浓厚的词语。试比较例[1]及其译文:

[1] 夏天里,大地一片<u>葱郁</u>,竹林的葱郁便<u>消融</u>于<u>秀山翠海</u>之中。(《竹》)

Summer saw the land bursting with *verdant* plants, *submerging* the bamboo grove in *a sea of luxuriant verdure*.

例[1]中的"葱郁""消融""秀山翠海"等都是文学用语,译文中与此对应的 verdant,submerging,a sea of luxuriant verdure 等也是文学用语,在语义和色彩上都基本相当。此外,这一句的译文还采用了"无灵主语 + 有灵动词"的搭配,即 Summer saw。所谓"无灵主语"指作主语的名词指称事或物,而所谓"有灵动词"则指描绘人或动物所发出的动作的动词。从修辞的角度来看,"无灵主语 + 有灵动词"的搭配是拟人的用法,经常出现在小说、散文、诗歌等文学作品或新闻报道中。汉语中也有类似的用法,如"<u>空虚和寂寞吞噬着他</u>""<u>我看到风在微笑</u>"等,但搭配的范围和出现的频率远没有英语等印欧语那么广,那么高。在译文中,适当采用类似的结构可以增加表达的文学效果,除了例[1]外,《石榴花》《汉墓健身之行》等篇目中也使用过类似的翻译技巧,读者可以留意。

当然,再现原文的文学性时应充分考虑译语的表达习惯问题。汉民族善于形象思维,语言表达中多用形象词语,而英语中形象词语的使用频率一般低于汉语,在汉译英时,应适当省略原文的形象表达。例如,《春风十里扬州路:人在扬州》中的"阳历的四月大约等同于阴历的三月,此时繁花似锦,桃红柳绿,莺歌燕舞,游人如织"这一句中的四个四字词语文学色彩浓厚,并列在一起,描绘了春光的无限美好,渲染了春天欢乐的气氛。原文的表述浓墨重彩,这是汉语的表达习惯,译文不必受原文形式的限制,"花""桃""柳""莺""燕""游人"等诸多意象无须一一再现,只要将主要的意义表达出来即可,这一句我们译为:
March in the lunar calendar, approximate to April in the solar calendar, is a time when *flowers and trees get their color back and bloom in full glory*, *infu-*

sing into every pore of a scenic place the hustle and bustle of tourists. 译文中保留了 flowers，trees，tourists 等主要意象，并且采用了拟人修辞格（如every pore of a scenic place 所示）、音韵修辞格（如 hustle and bustle 所示）等修辞手段，已经比较充分地表现出了原文的意境美。

原文作者的语言风格总体上偏向朴实，家常化的叙述散落各处，例如，"<u>管不了那么多</u>，童年爬树偷果子的情形一时<u>占了上风</u>"（《石榴花》）；"<u>说起我这尊'姜太公钓鱼'，可是有它来历的</u>"（《姜太公钓鱼》）；"之前倒是听人说过<u>野鸭野鸭的</u>"（《我有野鸭三两只》）；"这也是知识，<u>不懂就问呗</u>，吃要吃出个名堂"（《青岛记行》）；"<u>学英语、学文化，处处是知识</u>"（《别了，得州》）；"大家走<u>一路</u>，聊<u>一路</u>，照<u>一路</u>"（《温馨时刻：文友同游达拉斯》）；等等，比比皆是。但原文作者也擅用古色古香的词语或结构，这不但增加了文章的文学色彩，同时也使得表达简洁，节奏明快。例如，"童年<u>至今</u>，<u>屡次</u>相遇，竟不曾为其娇容<u>所动</u>"（《石榴花》）；"'粒粒皆辛苦'吗？<u>谬矣</u>"（《节俭意识与道德行为》）；"我<u>寄情于</u>得州云霞"（《得州云霞》）；"鱼竿不见踪影，或原为一节细竹，<u>抑或一截木棍</u>"（《姜太公钓鱼》）；"'扬州美女'样子若何？"（《春风十里扬州路：人在扬州》）；等等，也是随处可见。因此，原文的语言风格，不是单一的，在很多情况下，是朴实、典雅兼而有之，交错融合，但连贯得自然，没有斧凿的匠气。

语言风格是散文的一个重要方面，译者应把握得当。比较而言，原文朴实的语言风格在翻译时比较容易处理，我们一般采用英语中简单、常用的基本词语来传递，而原文典雅的语言风格则难以在译文中一一再现，尤其是来自古汉语的虚词，如"屡""抑或""颇""矣"等，一般在英语中是难以再现其古典色彩的。古汉语中的很多词语和结构一直沿用到现代汉语中，经常出现在文学作品或比较正式的非文学文体中，而英语中的古词语或结构沿用到现代英语中的数量不是很多，一般用于诗歌等文学作品或学术、法律等对严谨表述有较高要求的文体里。作为变通处理办法，原文通过典雅词语或结构来体现的风格色彩，我们主要使用英语中带有文学色彩或比较正式的词语或结构来弥补。试举两例：

[2] 童年至今，<u>屡次</u>相遇……（《石榴花》）

Ever since my childhood, I *have had different encounters with pomegranate flowers* …

[3] 前者节俭迫于<u>生活的压力</u>，限于物质层面；后者节俭则为美德，已<u>上升</u>到了一种精神境界。（《节俭意识与道德行为》）

> The former group does so as a daily necessity under *the pressure of subsistence*, suggesting a focus of their economy on material supplies, while the latter group does so as a virtuous trait, their conduct thus *ascending* to a moral altitude.

例[2]中的"屡次相遇",直白地说,就是"见过好几次"的意思。前者简洁而又典雅,而后者则明显是口语体。译文相应地采用了英语中正式的表达方式来翻译"屡次相遇",即词义比较虚的动词 have 和 encounter 这个名词化结构的搭配,译文缺失了表达上的简洁,但在语体上与原文相当,在色彩上也与原文接近。

例[3]中的"生活的压力"和"上升"是汉语中的日常词语,译文没有使用英语中对应的 the pressure of life, rise 等日常表达方式,而是采用了使用频率较低的 the pressure of subsistence, ascend 等表达方式,pressure, subsistence, ascend 等词来自拉丁语,后两个更为正式,属于"大词"一类。孤立地看,例[3]的译文在用词的风格上似乎超译了。但是,在翻译时,语体或风格上的"对应关系"除了以词为单位外,还可以句子、段落甚至更大的篇章为单位。例[3]所在的原文以说理、议论为主,总体来看,用词端庄,句法结构对称,带有文言色彩的词语或结构点缀其间,是非常正式的文体。上文我们提到,带有文言色彩的汉语词语在英语译文中往往难以再现其古典色彩,作为弥补,我们在译文的适当地方,增加使用语体上偏向正式的词语或结构,如例[3]的译文所示。这个策略在其他篇目的译文中也采用过,我们称之为"失之东隅,收之桑榆"策略。

二、修辞手段的处理

修辞是散文作者经常用来表达主题、内容、情感,增加艺术感染力的手段,是散文文学性的形式标志之一。本书的原文中使用了不同的语义和结构修辞手段,有比喻、拟人、夸张、借代、排比、对偶、设问、反问、引用、顶真等。除了顶真修辞格(《春风十里扬州路:人在扬州》中的"有了运输,便有了商贾,有了商贾,便有了财富,而有了财富,便有了招之即来的美女";《一轮舞阳照贾湖》中的"'贾湖'在'舞阳','舞阳'在'河南','河南'在'中国'";以及《盆栽》中的"盆栽藏乾坤,乾坤在心底"等情形)之外,原文中使用的其他修辞格在英语中都有对应的用法,因此在翻译时,绝大多数的修辞用法都能移植到译文中。我们把握的原则是,保留原文的形式,但假如保留形式与译语的表达习惯发生冲突,或出于表意更加明确的考虑,则采用变通处理的办法。例如,为了增强气势,《得州云霞》《下雪的季节》《汉墓健身之行》《别了,得州》等篇目中的排比修辞格用得很多,我们几乎一个不漏地将其移植到译文中,原文的比喻、拟人等修辞用法的处理也同此。但是,在细微处有变异。例如:

[4] 云时若炭火,块状堆积,从黑到红,再从红色走向沉寂;云时若金凤,似画笔画出的丝丝缕缕,好像在眼前飘飞;云时若波光,粼粼碎金洒满天西。(《得州云霞》)

Sunset clouds *look like* charcoal fires stacking up in lumps, and change in color from dark into red and from that eventually into a complete fade-out. Or they *resemble* golden phoenixes, floating as if just before the eyes like brush paintings of wispy strands. Or they *shine like* ripples, their shimmering golden fragments be sprinkling themselves across the western sky.

[5] 待到深秋时节,"白头翁"总会夸张地随着水波甩头作态。(《我有野鸭三两只》)

When it is late autumn, white reed flowers, *looking like grackles*, keep nodding exaggeratingly with the motion of water waves.

例[4]是一组排比句,以"云时若……"开始的三组句子,形象地描绘了晚霞时刻云的风姿,译文完全再现了原文的这个修辞用法,但用了三个不同的谓语动词(look like, resemble, shine like)来译原文的"若",这样表达既保留了原文的形式,又符合英语尽量避免在很短的上下文中同词重复的表达习惯。

例[5]中的"白头翁"是隐喻用法,指开着白花的芦苇,随着池水的荡漾而摇曳,像白头翁点头一样。这个例子的上文没有关于鸟的描述,而且"白头翁"置于引号中,读者自然明白这个"白头翁"一定另有所指。尽管如此,即使是原语读者,假如没有见过芦苇花,也未必能一下子明白修辞的用意。因此,为了表意直白显豁,译文保留了喻体"白头翁",同时添加了本体"芦苇花",译为 white reed flowers, looking like grackles,将原文的隐喻再现为译文的明喻。当然,这样处理,译文少了委婉含蓄,不如原文那么耐人寻味。

该文对原文的修辞格进行的微调还有多处,如《竹》一文中的"嗜竹之情已如竹笋萌生"、《得州云霞》一文中的"排山倒海"等情形,我们在翻译时也都采用了类似的变通处理策略。

我们在翻译时尽力保留原文的修辞手段,但并不是机械地保留形式而不加甄别。上文我们提到,汉语擅用形象色彩浓厚的词语。这些词语中往往包含夸张、比喻等修辞用法,如"瞠目结舌"(《节俭意识与道德行为》)、"黑云压城"(《得州云霞》)、"隔靴搔痒"(《竹》)等。这些词语已经成为汉语表达中的习惯用语,因此,修辞色彩就不一定非在译文中保留不可,根据不同的上下文,我们对这些词语做了灵活处理,在译文中舍弃了这些词语的修辞色彩。

三、音韵节奏的调节

音韵节奏的调节是文学作品的一个重要方面,优美的散文在音韵节奏上也必然具有美学特质。将语言成分有意识、有规律地排列组合,可形成语篇的音韵节奏。汉语和英语之间在语言文字类型方面差异显著,音韵节奏的调节手段和音乐效果迥异。汉语以单音节语素为主,语素之间的排列组合比较自由,讲究平仄相谐,在词语、短语、句子等各个层面都很容易制造重复、对仗、对称等工整的形式,工整和非工整的形式交替使用,使得汉语语篇的音韵节奏有抑扬顿挫的音乐效果。而英语以多音节语素为主,语素之间的排列组合远没有汉语那么自由,而句法结构又追求语法和语义上的完整性。因此,在表达中就不太容易构造类似汉语的整齐对称的形式,英语的音韵节奏讲究轻重音节交替,形成高低起伏、舒缓流畅、行云流水般的音乐效果。在英语中,形式上工整对称、语义上对仗对比的结构往往是修辞的手段,也能给读者带来独特的美感,如狄更斯(Charles Dickens)的小说《双城记》(*A Tale of Two Cities*)中的开头一段:

It was the best of times, it was the worst of times, it was the age of wisdom, it was the age of foolishness, it was the epoch of belief, it was the epoch of incredulity, it was the season of Light, it was the season of Darkness, it was the spring of hope, it was the winter of despair, we had everything before us, we had nothing before us, we were all going direct to Heaven, we were all going direct the other way—in short, the period was so far like the present period, that some of its noisiest authorities insisted on its being received, for good or for evil, in the superlative degree of comparison only.

在这一段文字中,it was the... 句式整整重复出现了 10 次,这也是排比的修辞手法。这 10 个 it was the ... 句子,结构上每两句两两对称,在语义上每两句中的关键词语形成两两对立。紧接的 we had ... 和 we were all going ... 句式,两两重复,四个句子在结构上和语义上也构成对称和对立。这些句子中对立的词语烘托了小说的背景,奠定了小说主题的基调,整个段落文采飞扬,音韵节奏高低起伏,如行云流水,读来令人震撼。

在汉语中,工整对称的结构既是修辞的手段,又是表达的习惯,在诗歌、散文等文学作品中尤其常见,形成了汉语独特的音韵节奏美感。和汉语相比,英语中工整对称的结构用作修辞手段的较多。整齐对称的结构在本书的多篇原文中都使用过,在翻译时,译文应尽量再现原文的音韵节奏美感。例如:

[6] ……<u>前头是果子,后头还是果子</u>,或红,或黄,或绿,就那么<u>玲珑有加</u>,就那么<u>剔透备至</u>。(《尝樱桃》)

Fruit is dangling *before the eyes* and *behind the back*, and is bursting with color in red, orange or green; *it makes a true delicacy*, and *it boasts a real luster*.

[7] 苍天精,统人生于须臾;大地能,拢万物于掌中。(《汉墓健身之行》)

The supreme Heavens condemn the multitude to a short life, and the mighty Earth clutches the world in his iron grip.

例[6]中的"前头是果子,后头还是果子",即"前后都是果子"的意思,但前者通过重复的方式,将一句话能表达的意思分成两个句子来表达,这样处理,句子在语义上没有增添任何新的信息,但在节奏上获得了一种平稳而又舒缓的音乐效果,提升了表达的文学性。翻译时,我们只是将表示方位的"前头"和"后头"表达成对称的结构,即 before the eyes and behind the back,而没有重复句子的谓语部分 is dangling,这是为了避免过多的重复,因为下一个分句中的谓语部分 is bursting 用的也是进行体形式,这样处理符合英语的表达习惯。例[6]最后两个分句中的"有加"和"备至"意思相近,译文中也使用了近义词 true 和 real 来对应,译文中这两个句子的谓语动词 make 和 boast,词形不同,但意思相近。如此,两个"主—谓—宾"句型的分句在形式上非常整齐对称,音韵节奏上的美学效果接近原文。此外,译文将 delicacy 和 luster 这两个抽象名词用作单数的形式,使语义的抽象程度有所降低,增加了文学性。

在例[7]中,分号前后各有两个分句,一长一短,错落有致,两组长短交错的句子并置,就获得了结构上两两对称的效果,两组句子中的名词、动词、形容词、介词短语等成分之间在语义上也工整对仗。因此,例[7]在节奏上抑扬顿挫,在音韵上和谐悦耳,读来朗朗上口、酣畅淋漓。

翻译时,我们将"苍天精"和"大地能"这两个主谓结构译成了短语,即 the supreme Heavens 和 the mighty Earth,形式和原文不同,但表达的语义相似。为了与原文对应,译文中还对原文中的其他句法成分进行了调整或添加,动词"统"的宾语为"人生",译文中添加了 the multitude,作为译文动词 condemn 的宾语,动词"拢"的宾语"万物"变通表达为 the world,"于掌中"译为 in his iron grip,该结构中添加的 iron 修饰语,是为了使译文和上文的 to a short life 达到结构平衡对称。这些调节均在音韵节奏上获得了与原文接近的效果。

但是,英语和汉语的语言文字类型不同,音韵节奏的表现方式和调节手段必然存在巨大的差异。在多数情况下,译文和原文的音韵节奏无法做到一致,为了准确传递原文的内容或者为了使得译文的表达符合译语的习惯,译者完全舍弃或部分舍弃原文语言形式上的美感,是无奈的选择。在表意的自然通顺和音韵美感之间,假如二者无法兼顾,我们也是优先考虑前者,不能为追求原文的音韵美感而因形害义。出于不同的考虑而舍弃原文音韵节奏美感的情形有很多,例如,下文的例[8]、例[9]都是整齐对称的情形,而译文在结构和音韵节奏上都和原文不对应,这是为了表意而不得不舍弃形式的做法。

[8] 盆栽藏乾坤,乾坤在心底。(《盆栽》)
Potted plants as a substitute embed wonder in the heart of the beholder.

[9] 路有坡度,才上顶巅,又下谷底。(《青岛纪行》)
The vehicle *lurched up and down* on the wavy road.

除了上文讨论的调节音韵节奏的策略外,英语中的语音修辞也是用来增强音韵节奏上整饬美和音乐美的手段,包括头韵(alliteration)、尾韵(end rhyme)等,常出现于诗歌、散文、谚语、警句、新闻标题中。头韵指相邻的两个或以上的词或重读音节以相同的辅音或元音开头,例如 as busy as a bee, a best buy, safe and sound, American Airlines 等,而尾韵则指以两个或两个以上的音节以相同的元音和辅音结尾,例如 fair and square, hustle and bustle, a white night, no pain, no gain 等。英语的语音修辞可增强语言的节奏感和表现力,在译文中适当使用,可弥补因无法再现原文的音韵节奏美感而导致的缺憾。例如:

[10] 凝视茶叶在茶杯里旋转,静观颜色在旋转时展现。(《喝茶与品茶》)
[I] began to appreciate better the sight of tea leaves unfolding and releasing color as they *steep and swirl* in the vessel.

[11] 零星几棵树,只是点缀于广袤……(《得州云霞》)

Trees grow there *sparsely and scantily* as the lone sign of life …

在例[10]中,动词"旋转"是一个双音节动词,译文中使用了 steep and swirl 这个并列结构来翻译,两个动词都以辅音/s/开头,属于头韵修辞法,其中的 steep 意为"浸泡",为译者所加,这个额外添加的成分所表达的意思与上下文相符。两个动词并列,增添了结构上的平稳感和节奏上的音乐感。

例[11]中的"零星"为双音节形容词,译为 sparsely and scantily,前者意为"稀疏",后者意为"稀少",二者近义,平行并置,重复使用,主要出于修辞的考虑。近义词并列,平稳厚重,同时这个并列结构中的两个英语词都以辅音/s/开头,都以相同的"辅音+元音"(-ly)结尾,融头韵和尾韵修辞于一体,节奏上优美动听,舒缓流畅。在英语中,语音重复是一种修辞格,表达不同的语用目的,偶尔为之,可以增加文字的美学色彩。

总而言之,汉语和英语都讲究音韵和谐,但程度不同,语用目的也不同。除了音节的构成以多音节为特征外,英语的句法还以形合为主,如此,语法和音韵节奏相比,前者往往高于后者,后者的使用一般以前者为基础。"相比之下,汉语的音韵节奏就显得更为重要。这种重要性不单单只体现在诗歌等精炼的文学作品中,其他作品亦如此,甚至可能为了节奏而牺牲语法的正确性,这点与英文恰恰相反。"(叶子南,2001:18)

四、诗歌的翻译

本书的多篇原文中都引用了汉语的古诗/古体诗(句),包括《节俭意识与道德行为》中的《悯农》(一、二)(唐·李绅)、《蚕妇》(宋·张俞)、《陶者》(宋·梅尧臣)等,《春风十里扬州路:人在扬州》中的《赠别》(唐·杜牧)、《寄扬州韩绰判官》(唐·杜牧)、《送孟浩然之广陵》(唐·李白)、《江夏行》(唐·李白)、《村居》(清·高鼎)、《田园乐》(唐·王维)、《忆扬州》(唐·徐凝)等,《盆栽》中的《鹿柴》(唐·王维),《下雪的季节》中的《沁园春·雪》(毛泽东),《喝茶与品茶》中的《和章水部沙坪茶歌》(明·杨慎),以及《别了,得州》中的《饮酒·结庐在人境》(东晋·陶渊明)。此外,《春风十里扬州路:人在扬州》一文中还有两处作者自己写作的古体诗句。

汉语古诗源远流长,集主题美、意境美、语言美、音韵节奏美于一体,是汉语言和文化的精华。上述篇目或多或少地引用了古诗/古体诗

（句），或是为了加强说理，或是为了增添意境，或是为了引出主题。古诗/古体诗（句）点缀在文章的行文中间，可提升文章的艺术性，丰富文章的表达和内涵。原文引用的古诗/古体诗（句）是构成原文文学性的重要方面，有必要对所引古诗/古体诗（句）的翻译策略做一梳理。在《逻辑性与艺术性的统一》《文学翻译的忠实度和文化传播的有效性》两篇评析里，我们已经专门讨论过古诗（句）的翻译问题，但针对的只是特定篇目里的古诗（句），本小节是对所有引用的古诗/古体诗（句）的翻译做一个归纳总结，探讨在不同的上下文中我们采用的不同翻译策略和方法。

　　诗歌是美的，汉语的古诗/古体诗更是如此。许渊冲（2006：81）为汉语古诗提出过"三美"说，他认为汉语古诗具有意美、形美和音美"三美"。"意美"指诗歌的内容美，"形美"指诗歌的语言形式美，"音美"指诗歌音韵节奏的音乐美。在翻译时，译者应再现原诗的各种美。在内容和形式上把原诗的艺术性再现出来，是译者的首要责任，孤立地看汉语古诗的翻译，这个原则当然是适用的，但翻译散文中引用的古诗/古体诗（句）就另当别论了。汉语古诗（句）被引用到文章里，被引用的语言文字就成为叙述、说理、议论等写作手法的论据了。因此，原文引用的部分古诗我们甚至借用了前人的译文，它们是李绅的《悯农》（其一）（许渊冲译）、杜牧的《赠别》（许渊冲译），以及李白的《送孟浩然之广陵》（陈君朴译）这三首，其余所引的古诗/古体诗（句），包括作者自创的古体诗句，都由我们自己翻译。

　　关于原诗（句）的形式、内容、音韵等方面，哪些需要在译文中再现，哪些可以省略，应根据原文的上下文来判断。在不同的上下文中，原文引用的古诗/古体诗（句），我们主要采用了以下几种翻译法：（1）传递意义的同时，尽量再现原诗/句的形式；（2）舍弃原诗/句的形式，只传递原诗/句的意义；（3）舍弃原诗句的形式和意义，只传递原诗/句传递的意境。这几种情形我们分别各举一例，以资证明。

　　[12] 李白并未着意描画扬州之美，他的《江夏行》有句佐证："去年下扬州，相送黄鹤楼。眼看帆去远，心逐江水流"……（《春风十里扬州路：人在扬州》）

　　The poet did not pen the beauty of Yangzhou at all in the above poem, nor did he in his another poem "A Song of Jiangxia": "When you went southward yesteryear to Yangzhou/At Yellow Crane Tower I bade you adieu/As I watched your sail till it vanished afar/My heart went after you with the river flow"...

[13] 如果把美国比作闹市,那么住在得州真有"结庐在人境,而无车马喧"之感。(《别了,得州》)

In spite of that, for its residents it (Texas) is "*an oasis of serenity amid the hubbub of the outside world*" if the whole country could be likened to a bustling cosmopolitan city.

[14] 久而久之,我已能深入"空山不见人,但闻人语响"的境地。(《盆栽》)

Gradually, I start to visualize in potted plants *the same vast serenity that goes with grand forests*.

例[12]中引用了李白的长诗《江夏行》中的诗句,韵律模式是 aaba 型,押 ou 韵。原文引用这几句诗是为了证实,李白的诗歌并没有着意描绘扬州的美景,因此,译出引用的全部诗句是必要的,包括形式和内容。李白的这首诗以女主人公的口吻进行叙事,引用的这四句诗用词简单朴实,偏向口语,译文从总体上把握了这几句诗在语体上的用词特征,只是 bid you adieu,vanish 等词语的语体略偏向正式,这是因为译文在把握词语风格特征的基础上,还要考虑译文在音韵节奏方面应接近原诗句。使用 bid you adieu 这个结构,是为了和第一行、第四行的韵尾 ou 保持一致,而使用 vanish 一词不用 disappear 等,主要是为了使 vanish 所在的诗行在音节数量上和其余诗行保持一致。

例[13]中的诗句来自陶渊明的《饮酒·结庐在人境》一诗,全诗为:"结庐在人境,而无车马喧。问君何能尔?心远地自偏。"韵律模式为 abcb 型,押 an 韵。引用的两句意为"居住在人群聚集的地方,却一点也感觉不到车马的喧闹声"。简单地说,是"心静自然感觉不到喧闹"的意思。在这个上下文里,作者引用这两句诗是为了说明,得州是美国南部要塞,但闹中取静。如此说来,诗句的形式就不是那么重要了,译文也不必追求与原诗句在形式上的对应,只要表达出内在意义即可,因此,诗句所在的句子译为:It (Texas) is an oasis of serenity amid the hubbub of the outside world … 译文中的 oasis,serenity 等词都带有浓厚的文学色彩,与这两句诗句描绘的意境契合。

例[14]中的诗句来自王维的《鹿柴》,全诗为:"空山不见人,但闻人语响。返景入深林,复照青苔上。"韵律模式为 abcb 型,押 ang 韵。引用的这两句诗意为"空山之中看不到人影,但可以听到人说话的声音",以声响来烘托一种幽静的意境:森林空旷,偶尔传来人的说话声,反而更能衬托森林的幽静。作者此处引用这两句诗,是为了说明作者因喜爱森林而移情于盆栽植物,久而久之,能把盆栽植物想象成森林,从盆栽植物中领悟到和伟岸森林一样的幽静意境。因此,这两句诗不按照字面意思进行翻译,而诗句的形式更无必要再现,表达出作者引用这两句诗所传递的实际意思即可,其意境可简明地表达为 the same vast serenity that goes with grand forests。原文引用古诗句来描绘一种意境,含蓄而耐人寻味,而译文通过 serenity 一词来点明作者的语用意图,则多了一分直白明了。我们这样处理,主要是考虑到译语读者对于原诗可能不熟悉,不一定能明白其中的意境美。

从上文简单的举例分析可以看出,假如原文所引古诗(句)比较完整,能看出韵律(或格律)模式的情况下,我们采用同时再现意义和形式的翻译策略;假如所引古诗句比较简短,显现不出韵律或格律模式,或者作者引用古诗句主要为了取其意义,则一般以再现诗句的意义为主;假如引用诗句是为了其他的语用目的,则再现诗句的意义或形式就无关紧要了。

五、结束语

散文的美学价值构成了其文学性,假如不美,读来便索然无味,也就不能称其为散文。翻译散文时,一个重要的方面就是再现或"美化"散文的各种美学因素,语言美是其中一个重要的方面。在翻译的过程中体现原文的语言美时,假如译文在词、短语、句子层面上能与原文对应,当然理想,否则就要力求在段落甚至更大的语篇范围内再现原文的文学性,将原文的主题、内容、意境、音韵节奏等不同层面上的美感全面地、多角度地再现出来,正如许渊冲(2006:5)所说的那样,"文学作品应该是美的,如把美的文学作品译得不美,那也不能算是忠实,不能算真,所以似而不美的译文不能算是文学翻译,更不能算是翻译文学"。

II · 散文英译实践

原文

一只麻雀

"爸爸,快,有只小鸟飞到阳台上了[1]。"

"噢,在阳台外面吧。"

"不,飞到阳台里面了,我放学把玻璃窗拉开了。"

"真的?"

转身。猛冲。关窗。堵门。[2] 我独自站在封闭的阳台上,喘息着,两眼贪婪地搜寻着猎物。

"爸爸,看,在墙角。"8岁的儿子在玻璃门后帮战助威,"啊,还是只麻雀呢!"

我喜不自胜,顿觉眼前一亮,胸口怦然作跳,其神情定不亚于见到了一只稀世珍禽。我扑,它闪;我跃,它冲;[3] 我用盆子扣,竟听到它在我的头顶扑腾。不知多少个回合[4]过去,只见麻雀张着嘴,紧贴着玻璃,惊魂不定。我蹲在地,喘着气,怒目而视。扑、闪、跃、冲[5],又开始了新一轮攻守行动。终于,深陷囹圄的小麻雀被狠狠的我按于股掌之中。

说实在的,我早想给儿子买只小鸟,最好是色彩鲜艳的,老家开封市的宠物市场上光鹦鹉就有许多种,色彩斑斓,而且便宜。儿子幼小,手没个轻重,我在市场犹豫了几次,狠狠心[6]买回一只小鸡,5角钱,只顶一个茶叶蛋的价,有几次儿子差点让小鸡命归黄泉。我不忍,怜惜它是个性命,不得已割爱送了个人情。待儿子稍大一点,懂得珍爱生命时,我们举家迁到了扬州。扬州接近南方,有不少鸟我只在家乡的山里见过,很是稀罕。天刚蒙蒙亮,各色小鸟就在窗前[7]的树枝上啁啾不止,甚是悦耳。曾目睹"鸟的天堂",但不在巴金的故事中[8],而就在扬州大学师范学院那片竹林里,叽叽喳喳,追逐嬉戏。我为小鸟庆幸,若在北方,众鸟恐怕早已成了网中之物。

小时候,晚上用手电筒在草堆中找鸟,一抓一个准[9];用弹弓打鸟,也有射中的时候。后来受教育,才认识到小鸟是人类的朋友。自此,我恨那些卖鸟的,为食;恼怒那些养鸟的,为赏。小鸟纯粹是大自然的尤物,怎么命运就被人类裁定!

年龄渐大,早失捉鸟的本事[10],问遍同事,也难觅鹦雀之人。而今老天佑我,一只麻雀主动送上门来,怎不叫我喜从中来!麻雀虽无五彩衣裳,但有此一鸟在手,更胜百鸟在林。我手握麻雀,却感到它那毛茸茸的躯体在瑟瑟发抖。儿子瑟缩在身后,惴惴然,一语惊人:它有妈妈吗?

是呀。它有妈妈在等它回家去。默默地,我把麻雀塞到儿子手里,他抚摸着麻雀的羽毛,一遍又一遍,显得爱不释手,但毕竟打开了玻璃窗户。我们交换着目光,坚定地,吐出两个字:飞吧![11]

译文

A Little Sparrow

"Daddy, come over here quick! There's a bird on the balcony."

"You mean outside it?"

"No, inside. I opened the windows after school."

"Seriously?"

I sprang to my feet, dashed to the balcony, shut the windows and blocked the passage. I stood alone on the balcony, gasping for breath, and eagerly searched for the trapped bird with my eyes.

"Look, daddy, it's in the corner!" My eight-year-old son whooped behind the glass door of the balcony. "What! It's a sparrow!"

Delirious with delight, I felt my eyes brightening up and my heart beating faster, as if I were seeing a rare bird. I leaped forward and it ducked back. I sprang at it and it bounced up. I tried to catch it with a basin, only to hear it fluttering over my head. After a number of such captures and escapes, the bird was thrown into panic and stayed clinging to the window glass, its beak kept open, while I squatted on the floor, glaring furiously at the bird, panting. Immediately a new round of captures and escapes began: leaping, ducking, springing and bouncing. At last, I caught the trapped little bird in my clumsy hands.

Honestly, I had long wished to buy a bird for my son, preferably one of colorful feathers. The pet market in my native place Kaifeng City had for sale a wide variety of pets, and parrots alone came in different species, all bright in color and low in price. My son was still small and did not know how to handle a bird gently. It was with much hesitation in the pet market that I was resolute and bought him a chick for 50 cents, which only amounted to the price of a tea egg. Expectedly, many times he almost crushed the chick to death. I did not have the heart to see the bird killed, and grudgingly gave it away as a gift. When my son was big enough to show respect for life, the whole family moved to settle down in Yangzhou. A city in close vicinity to the south, Yangzhou was home to rare species of birds, many of which could only be seen in mountainous areas back in my native place. Early at dawn, birds welcomed the day by twittering musically in the trees outside the windows. I once came upon the sight of a "birds' heaven", not the one written about by the well-known Chinese writer Bajin in his essay, but the one found in a bamboo grove growing on the campus of the Teachers' College of Yangzhou University. Twittering and sporting happily among the bamboo plants, these birds were lucky ones. If they had been living in a northern place, they would have fallen victim to nets.

When I was little, I often went out at night, carrying an electric torch, in search of birds nesting in haystacks, and I never missed my target. If I used the catapult to hunt birds, it also found its mark sometimes. Later I was educated that birds were the feathered friends of humans, and began to resent those who sold birds for profit or those who raised birds in cages for delight. Ranked among the most beautiful creatures on earth, why should birds have their life controlled by human hands?

When I was older, my skills in catching birds were all rusty. I asked my colleagues for information about where to find a bird seller, but it was in vain. Today the heavens showed mercy on me and sent a sparrow to my door. How happy I was! Though sparrows are not colorful, a bird in the hand is worth two in the bush. I held the bird in my hand, its feathery body shivering timidly. My son huddled behind me nervously, and got me electrified with his words, "Does it have a mom?"

Yes, of course. Its mom was waiting for it to return home. Quietly I tucked the bird into my son's hands. He stroked its feathers caressingly with his fingers, again and again, before he opened the windows. We exchanged eyes, and resolutely and simultaneously spoke out, "Go home!"

注释

［1］在这个句子中，动词"飞"描述的是一个眼前可见的事实，表达的是一种结果性状态，即动作"飞"完成后的结果。在英语中，除了"A bird flew onto the balcony"之外，还可以说成"There is a bird on the balcony"。译文用了后者，如此可减少英语动词的使用频率，使之更加符合英语的表达习惯。

［2］"转身""猛冲""关窗""堵门"这四个双音节的动词短语组成了四个句子。汉语的句法不要求句子结构的完整，动词的必要语义成分常可省略或隐含，而英语则相反。因此，这四个动词短语句译成英语时，需要将隐含的语义成分表达出来，可译为：I sprang to my feet, dashed to the balcony, shut the windows and blocked the passage. 译文不仅补充了动作的施事，即 I，还添加了其他一些必要的成分，例如动作的目的地(to the balcony)，以及最后两个分句之间的衔接性词语 and。这样处理，原文简洁生动的戏剧性效果在译文中就有所丢失，这是由汉语和英语之间在句法、篇章衔接方面的差异造成的，实为难免。

［3］这几个小句所表达的形象效果和节奏感与注释［2］中讨论的句子类似，可译为：I leaped forward and it ducked back. I sprang at it and it bounced up. 译文中的副词小品词和介词短语(forward, back, at it, up 等)补充了动作方向的信息，这些信息是原文的动词所隐含的。此外，两个分句之间各添加了衔接词 and。原文和译文之间在色彩方面显然是有差异的，原因见注释［2］。

［4］"多少个回合"隐含的意思是"多少个回合的抓与逃"，补充隐含的意思，可译为 a number of such captures and escapes。

［5］原文此处以更加简洁的方式，即用四个单音节动词，来描述人鸟之间的攻守之势。上文已经将"我扑，它闪；我跃，它冲"译为完整的英语句子，读者已经明白原文隐含的信息。因此，这几个单音节的动词在译文中也可用简略的形式来表达，译为 leaping, ducking, springing and bouncing。

［6］这句中的"狠狠心"并不是"硬下心肠"的意思，而是指"下定决心"，译为 make up one's mind, be resolute, determine 等都可。

[7]"窗前"可译为 outside the windows。按照常理,天刚蒙蒙亮的时候,人还未出门,所谓"窗前"即"窗外",观察的视角在室内。翻译时不必过分拘泥于原文的用词,"窗前"不一定非译为 in front of the windows 才算对应。

　　[8]广东省有一座小岛,小岛上榕树繁茂,栖息了数万只鹭鸟,成为一道美丽的天然风景线。20世纪30年代,著名作家巴金游览了该地,写了一篇散文,题目叫作《鸟的天堂》。所以,这句中的"但不在巴金的故事中"译为 not the one written about by the well-known Chinese writer Bajin in his essay,译文中对巴金这一人物也做了必要的信息补充。

　　[9]肯定表达和否定表达之间,经常可以转换,"一抓一个准"意为"从未失手过",可译为 I never missed my target。

　　[10]"早失捉鸟的本事"表达为 I lost all my skills in catching birds 或 My skills in catching birds are all rusty 都可。译文采用了第二种表达法,比较形象,rusty 意为"生锈的",可喻指能力、技能等因少用而生疏或丢失。译文中适当增加原文没有的形象色彩,可弥补在其他地方丢失的形象色彩。

　　[11]"飞吧!"变通译为 Go home! 契合上文提到的"它有妈妈在等它回家去"这个句子的描述。当然,直译为 Take flight! Fly free! 等也是可以的。

原文

我有野鸭三两只[1]

　　初识野鸭是在离开北方家乡、走近南方水泽大约十多年之后的事。之前倒是听人说过野鸭野鸭的,不过想当然地认为,家鸭和野鸭所不同者,无非前者系人工所养,后者是大自然的尤物罢了。

　　就在几年前,在临近长江的一片水域,我看见几只鸭子在远离村庄的一座湖面上闲游。有一老翁,可能是刚刚做完了水中活计,驾着一叶小木舟,擦着那群鸭子,吱吱呀呀[2]朝着岸边划来。

　　"喂,那是野鸭吗?"我指着那几只鸭子,心中不无疑惑。但愿是,毕竟可以还愿般满足我长久以来想一睹野鸭芳容的好奇。

　　"是野鸭。"老翁作司空见惯状[3]。

　　"你们为什么不捉呢?!"我这样发问,因为原本从小到大,见到野生动物,只要能捉,就没有不捉的道理,或可捉来做宠物饲养,或可食用以饱口福,说不定还能换个钱花。总之,动物是野生的,不捉白不捉,这可是一笔可遇也可求的财富呢。

　　"野鸭会飞,不好捉。"老翁的答话和着我的问话,倒也和谐。

　　野鸭会飞? 这可是我始料未及的。会飞的野鸭,就该称作"鸟"吧[4]。对了,"鸭"字就是由"甲"和"鸟"组成的[5],应该是典型的水鸟无疑。但家鸭翅膀退化了,实在不配延续这一称谓。我这么瞎想着,随手捡起一枚石子朝野鸭抛去,不偏不倚,正中鸭群,陡见几只野鸭扑棱棱飞向岸边的大树,并稳卧于颤颤悠悠的枝头。可真是开眼了,老翁说得不错,怪不得他们不捉呢。原本不是想捉不想捉,而是在能与不能之间啊。

　　因此偶然的艳遇,我每每走近水边,总怀着这份好奇。野鸭不负我心,长江沿岸的坑坑洼洼,总不乏它们的身影,三三两两,好不逍遥。

　　几年之后的今日,当初"偶然的艳遇",已经变成了生活中普普通通的一件事。

　　说这话,也不过三四年的光景。我工作的单位搬到了远离闹市的新校区。新校区开挖了几亩水塘[6],碧波荡漾。周围水草茂盛,春天一来,五颜六色的野花,次第开放,名字叫不上来,不过芦苇还识得,待到深秋时节,"白头翁"总会夸张地随着水波甩头作态。冬天没花,留下的是草木密密麻麻的枯根,一直延伸到水塘一米见方的地方。我自忖,水塘莫不是剥掉了上层浮土就露出了水的天地?那可是又一个充满生灵而灵动的世界啊。

　　看到水就想到鱼,"有水就有鱼"[7]嘛,有几次还见到有斤把重[8]的大鱼在芦苇的枯根间扑腾。既然有鱼,会不会有野鸭呢?想到野鸭,就兴奋起来。我搜寻着水面,真有两只,不,是三只,走近才看清楚有一只是刚孵出的小鸭。我忍不住,对着野鸭喊两声,它们竟钻入岸边的草丛里,好久不见出来,大概不受到过度惊吓,它们是不会飞走的。要是当年,我早就下水捉了去,就算捉不到老鸭,小鸭也会落入毂中。网、箭、马尾毛等捕捞神器,早已烂熟于心,我算得上是捕捞的一个行家里手。

　　我观察过,三五成群的人们经过,都那么泰然处之。我每有"捉"心,总还要做贼似的环顾左右。我当初是童心无知,睁眼再看今天的世界,早已变了模样。

　　我在美国居住时,小区里就有一个野鸭湖。几只野鸭旁若无人,鹅行鸭步于马路之上,即使路过的汽车也要停下脚步[9]。野鸭湖边的马路上,就立着一个牌子,画着野鸭跨越马路的景象,时刻提醒司机避让。新闻里还说过,一位女士开着车还因避让野鸭而身亡。

　　现在,我几乎每天都要走在水塘边,看野鸭潜水觅食,憋口气再上来透透气;观野鸭蹒跚于水草上,一个趔趄再继续徜徉。不见它们何时飞入,也不见它们何时离去,这水塘,俨然成了野鸭一处固定的家。

　　"我有野鸭三两只",人人皆以"我"自居。

译文

Wild Ducks Show Up There for Me in Twos and Threes

　　It was more than ten years after I left my northern homeland and moved to live in the southern water region that I encountered wild ducks for the first time. Previously when I heard people talk about wild ducks, I took it for granted that wild ducks differed from their domestic counterparts only in that the former were nature's untamed creatures while the latter were a cultivated species.

Several years ago near the Yangtze River, I caught sight of some ducks swimming lazily on a lake quite away from a village. An elderly man, who might just have finished his work in the water, was rowing his canoe past the ducks towards the shore, the oars creaking all the way.

"Hi, there. Are they wild ducks, please?" I pointed to the ducks, inquiringly. I hoped they were, and if so, it could satisfy a curiosity that I had long had about what wild ducks looked like.

"Yes, they are." The elderly man put on an air of familiarity with the scene.

"Why don't you go and catch them?" I was curious. As far as I remember, ever since I was a child, if I could make it, I had never wasted any chance of catching wild animals whenever I saw one. They could be kept as pets, cooked for food or traded in for money. In short, wild animals being wild, they were an easy and lucky treasure and it was stupid not to have them for free.

"They can fly. Not easy to catch." His reply was quite in tune with my question, though.

What? I never expected to hear that. As they can fly, wild ducks ought to be referred to as "niao" in Chinese, meaning volitant birds. Truly, the Chinese character for "duck" has two components in it: the left part "jia", suggesting the sound of the character, and the right part "niao", its meaning, i.e. "bird that can fly". From the motivation for the coining of the character, ducks are typical waterfowl for sure. However, domestic ducks are unworthy of the name now, for their wings have degenerated with time. As I was thinking along this line, I picked up a pebble and tossed it at the flock of birds. It went right into them, very accurately. All of a sudden, the birds took flight, fluttered towards the trees on the shore and securely balanced themselves on the swaying branches. What a spectacle! The elderly man was right. I knew now why people ignored those wild ducks: it was not that they were not interested in doing the catching, but that it was not in their capacity.

After this accidental encounter, I grew to be more curious to see wild ducks whenever I approached a water area. Wild ducks, on the other hand, didn't let me down, either. They often showed up in bumps and hollows near the Yangtze River, flocking happily together in twos and threes.

The occasional sight I caught years ago of wild ducks is now a commonality in daily life.

This change took place only in a few years' time. The Foreign Languages College, where I teach, moved to the new campus on the outskirts of the city. The new campus had a pond, about half an acre in extent, dug up within its limits. Its water ripples in the breeze and fondles the lush waterweeds growing around the perimeters of the pond. In spring, wild flowers bloom vigorously in a riot of colors. These wild plants are all unknown to me except the reeds. When it is late autumn, white reed flowers, looking like grackles, keep nodding exaggeratingly with the motion of water waves. In winter flowers are all gone, and plants also wither away with only their roots left, thickly matted together, extending as far as one meter off the pond's edge. Isn't a pond, as I often think to myself, simply a watery realm after the upper layers of earth have been removed? It is such a dynamic world alive with living creatures.

The sight of water always reminds me of fish; "where there's water, there's fish". Sometimes I could see big fish flopping among the bottom ends of withered reeds. Were there wild ducks too where there were fish? This thought lifted my spirits. My eyes began to search the water surface. There they were. I saw two wild ducks there, no, three. I moved a bit closer and made out that the third one was a newly hatched duckling. I shouted to them involuntarily. At this, they ducked into the thick growths of grass at the edge of the pond and would not come out. I guessed that they would not take off in flight unless frightened. Had it been earlier, I would have gone for them in the water. If I should have failed to capture the parent ducks, I could at least have got the baby duck in the hands. I used to be an old fishing hand, good at using those magic catching tools like nets, arrows, hairs of the horse tail, etc.

I noticed that these wild ducks were human friendly, remaining calm and unafraid of people who passed by in small groups. Every time when I had an impulse for setting my hands on them, I would have to steal guilty glances around me before I tried to do so. That childlike behavior of mine was propelled by mere ignorance, of course. A look at today's world, however, shows that it has changed to my surprise.

In the residential area where I lived during my stay in the US, there was a wild duck lake. Wild ducks often waddled on the street, having little regard for people, and the traffic had to stop to give them way. At the roadside near the lake stood a road sign, which depicted on it wild ducks crossing the street, warning drivers to stay alert. A news story once reported that a female driver even got killed in a car accident while she was attempting to avoid wild ducks.

Now, I need to pass by the pond almost every day, and those wild ducks are a good sight to see. Look, they extend their neck under the water in search of food and after a while pull it out for breath, or they toddle on the grass floating on the water surface and with a slip of the foot go back to paddling in the water again. Never seen to come or go, they just take the pond as their permanent home.

Wild ducks show up there for me in twos and threes, and for everyone else.

注释

[1] 原文的题目和最后一段在语义上是呼应的。在最后一段，作者重复题目，并以"人人皆以'我'自居"点明主题。言下之意，野鸭属于大家共同所有。假如根据字面意义，将题目直译成 I Have Several Wild Ducks，则最后一段中的"人人皆以'我'自居"这句就不容易和上句接得自然，接得明白易懂，不利于点明文章的主题。作者向往野鸭，并且总能在水边见到它们三三两两的身影，似乎野鸭与人有心灵相通的感应，因此，译文舍弃题目的表面形象，将题目意译为"Wild Ducks Show Up There for Me in Twos and Threes"，契合原文中"野鸭不负我心，长江沿岸的坑坑洼洼，总不乏它们的身影"的表述，而最后一段中的"人人皆以'我'自居"这一句也顺势译为 and for everyone else，在句法和语义上都能和"我有野鸭三两只"这一句的译文紧密地衔接起来。

[2] "吱吱呀呀"，只是象声词，指划桨声，需添加逻辑主语译为 the oars creaking all the way。

[3] "作司空见惯状"指老翁常见湖面上的野鸭，已经习以为常，可译为 put on an air of familiarity with the scene。

[4] 汉语中鸟类的总称叫"禽"，能飞的叫"飞禽"，已经驯化的叫

"家禽","禽"也可指"兽"。"禽"为书面语,"鸟"为日常用语,后者主要指能飞的。英语也类似,能飞的(volitant)鸟类称为 bird,不能飞的(flightless)鸟类,包括家禽、企鹅等,也称为 bird。可见,汉语的"禽"和"鸟"与英语的 bird 之间在指称意义上是不对应的,"鸟"仅和能飞的 bird 相当。当然,在孤立的语境中,汉语的"鸟"和英语的 bird 一般都指能飞的。因此,在翻译此句时,译文用了拼音的形式来翻译该句中的"鸟",即 ought to be referred to as "niao" in Chinese,并添加 meaning volitant birds 这个解释性成分,以表明此处所说的"鸟"是指能飞的鸟。

[5] "鸭"字是形声字,"甲"表示读音,"鸟"表示外形,同时也传递意义。对于原语读者来说,理解不成问题,但对于译语读者,假如不补充必要的信息,仅按照字面意义翻译,就可能造成理解困难。因此,译文以拼音的形式表达"甲"和"鸟",同时补充这两个构字部件的功能,译为 the left part "jia",suggesting the sound of the character,and the right part "niao",its meaning,i. e. "bird that can fly"。

[6] 汉语中的"亩"是计量土地面积的单位,翻译时,可用拼音 mu 来表示,但一般的英语读者不了解这个意义,可将亩换算成英美制面积单位"英亩",一英亩约等于 6.07 亩,"几亩水塘"大约相当于 0.5 英亩,可译为 about half an acre in extent。假如换算成"平方米"等公制面积单位,"几亩"大约是 2 000 平方米,数字似乎太大了,表达不简洁。

[7] 英语中有一个谚语,Where there's a will,there's a way. "有水就有鱼"可仿此结构,表达为:Where there's water,there's fish.

[8] "斤"是中国使用的重量单位,一斤等于 0.5 千克。上文的"几亩"进行了单位的转换,"斤把重"是否有必要翻译成 about half a kilo in weight? 这句中的"斤把重"是为了形象地说明鱼大而已,译为 big fish 即可,简洁明了。

[9] "停下脚步"为形象表达法,且动作隐含了一个目的,即"让路""让行""让路""让行"在英语中习惯表达为 give … the right of way to … 或 give way to …,整个小句可译为 and the traffic had to stop to give them way。

原文

竹

从小爱竹,却又难得一见。说爱竹,倒不如说是对竹的一种渴望。我家住河南农村,村里无竹,倒是邻村有一片小竹林,就在村西头,与我上学每日必经之路隔着三四块地,似乎很遥远,像远古的童话,可分明又看得到小鸟在茂密的竹林上空盘旋。夏天里,大地一片葱郁,竹林的葱郁便消融于秀山翠海之中。冬天里可别有景致,万木凋零,麻雀一类的小鸟在田头干瘪的草间觅食,老鸹之类的大鸟便呼啸着结群飞上枝头,嗑食冬日里未及被野风吹落的楝子类的坚果[1]。这景象于萧瑟中又平添几分孑然孤独,本能地,对春的渴望便在胸中涌动。在沉沉的、霭霭的气氛里[2],我背起书包,便匆匆地踏上上学的路。

上学的路,朝南,我常目视东方。我放缓脚步,凝神遐思,眸子里却分明在寻找春的足迹。看到了,春就在临村西头那片小竹林里。那竹子虽绿中有些泛黄,翠中稍带干瘪,但在万木萧瑟的季节里,竹便是勃发的生命,是不畏严寒的战士。竹子号曰修竹[3],修长、苗条,恰似单薄的少女。瘦弱吗?不,一节一节的,棱角分明,不屈地挺拔向上,柔弱中透露出刚强。巨木尚凋敝,修竹傲寒霜。我虽孱弱,却志在学竹[4]。

那片小竹林是我心中的向往,虽不算远,在幼年却昭示着一种理想。我壮着胆与伙伴们夜间到竹林边看电影,亲手抚摸过那片竹子,久久地,爱不释手。我思索,若有所悟,日后铸就的是今日的理想[5]。

我上了大学,又留校工作,邻居是一位美籍华人,他的院中有一片竹林,虽未涉足门内,但修竹出墙,每日经过,其距之近,早已满足了心中那份奢望。几次口中上火,熬些竹叶水,和一把冰糖,甜中洋溢着竹香[6]。因情所致,爱屋及乌[7],吃粽子就爱吃那竹筒粽子,饮酒也喜欢饮个竹叶青,买大米就爱买那泛着绿光、浸着竹香的竹香米。虽后来媒体上说那竹香米与竹子无缘[8],属有毒大米[9],恍惚间有为竹子所累之惑[10]。累则累了,却为再也见不到那绿莹莹的"竹香米"而多少生出一些惋惜。

如今来到扬州,却满眼翠竹。公园里办个年票,便能与儿子经常光顾。走在瘦西湖的竹林里,有几次差点绊倒,细查看,原来是那可爱的竹笋破土而出。来扬州后才亲见竹笋,当初那种雾里看花、隔靴搔痒[11]之感顿时烟消云散。在家乡的饭店里吃过所谓的"玉兰片"[12],那是经常与鱿鱼搭配在一起烧的一道菜,黄黄的、脆脆的,让我津津乐道,有人说那就是竹笋。疑虑冰释,爱竹之意更浓。竹子满身是宝,国宝熊猫食竹莫不是因竹貌美、味美之故?

　　竹子种类繁多,这多半是来扬州后才知晓的。才听说个园,不知"个"为何意,探究竟时才知主人爱竹,取"竹"之半[13]。个园竹多,怎一个"个"字了得?古人有以三喻多的,甚至有些店面的招牌上还有用三个"羊"或"鱼"生造的字,真不知这独独的"个"字出自哪位谦谦君子之手。

　　松竹梅岁寒三友[14],而我偏爱竹。"三八"节,夫人与图书馆的女教工参观了溧阳之南山竹海,壮辞所及,尽述竹之茂、之秀、之广、之美,嗜竹之情已如竹笋萌生[15]。于是,冥冥中又生出一分向往:观竹海。

译文

Bamboo

I began to love bamboo as early as my childhood, yet it was a rare sight. As I loved it, I craved to see it. I grew up in rural Henan Province and lived in the village where there were no bamboo trees. Fortunately, a neighboring village had a bamboo grove at its west border, just about three or four patches of field away from the route of my daily school run. The bamboo grove looked far away, growing as if in a fairyland, yet birds could be clearly seen hovering over it. Summer saw the land bursting with verdant plants, submerging the bamboo grove in a sea of luxuriant verdure. Winter, a season of fading colors and falling leaves, took on a completely different look. Smaller birds like sparrows foraged busily in the dried grass in search of food while bigger ones like crows whooshed in flocks into trees and pecked at the nuts that hung onto the branches into winter. The winter scenes, bleak and dismal, cast a lonesome shadow over the heart and set off an instinctive craving for spring. In this gray and gloomy twilight of winter, the day began with my hurried pace to school, my school bag on the back.

On the southbound road to my school, now and again I slowed down and turned my gaze to the east, the mind lost in thought, the eyes looking for the signs of spring. There was the spring, hiding in that bamboo grove at the west border of the neighboring village. In a season when most trees are bare, those green bamboo plants, though speckled with yellowish tints or dry patches, stood upright, battling against the wintry cold with vitality. Bamboo boasts a name in Chinese culture, known as "slender bamboo" for its shape, lean and slim like a teenage girl. Is it weak then? No. Its clear-cut joints bunching up one on top of another, bamboo thrives straight up defiantly, incorporating a toughness in its pliability. When even giant trees wither periodically, slender bamboo can well withstand the cold. Though lacking in physical strength, I had my mind set on acquiring a spirit as unyielding as bamboo.

The bamboo grove, not distant from my home, kept me attracted and it nurtured my childhood dream. Once I went daringly with little friends to a night movie shown in an open space by the bamboo grove, and had the chance of giving the bamboo stalks a long and loving touch. They set me pondering and the wisdom I gained gave birth to the dream I was to realize in my later life.

Later I attended university and worked in the same university after my graduation. I lived next door to a Chinese-American, who had some bamboo plants growing in her courtyard. The bamboo stalks towered higher than the fencing wall that I did not even have to go inside for a look. Whenever I passed by them, they were so close to me and filled my heart with content. Occasionally when my mouth got inflamed from the excess heat accumulated inside the body, I would stew some bamboo leaves in water. The liquid, added with crystal sugar, was a sweet and fragrant remedy. English has a saying that applies to me, "Love me, love my dog." As I loved bamboo, I always showed a special preference for items related to it, for example, the Zongzi cooked in a bamboo cylinder, the liquor by the name of "Green Bamboo Leaf", the shining rice scented with a bamboo flavor. The bamboo-scented rice, however, as it came out in the mass media, mostly did not contain any bamboo extracts, and was even harmful for health, contaminated by process chemicals. I felt as if I had been tricked by bamboo itself. In spite of that, I somewhat regretted that the greenish "bamboo-scented" rice was no longer available on the market ever after.

Now I live and work in Yangzhou, where lush bamboo plants meet the eyes everywhere. If I purchase an annual pass to the Slender West Lake Park I can go there with my son whenever I want to. Many a time, I was walking in the bamboo grove of the park when my feet tripped on something. Upon a closer look, I found it to be a bamboo shoot, breaking cutely through the ground. Only in Yangzhou did I get to see bamboo shoots for the first time, which once and for all cleared away all my previously vague conception about them. I remembered a dish that I tasted in a restaurant back in my hometown, called "Yulan Slices", literally "slices looking like magnolia flower petals". The luscious yellow, crisp slices in the dish, which normally went with squid fish as a filler, were actually slices of bamboo shoots, as I was told. With a clearer picture in mind about bamboo, I came to love it even more. Every part of bamboo has its use. And bamboo is awesome in both looks and taste; I even wondered if the giant panda, China's national animal, loves eating bamboo because of that.

Bamboo varies widely in species, a knowledge I gained after I was here in Yangzhou. When I first heard about the bamboo garden in this city, "Ge Garden", so far the best-preserved in the country and the longest in its history, I was bewildered by the character "ge" in its name, literally "one" or "single" in Chinese. I investigated and learned that, as the garden owner was a bamboo lover, half of the Chinese character for bamboo, which is composed of two "ge", was taken as the name for his garden. Could "ge" honestly feature the abundance of bamboo plants in the garden? The contributor of the garden name actually contrasted the traditional Chinese conception, in which the numerical value "three" represents greatness in quantity, and for that reason a food business, for example, likes to put on its signboard an invented word formed by three same characters going together, like three same characters for sheep or fish.

Of pine, bamboo and plum trees, known in Chinese culture as "three companions in winter", I love bamboo the most. After my wife described in detail the Nanshan Bamboo Forest in Liyang City of Jiangsu Province she visited together with her female colleagues on a Women's Day as exuberant, elegant, magnificent and charming, a rush of love for bamboo was surging up in my heart like a fountain, and a new wish sprouted inside me as well: I want to see the bamboo sea, too!

注释

[1] 这个小句译成 the nuts that hung onto the branches into winter。原文用的是否定结构"未及被野风吹落",译文用的是肯定形式 that hung onto the branches,肯定与否定转换自如。

[2] 上文描述的是冬日的景象,这个"在"字结构紧接上文,描绘的是冬天早晨的氛围,因此,这个介词短语的译文中增加了指示词 this,以及修饰语 of winter,即 In this gray and gloomy twilight of winter,以明确原文所表达的实际意思。

[3] "修竹"是汉文化中的意象,因此,这句的译文中添加了 in Chinese culture。

[4] 上文提到竹子"柔弱中透露出刚强"这个特性,这句中的"学竹"意为"学习竹子坚韧不拔的精神",译文应添加这一隐含的信息,而不宜直译,可译为 I had my mind set on acquiring a spirit as unyielding as bamboo。

[5] "日后铸就的是今日的理想"指"今日受竹子精神的启发而立下的志向,在以后的人生中实现了",可译为 the wisdom I gained gave birth to the dream I was to realize in my later life。

[6] 这几个小句说的是一种民间土法,利用竹叶治疗口腔上火发生的溃疡,因此,"甜中洋溢着竹香"译为 a sweet and fragrant remedy。Remedy 一词是为了明确传达原文隐含的信息所添加的。

[7] 汉语成语"爱屋及乌"大致相当于英语的"Love me, love my dog"这一习语,为了上下文连贯,应适当添加一些铺垫性信息,可译为 English has a saying that applies to me,"Love me, love my dog"。

[8] 所谓的"竹香米",指添加了从竹子中提取的天然色素加工而成的大米,但厂商为了牟利代之以对人体有害的人工色素。因此,"与竹子无缘"意为"没有包含任何从竹子中提取的成分"。在翻译时,应了解这一背景信息,可将"与竹子无缘"译为 mostly did not contain any bamboo extracts,译文中添加的 mostly 是为了避免话说绝对,因为市场上还是可能有正宗的"竹香米"出售的。

［9］"有毒大米"指含有人工色素、化工原料或重金属成分而影响健康的大米，吃了不一定即刻中毒，按照字面意义译成 poisonous rice 就不是很恰当，比较符合英语表达习惯的说法是 contaminated rice。

［10］这个小句的意思是"似乎有被竹子牵累的感觉"。作者原本是喜欢竹子才买"竹香米"，结果买到了毒大米，似乎是被竹子害了，这个小句可译为 I felt as if I had been tricked by bamboo itself。

［11］"雾里看花"和"隔靴搔痒"这两个成语在上下文里表达的意思近似，两个结构共现并置，主要为的是音韵节奏上的平衡，此处侧重叙事，用一个英语词即可，合并译为 vague。

［12］"玉兰片"这个菜名包含了一个隐喻用法，即"像玉兰花瓣一样的切片"，译文取音意合译法，译为 Yulan Slices，并以同位语的形式，添加解释性成分，即 literally "slices looking like magnolia flower petals"。

［13］"竹"的一半即"个"，对于"竹"字的构造，译文通过 which 引导的关系分句做了必要的信息补充，即 half of the Chinese character for bamboo, which is composed of two "ge", was taken as … 以方便译语读者理解。

［14］"松竹梅"为中国文化中的意象，添加 in Chinese culture 的表述是必要的。"岁寒三友"直译为 three companions in winter，并置于引号之中，以表明这是拟人的用法。

［15］翻译这个小句需要注意两个方面。(1) 这个小句描写的不是上文的"夫人"的心情，而是作者盼望看竹海的心情。(2) 汉语中，"竹笋""春笋"等意象常用来比喻事物生长、发展迅速，而英语一般不用这类喻体；在翻译以"笋"为喻体的比喻用法时，我们将原文的"竹笋"替换为 fountain，"萌生"替换为 surge up，使之相互呼应，将整个小句表达为 a rush of love for bamboo was surging up in my heart like a fountain。

原文

尝　樱　桃[1]

　　五月里[2],正是樱桃树挂果的时节;挂果的时节里[3],我们回到了挂满樱桃的故乡小院。

　　老家有个小院,院子里有树,层层叠翠,唯有那两棵樱桃树,满身裹着霞帔[4]。樱桃树的树干并不十分粗壮,但其盖如云,枝枝丫丫,挂果的时节更有琼果处处压枝低的感觉。两棵树就立于院子里那条唯一的水泥路[5]的两侧,相互交错,若不躬身,委实难以前行。置身于樱桃树下,宛如置身于百果园中,前头是果子,后头还是果子,或红、或黄、或绿,就那么玲珑有加,就那么剔透备至。

　　见过马奶子葡萄吧,但樱桃明显多了一分光鲜;见过玛瑙吧,但樱桃明显多了一分酸甜[6]。新鲜水果上市,人人都要尝尝鲜,只是今年,我才身临其境,有了真切的体验。"五一"期间适逢下雨,阵雨过后,便是细雨蒙蒙。每棵樱桃上都挂着那么个小水珠,闪着晶莹。那就品尝个免洗[7]的樱桃吧！摘一颗鲜红的,放在嘴里,甜而不酸;摘一颗泛黄的,酸中带着一股一股的甜。绿的可不要碰[8],吃上一颗开胃,多吃几颗,就尝不出饭菜的滋味是淡还是咸[9]。

　　这才是尝鲜,却不是尝鲜的最佳体验。

　　背着手,用嘴将樱桃从树枝上叼下,一颗,两颗……闭着眼,咬住樱桃,一串,两串……酸甜和着雨珠,爽而解渴,闲情逸致中,令人心驰神悦。

　　樱桃树是父亲栽种的,自然要请教一句流传很久的话:

　　"不是说'樱桃好吃树难栽吗'？"

　　"樱桃树并不难栽,是樱桃熟了难看护。"

　　父亲一边说着,一边指着周围几棵上蹲着的大老鸹。说话间,就见这几只老鸹向树上的红樱桃俯冲过来。父亲急忙吆喝,但见黑鸟掠过,几颗熟透了的红樱桃飘然滑落。母亲端着饭碗,手里还要拿着根驱赶鸟儿的竹竿。

　　樱桃不光诱人,也诱得小鸟们偷着尝个鲜。

{译文}

The Cherry Feast

May, the very season when cherry trees are in full swing, brought us back to my hometown abode, where cherries were hanging heavy on the trees in the courtyard.

In this courtyard trees grow and thrive. And amidst the masses of their lush verdure are interspersed two cherry trees, blazing in a sheen of colors from their ripening fruit. Though not stout in the trunk, each is vibrant with a canopy of profuse branches and twigs, which droop lower when the tree is loaded with fruit. Opposing each other, one by each side of the only cement path in the courtyard, the two trees have their branches entwined and entangled over the path, making passage difficult without bowing the body. Standing under them, you would find yourself as if in an orchard: fruit is dangling before the eyes and behind the back, and is bursting with color in red, orange or green; it makes a true delicacy, and it boasts a real luster.

You must have seen elongated grapes, but cherries defeat them with their brighter shine. Or you may have seen carnelians, but cherries are luscious, with a flavor absent in the former. Fresh fruit in season will as a rule tempt people to scramble for a taste. It was only this year that I could feast on cherries right off the trees on site. There happened to be rains during the May Day holiday. Showers and drizzles, coming in succession, painted cherries with teeny-tiny raindrops, sparkling clean and clear. Why not have a snack of naturally rinsed cherries? I crunched a red one, it was so sweet. I chewed on an orange one, it was sour and sweet. As for the green ones, they were not to be overeaten, for one could be appetizing while more than one would be too sharp for the taste buds to appreciate meals.

That was a good experience of tasting seasonal cherries and it could be done for greater fun like this.

Placing my hands behind my back, I plucked cherries with my mouth, one after another, off the branches. Keeping my eyes closed, I caught the fruit between the teeth, one bunch following another. In this leisurely fun, the sweet sour juice, diluted with raindrops, satiated the thirst, and invigorated the mind as well.

As Father was the cultivator of the cherry trees, I went to verify with him a long standing saying.

"They say cherry trees are not easy to grow. Is that so?"

"Well, it's not the trees. It's the ripe cherries. They are hard to keep."

As Father was saying so, he pointed to the several crows perching in the nearby trees, who almost simultaneously pounced down on the red fruit, and startled by Father's shouts of warning, fluttered away, slipping a couple of ripe fruit down onto the ground. Mother had to be on the alert even at mealtimes, holding in the hand her meal bowl and at the same time a bamboo stick for scaring birds.

So cherries are not only inviting to people, but also tempting to birds for a sneaky tasting.

注释

[1] 题目"尝樱桃"译为"Tasting Cherries"或"A Tasting of Cherries"固然没错,但"尝"字看似普通,实则隐含了"尽情享受"的意思,用 savor 或 feast 等词语是不错的选择。根据 *The American Heritage Dictionary of the English Language*(1992)的释义,动词 savor 意为 to taste or smell, especially with pleasure; to appreciate fully, enjoy or relish, 而名词 feast 则意为 a meal that is well prepared and abundantly enjoyed, something giving great pleasure or satisfaction。除了丰盛的饭菜可用 feast 表达之外,凡是可吃之物,只要能尽情享受者都可称为 feast,例如 a fruit feast, a fish feast 等。因此,我们将原文的题目译为"The Cherry Feast"。

[2] 首句以"五月里"开始,这个时间词语提供了一个描述的时间框架,译文的首句也以时间词语开始为好。此外,原文文学色彩浓厚,译文也可适当采用一些文学色彩浓厚的形式,例如时间词语与有灵动词的搭配,开头的"五月里……我们回到了挂满樱桃的故乡小院。"这句,可译为: May ... brought us back to my hometown abode.

[3] 在原文里,"挂果的时节"这个时间词语重复出现,在节奏上制造了一种舒缓流畅的阅读感受。因汉英语言之间在表达习惯方面的差异,译文舍弃了原文中这个重复的时间词语。

[4] 霞帔,指古代妇女的一种披肩服饰。在上下文中,"霞帔"也可理解为"彩霞般的光彩",指不同成熟程度的樱桃五颜六色,樱桃树就像裹着五彩衣裳一般。"满身裹着霞帔"可译为 blazing in a sheen of colors from their ripening fruit。

[5] 汉语中的"路"可对应英语中的 road, path, track 等不同词语。根据上下文,这个小句中的"路"应该使用 path,指专供人行走的小路。而 road 指既可供人行走又可供车通行的路,track 指崎岖不平、未经铺砌的小路。

[6] 原文的这几句将"樱桃"分别与"马奶子葡萄"和"玛瑙"相比,从"光鲜"的角度看,马奶子葡萄光鲜,樱桃更光鲜;从"酸甜"的角度看,"樱桃"酸甜,而"玛瑙"则根本没有"酸甜"的特征。因此,原文看似两个相似的比较结构,却不能做简单处理。"樱桃"和"马奶子葡萄"的比较可用比较结构,因为二者同为水果,可译为 defeat them with their brighter shine;和"玛瑙"的比较则不可用比较结构,因为二者不是同类,没有比较的基础,可译为 cherries are luscious, with a flavor absent in the former。

[7] 上文提到,阵雨、细雨过后,樱桃上都挂着水珠,已经得到大自然的洗刷。因此,这句中的"免洗"不是不洗,而是不必自己动手清洗,有多种不同的表达法,可译为 naturally rinsed, washed by mother nature 等。

[8] 根据下文的描述,指"绿的不要多吃",一颗已经足够,可译为 they were not to be overeaten。

[9] "是淡还是咸"是为了描述生动形象而添加的味觉意象,同时传递一种平衡稳重的音韵节奏感,并不是真正表达饭菜中盐量的多少。所以,只需译出"尝不出饭菜的滋味"这个前半部分即可,即 would be too sharp for the taste buds to appreciate meals。

原文

盆　　栽

我对森林钟情有加。喜欢森林,便是醉心于植物,但我对于盆栽的植物,以前却从未提起过真正的兴趣。

森林多木,木繁为林[1],恣意生长,自由存在于天地。盆栽植物有木而无林[2],被"囚"于狭小的盆中,若鸟置于牢笼,若人投于监舍[3],根系得不到尽情舒展,希冀参天,莫若妄言。

森林地阔,可任人游走于其中,脚踩积年落叶,听"泉声咽危石"的声响,赏"日色冷青松"的秀色[4],若还年轻,即使缘木而上,定也不在话下。而盆栽植物,大能揽入怀,小可玩掌中[5],俯视足可透底,甚或一览无余。

森林之长,难以穷尽。如今旅游,森林早已成就了一个极好的卖点[6],被赋予"天然氧吧"和"森林浴"之谓,而"森林浴"竟是从"桑拿浴""日光浴"等称谓派生出来的新新时尚之语。游人陶醉于"天然氧吧"和"森林浴"的洗礼,徜徉于清新自然的空气,即使流连忘返[7]于闹市,想必也并不稀奇。

盆栽植物难以望森林之项背,料想没有人愿意为此打赌辩理,但万事万物皆是有备而来[8]。喜欢森林,却无力把森林搬进房间,这是房间之短抑或森林之弊?"一鸟在手,胜过百鸟在林。"于是,盆栽植物更有了发挥优势的天地。

旷野森林伟岸大气,盆栽植物小巧精致。有些盆栽植物还可变身为盆景,其精巧别致的外形,常常让人叹为观止,免不得充作人们茶余饭后的谈资。有人以此为业,谋生兼及怡情,自然乐此不疲。

盆栽植物是另一种别样的森林,不仅在于它也具有森林般净化空气的实用之功,更在于它能给人森林般的遐思,让人跨越了"只见树木,不见森林"的伤感。你瞧,一盆文竹,弱不禁风,可我凝神枝干,它竟可幻化为参天巨木,硕大无比;我蜕化为蝼蚁,竟能缘木而上,直至梢端;我变身为猿猴,竟在相邻的枝干间,跳跃攀飞。[9]目之所及,心向往之,踵也似接而至。[10]盆栽植物就是缩微版的森林呢,久而久之,我已能深入"空山不见人,但闻人语响"的境地。"境由心造,景由情生"[11],想必就该是这个道理。

我从森林移情于纤小的盆栽植物,一是出于客观世界的无奈,二是出于精神世界的诉求[12]。我道是：
盆栽藏乾坤，乾坤在心底。[13]

译文

Potted Plants

I am an ardent lover of forests. This means I am virtually enthralled by plants. To those growing in planters, however, I never took a genuine liking before.

Forests are lush assemblages of trees growing unhindered in the open wilderness, while potted plants are arboreal entities that live in isolation and, wedged in containers like incarcerated birds or humans with little room to stretch their roots, will never possibly grow into towering giants.

Vast forests are ideal sites where tourists are free to roam as they please, stepping on the thick layers of fallen leaves, drinking in the soothing sound of creeks gurgling over rocks or the somber chill of pine trees intensified by the sun piercing through them. If one is young enough, it should not be too physically demanding for him to ascend a tree. By contrast, potted plants vary in size, from as large as can be taken in the arms to as small as can be held in the hand. A single vertical view can capture their full features from the top down to the root.

Forests are credited with conferring a multitude of benefits. They have now been promoted as a best tourist attraction by the concept of "natural oxygen spa" or "forest bathing", the latter derived by analogy from the trendy term "sauna bathing" or "sunbathing". Tourists, immersing in the invigorating fresh air, get intoxicated by the amenity of the "natural oxygen spa" or "forest bathing". And it is not an uncommon sight that urbanites make frequent escapes into distant forests from metropolitan cities.

It may be undisputed that potted plants are not at par with forests. However, everything has a base for their existence. Much favored as forests are, they are impossible to have in people's indoor living spaces. Is it a weakness on the part of rooms or of forests? Anyway, a bird in the hand is worth two in the bush. This is where potted plants have their strengths coming into fuller play.

In contrast to majestic forests, potted plants are exquisitely petite, and certain species can be manipulated into bonsai, dwarf trees that are often awe-inspiring for their tasteful ingenuity in design, making good fuel for their admirers' leisure chats. When cultivation of bonsai trees is taken up as a profession, it brings a gratification to its practitioners by giving them a living and enjoyment as well.

Potted plants are container-grown "forests" in that they serve not only as an air purifier as natural forests do, but also more as an open source of imagination that alienates one from the regret of "not seeing the forest for the trees". You see, the asparagus fern, for example, looks so delicate living in its container. Under my illusionary gaze, its slender limbs seem to be turning into lofty trunks, and I envision myself being a tiny ant, engaged in an ascent to its top, or being an agile ape, flying between its trunks with the feet following the eyes to wherever the heart wishes to go. Potted plants are indeed miniature forests so to speak. Gradually, I start to visualize in potted plants the same vast serenity that goes with grand forests. This may well be described by the Chinese maxim, "The heart makes the scene, and love makes beauty".

I am getting attached to diminutive potted plants for my love of forests, which are mesmerizing but are not easily accessible in my physical world.

Potted plants as a substitute embed wonder in the heart of the beholder.

注释

[1] 翻译这两个小句,不必拘泥于原文的形式,将意义体现出来即可,合并译为 Forests are lush assemblages of trees。在原文中,两两相对的结构比比皆是,这类结构制造了稳定和谐、整齐对称的形式美,体现了汉文化求偶对称的审美诉求。而英文化则并无类似的审美诉求,除非为了修辞,英语的表达并不崇尚形式上的整齐对称。此外,因为语言文字上的特征,英语的句法构造也难以获得像汉语那种整齐对称的效

果。因此，在多数情况下，汉语特有的音韵节奏在英语中再现是不易的。

［2］同注释［1］，不宜直译，能表达意思即可，即 potted plants are arboreal entities that live in isolation。

［3］这两句可合并译为 like incarcerated birds or humans。Incarcerated 一词可同时与表示人和鸟的名词构成搭配。

［4］译出"泉声咽危石""日色冷青松"这两句古诗的意义即可，不必考虑诗句的形式。

［5］"大能揽入怀，小可玩掌中"这两个小句可用英语的比较结构来表达，可译为 from as large as can be taken in the arms to as small as can be held in the hand。在英语中，比较状语从句中的主语常可缺省，这些缺省的主语通常是语义比较虚的成分，如 it，there，what 等。再举几例：The apartment was as spacious as was advertised. / This is more extreme income inequality than exists in the rest of the country.

［6］"卖点"在英语中可表达为 selling point，原指产品吸引人购买的某个方面，此处指森林是吸引人去旅游的胜地，可译为 a best tourist attraction。

［7］按照一般的理解，"流连忘返"指在一个地方逗留很久，忘记返回，在这个上下文中，指在森林和闹市之间来回往返，说明都市人喜欢森林，不嫌路远。"流连忘返于闹市"可译为 make frequent escapes into distant forests from metropolitan cities。

［8］这句意为"但万事万物的存在都是有理由的"，可译为：However, everything has a base for their existence.

［9］"你瞧，一盆文竹……跳跃攀飞"这几句描写的是作者的想象，"幻化""蜕化""变身"等动词表达的都是"想象"的意思。两个分号分隔的3组句子在语义上是并列的关系，但是可以分出层次，将第二和第三组句子译成并列关系，然后再将其和第一组句子译成并列关系，即 Under my illusionary gaze, its slender limbs seem to be turning into lofty trunks, and I envision myself being a tiny ant ... or being an agile ape ... 这样处理，既充分表达了原文的意思，又可使译文句子的结构富于变化。

［10］这几个小句形容身手十分敏捷，意思是"眼睛看到哪里，心里就想去哪里，脚也跟着过去了"，可译为 with the feet following the eyes to wherever the heart wishes to go。

［11］这两句意为"用心才会产生美丽的风景，有情才能感受其美丽"，可译为：The heart makes the scene, and love makes beauty. 原文的

结构整齐对称,译文也采用了整齐对称的结构,力求在形式上贴近原文。

[12]"客观世界的无奈"指森林地处偏远,作者难以常去;"精神世界的诉求"指作者喜欢森林,但无法接近,只好移情于盆栽植物。这两句不宜直译,可通过 which 引导的关系分句,变通译为 which are mesmerizing but are not easily accessible in my physical world。原文是对称的结构,译文出于表意的简洁而舍弃形式上的对应。此外,"一是……二是……"表达的是原因。英语有多种手段来表达原因,which,who 等关系词引导的关系分句就是其中之一。英语的关系分句可表达原因、条件、让步等多种语义,功能上相当于状语从句,用于比较正式的语体。关于英语关系分句相当于状语从句的用法,详见章振邦编《新编英语语法教程》(第 5 版)(上海外语教育出版社,2013 年版)。

[13]这两句意为"盆栽里潜藏的玄妙,只有用心才能体会到",可译为:Potted plants as a substitute embed wonder in the heart of the beholder.

原文

温 情 电 梯

  我爱乘坐电梯。我工作的扬州大学中心校区主楼就有四部电梯,每天忙忙碌碌,迎来送往,教师、学生川流不息。我穿行其间,一次次感受着温馨,享受着惬意。
  电梯方便、快捷自不用说,可也有不尽人意之时。明明快到了上课的时间,可电梯显示的数字[1]还在高层,让人好不着急;有人到二层以下也乘坐电梯,情急里,眼睁睁盯着那恼人的红色数字[2]。此时唏嘘声一片,我看着急的就不仅仅是我自己。
  更多的时候还是感受到电梯的善解人意。关门时,她就那么"犹豫",即使门关到了一半的位置,只用手那么轻轻一挡,她便柔情地撤回原地。即使有时超出了自身的负荷,警报蜂鸣,其中一人就不得已而退让出去。可爱的是,有几次电梯工作人员示意退出之人再悄悄进来,真神,电梯竟多情地收回"成命"[3],乐哉乐哉将大家送往目的地。不过,有时她也很倔强,分明让人感受到了她的娇气。有一回风大,到了该到的楼层时她就不放行,没办法,还是几个人合力掰开了她的"双手",挤了出去。
  电梯间充满了人间温情,熟人相见,免不了要打声招呼,遇到上了年岁的教师,还免不了彼此谦让,让进让出[4]。温情的电梯此时竟免不了流露出一点愠怒,半关的门在催促人们加快脚步。单纯的电梯呀,你哪里知道人间之情更多更浓?但愿情常在,慢嫌礼繁缛。
  电梯里有时很热闹,热闹的多是那些成群结队的女同学,叽叽喳喳,一路歌声,满间都是笑语。有时又静得出奇,特别是当与异性独处时,那小小的"房间"里竟死一般沉寂,少了份自在,空气也有些凝滞。此时,巴不得赶快赶到该去的楼层。或许有人宁愿电梯放慢脚步也未可知。
  我爱电梯,就愿使电梯面貌"更上层楼"。悬挂一面钟?提醒人们惜时;镶上一面镜?让人们注意尊容[5]。我看最好在红色数字的上方嵌一面五星红旗,人们在举目凝视数字时,情感更添厚重。虽说电梯有升有降,但电梯间里的五星红旗一如既往,岿然不动。
  电梯间里有几多温情?让我尽情享受此时此刻的人生。有时独自一人从高层直下 B(basement)层,让人恍若隔世[6],乘坐之人便多一层对生命的珍重。

{ 译文 }

Warmth in the Elevator

  I love riding elevators. There are four elevators installed in the main building on the main campus of Yangzhou University where I work. They go up and down every day, busily taking teachers and students to their floors. Whenever I am in one, I can always perceive cozy warmth in the small space.

  The elevator offers quick and convenient transportation, but it could also be disappointing sometimes. For example, if one is waiting to take an elevator close to class time, he will most likely fall into impatience when the indicator shows that the elevator is still stopping at a high floor. Or, if one is in a hurry, he can possibly get annoyed at the sight of a passenger taking the elevator to a floor lower than the second, and the only thing he can do is to stare helplessly at the red numeral on the inside indicator. The audible impatient sighs from others tell me that I am not the only one that cannot take it easy in such cases.

  In more cases, however, the elevator is considerate. She seems to be so hesitant when she closes her doors. Even when the doors are already half closed, she will gently have them retreat back to their fully open position if a hand is raised and goes between them. Occasionally the elevator buzzer gives off a loud warning, alarming an overload of capacity, and one of the passengers has to go out. Many a time when the operator motions to the passenger to slip in, quite amazingly, the elevator resumes its work and cheerily takes the passengers to their destination. Sometimes she is unruly and unyielding. On one occasion when it was windy, she reached where it should be, but refused to open. The passengers had no way but to force the doors apart with their hands to squeeze their way out.

The elevator is a space brimming with human warmth. When one meets an acquaintance there, naturally they will go into an exchange of friendly greetings. When one runs into a senior teacher there, either side will courteously give the other the right of way. The elevator that is normally good-tempered shows a bit of annoyance at this and urges the passengers to quicken their pace by closing her doors halfway. Lovely elevator, don't you know that humans are beings that hold greater and deeper love for each other? May the social etiquette promote a lasting attachment between them!

Sometimes the elevator is lively when noisy female students go in groups, chattering and singing all the way, filling the whole space with happy laughter. Other times it is embarrassingly quiet, especially when one rides alone with another of the opposite sex. In such a small "room" of deadly silence, there is less comfort and the air seems to be stagnant. One's only wish may be to reach his or her floor as quickly as possible. Or, there may be someone who oppositely wishes the elevator to slow down her pace on an occasion like this. Who knows?

As a lover of elevators, I would like them to take on a nicer look. How about fixing a clock on one of the walls so that people could be reminded to make a better use of time? Or, a mirror so that people could check their appearance by looking into it? It might be best to have a national flag hung above the inside indicator so that it could inspire more patriotism in people when they look up at the indicator. While the elevator makes its way up and down, the flag would stay as unshakable as ever.

How much warmth I have felt in my elevator rides! It makes me enjoy these moments of life to the fullest. Whenever I take an elevator alone from a high floor right down to the basement level, I feel as if it was taking me into a world of confinement, which prompts me to treasure life with a greater respect.

注释

[1]"电梯显示的数字"指电梯门外上方的显示屏上显示的数字,译为 the indicator shows。

[2]这句中的"红色数字"指电梯内上方显示屏上显示的红色数字,译为 the red numeral on the inside indicator。

[3]"收回'成命'"指重新开始工作,原文将电梯拟人化,译文保留了这一修辞格,但适当减少了原文的形象表达,省略了原文的一些形象色彩,更加符合英语的表达习惯,例如将"收回'成命'"译为 resumes its work,下文的"合力掰开了她的'双手'"译为 to force the doors apart。

[4]"彼此谦让,让进让出"指"双方都谦让,让对方先行",可译为 either side will courteously give the other the right of way。

[5]"注意尊容"指照镜子而整衣冠,不可机械地照字面译为 remind people to pay attention to their appearance,可译为 people could check their appearance by looking into it。

[6]"恍若隔世"不应理解为阴阳隔世或类似的意义,而是指"仿佛进入一个与世隔绝的世界",可译为 as if it was taking me into a world of confinement。

原文

下雪的季节

下雪的季节,稀罕的,也就是那个雪哟!

"千里冰封,万里雪飘"的世界晶莹剔透,银装素裹;"山舞银蛇,原驰蜡象"的大地玉洁冰清,清爽而浪漫[1]。

我喜欢下雪,喜欢看那悄无声息、飘然而至的漫天飞舞的大雪;喜欢在飞雪中傻站着,看自己转眼间变成须发皆白的耄耋老翁;喜欢看棱角分明的雪花飘落于掌心又转瞬消融的踪影;喜欢看雪天在白皑皑一望无垠的原野上村庄房屋被大雪"淹没"而显露出的只是冒烟的烟囱。大雪纷飞里,总能瞥见人们堆雪人找鼻子、装眼睛忙碌的身影,老远就能听到大人小孩借东讨西[2]的那份激情。春节了,还能看到雪帘中通红的春联透出的那份喜庆,正月里最好看的,是远处雪地里走亲串友在雪白的背景上游动的点点绿红。我喜欢走在雪地里,感受那咯吱咯吱的响声;喜欢看小鸟成群结队飘落而至匆忙觅食转眼间又扑棱棱飞走的身形……抓一把雪,揉成蛋儿,塞入同伴的衣领;邀同学于树下,朝树身上跺一脚,看雪面儿抖落的壮观,听人家数落还要提防对方的"报复"行动。农民盼下雪呀,盼它个"正月十五雪打灯""瑞雪兆丰年"[3];城里人盼下雪呀,盼它增加湿润、减少疾病。孩子们盼下雪,盼的可是雪地里的嬉戏;青年人盼下雪,玉树下相机里留下的是芳姿倩影。

小时候,那个雪下得就格外的大。一夜无声,感觉天不该亮的时候窗户却已发白,窥视窗外,谁知早已是大雪封门。白雪映着青光[4],满目都是玉雕的枝枝丫丫。裹在被窝里,就喜欢听大人在院里扫雪,也喜欢跟着大人手托竹竿、拴上笤圈将积雪从草房子上刮下。大人们望着雪,说要是雪变成白面可就不忍饥了;小孩子们望着雪,说要是雪能变成白糖,想啥时候解馋就能解馋。房檐下常常挂着冰柱,小孩子用力地咀嚼,牙冰木了,嘴却不闲,还说自己吃的是冰棍儿,人家吃的冰棍儿也不过就是多了一点点甜。漫天雪地里,最多的感受还是浪漫。带着狗,在沟沟坎坎的雪地里寻找黄色的出气孔[5]。陡然间,看到一只野兔从雪底下窜出来,惊愕之余,孩子和狗就拼命地在雪野深一脚浅一脚地狂奔,嘴里哈着白气,身上冒着热汗。捉到了,是惊喜;捉不到,也乐此不疲。茫茫的原野上,到处似乎都是一个模样,迷失方向也是常有的事,有时还要驻足观瞧,想努力找到人的足迹。

在乡下,大雪天围着火堆烤火也别有一番情趣。烤一把粉条,眼见粉条在火苗中由细变粗;执一把铁勺,听黄豆爆裂的声响,享受满屋飘着的香气。想吃咸的吗?就有人积极,撒入的却是一把盐似的雪[6]。看哪,孩子们闹翻了[7],旋即重归于好,一起凝视雪水如何在铁勺里、在那嗞嗞声中消逝。烤火?还想长点见识。听大人们侃大山,侃中原比不上大东北,那里雪更大,天更冷,尿出来的干脆就是冰棍棍儿,掉地上也不烂,之后准能听到唏嘘声[8]不断;侃冰河里刨个洞,就有鱼儿往上跳,之后还能听到咂嘴声,说鱼肉有啥好吃,刺又多又乱[9];侃冰河上能开坦克车,就忍不住再尝试到池塘的冰面上沿冰去寻找那份惊险。

正月一过,就很难觅到雪的踪迹。不过,苍天或许有情,在桃花烂漫的初春时节,差不多还要恩赐人间一场与桃花共舞的飞雪。"三月还下桃花雪呢"[10],也就成了缠绵于雪的人们新的希冀。

又是一个下雪的季节。我渴望感受多雪的故乡和我那风情万种的北国。

译文

The Season of Snow

For the season of snow, a most welcome sight for the eyes is the snow itself.

Ice-bound and snow-covered, the vast landscape is a crystal white with all colors drained away from it, and the undulating plain a romantic purity of icy powder with white mountains meandering their way across it.

I love snow. I love to watch fluffy snowflakes swirling and twirling down gently and silently from the heavens. I love to stand in the fluttering snow and to be dusted white shortly over the hair and beard like an old man. I love to catch pointed snowflakes on the palm and see them melt instantly. I love to gaze upon the village houses that are submerged in a white mantle of snow, with only their smoking chimneys being distinctly visible. Amid snow flurries there are always people who are busily immersed in building a snowman, adding a nose here, putting eyes there, or are loudly enthusiastic in borrowing items from one household to another. Shining through the fringes of snowy icicles hanging off the eave is the festivity of the red couplets pasted on the front door for celebrating the Chinese Spring Festival. The most pleasing sight for the Chinese lunar January is the tiny human figures of different colors moving about in the distant snow. I also appreciate the crunchy protest of the snow beneath the boots, or the sight of little birds that land on the ground in flocks in a hurried forage for food and then flap away in a rush of wings. And the snow tricks, too. One scoops up some snow, shapes it into a ball and slips it into the collar of a playmate. Or one induces a pal to go under a snow-coated tree, and stomps at its trunk, sending snow cascading down onto the victim; while he is enjoying the spectacular scene, he is bombarded with complaints from his adversary and at the same time has to watch out for a counterstroke. Snow is a blessing, expected by farmers for the bountiful harvest it can herald for the coming autumn, by urban people for a moistened air and a reduced spread of diseases, by children for play and games in the snow, and by young people for the pictures they can take of themselves against snow-laden trees.

  I used to see much heavier snowfalls when I was small. Snow drifted down, soundless, during the night, and dawn awoke early to reveal a white world outside the window and unexpectedly a snow-blocked front door as well. The snow was glowing white with a bluish tint, and turned trees and their branches all into statues of white crystal. It was a joy snuggling warm under the cozy bed cover and listening to my parents clearing snow in the courtyard, or sometimes helping them scrape snow off the roof of the thatched house with a bamboo pole attached with a flat basket on its top. Snow being so white, how parents wished it were flour that could satisfy hunger, how children wished it were castor sugar that they could taste whenever they wanted to. There were often icicles dangling from the eave and they were a tasteless delicacy for children. Though their teeth got numbed from chewing on these icicles, they did not forget to pretend that they were eating popsicles, ones that were just lacking in a sweet flavor. In the vast stretches of snow, the most frequent sensation was the romantic ambiance.

Out in the lumpy snow, followed by a dog, children were trying to stalk hares by way of locating their brownish breathing holes; at any moment a hare could suddenly burst into view from beneath the snow. Immediately the children and the dog limped along in their desperate chase after it, breathing frostily and sweating heatedly. It was a delight if they managed to catch it, and if not, they would never feel frustrated. As the immense snow blanket seemed to be disguising the world in the same uniform, losing the sense of direction was not uncommon, and one had to stop from time to time to look for human trails to follow.

In rural villages, snow days were also happy moments when villagers sat around a fire warming themselves. Bean starches swelled thick over the fire in no time. And beans, frying in an iron vessel over the fire, gave off crackling sounds and an inviting aroma as well. What about adding a salty taste to the beans? Someone mischievously sprinkled some snow into the vessel! Alas, children fell out with each other for that, but they reconciled instantly, watching together the sizzling evaporation of the snowy water in the vessel. Around the fire for warmth only? No. Something eye-opening would enhance the fun. Adults shot the breeze about how much colder it was in the northeast than in the central region for heavier snows and lower temperatures. They said in the northeast pee would come out frozen and remain unbroken even when hitting the ground, which was followed by disbelieving hisses from the listeners. Hearing that fish would jump right out of a river through the hole cut into its frozen surface, someone smacked his mouth hungrily but comforted himself by saying what was the good in eating fish with so many tiny bones in it. And the frozen rivers there, as adults said, could even support a tank driving across, and that sparked a craving in the child listeners for an adventure of skating on a frozen pond.

After the lunar January, snow is a rarity. However, the heavens may shed mercy on snow lovers and shower down in early spring when peach flowers are in brilliant bloom an occasional snow, whirling in the air together with flying peach petals. Thus the wish for snow lingers into March in the heart of people loving snow.

It is another season of snow now. I yearn for the snow in my hometown and the wintry charms of my central north.

> 注释

[1] 这一段描写的是北国雪景的壮观景象,作者将毛泽东《沁园春·雪》一诗中的诗句引用到原文中,作为"世界"和"大地"的修饰语,来增强表达气势,以获得更好的表达效果。译文将诗句中的"山""银蛇""蜡象"等意象加以整合,将"千里冰封,万里雪飘"意译为 ice-bound and snow-covered,将"山舞银蛇,原驰蜡象"意译为 the undulating plain (is) a romantic purity of icy powder with white mountains meandering their way across it。

[2] "借东讨西"指村人走东串西借东西,可译为 borrowing items from one household to another。

[3] "正月十五雪打灯"和"瑞雪兆丰年"是中国文化中的农谚,前者完整的表述是"八月十五云遮月,正月十五雪打灯",意思是说,农历八月十五这一天如果是阴天或者下雨,则来年正月十五这一天就会下雪。原文引用"正月十五雪打灯"这一句,只是借用了其中的"雪"的意象,来增强话语表达的气势,简单地说就是"农民盼下雪"的意思,译文不一定非得把这个农谚完整地表达出来不可。因此,译者将意义加以整合而译为:Snow is a blessing, expected by farmers for the bountiful harvest it can herald for the coming autumn.

[4] 白雪为什么会映着青光?雪越厚,吸收的红光越多,从而显出蓝色,天刚蒙蒙亮时,光线暗淡,厚雪越加显得发蓝,"白雪映着青光"可译为 the snow was glowing white with a bluish tint。

[5] "黄色的出气孔"是野兔在雪地里活动时留下的痕迹,野兔躲在厚雪底下,需要呼吸,洞口因野兔出入而沾染黄色的痕迹,可译为 their brownish breathing holes。

[6] "就有人积极"是反语,译文中添加 mischievously 一词,表达了这个反语的言下之意。

[7] 孩子们闹翻是因为有人恶作剧,在炒豆子的锅中撒了雪,可译为 children fell out with each other for that,译文中添加介词短语 for that,以明确"闹翻"的原因。

[8] "唏嘘声"描述的是听者难以置信的反应,可译为 which was followed by disbelieving hisses from the listeners。

[9] 听者听到"鱼"嘴巴就馋,咂嘴巴,但吃不到,只能自我安慰说

"鱼肉有啥好吃",这是酸葡萄心理,可译为 someone smacked his mouth hungrily but comforted himself by saying what was the good in eating fish with so many tiny bones in it。

[10]"三月还下桃花雪"是中国文化中的农谚,说的是桃花盛开的春天还有下雪的可能。在上文,原文对于三月的下雪美景已经做了描述,译文也充分表达了原文描述的桃花雪的美景。这个农谚表达的意思与上文相同,此处引用属于语义叠加,因此,译文可省略这个农谚的形象。

原文

一轮舞阳照贾湖[1]

"贾湖"在"舞阳","舞阳"在"河南","河南"在"中国"[2]。这一连串富含诗意的地名,如今都被第8次试掘的"贾湖"文化遗址[3]紧密地串在一起。

贾湖在河南。提起河南,其文化底蕴之丰厚,足令诸多雅士如数家珍般娓娓道来:安阳之殷墟(甲骨文发现地)、洛阳之白马寺(唐玄奘白马驮经处)、开封之开封府(宋代开封府尹"青天"包拯府衙)、焦作之云台山("竹林七贤"隐居地)……贾湖,准确地说位于舞阳境内,一处因城在舞水之阳而得名的县级所在地[4]。

河南下辖舞阳,而舞阳群聚了诸多河南文化之圣。君可见"项庄舞剑,意在沛公"的鸿门宴和西汉刘邦大将樊哙的生性猛烈吗?樊哙被封为"舞阳侯"而长眠于封侯之地。君可知三国时的司马懿曾在舞阳封侯拜帅吗?君可闻五代十国的前蜀皇帝王建生于斯而北宋平西王狄青葬于斯吗?凡此种种,令舞阳享有"帝国侯乡"之谓,也就不足为奇了[5]。

但此时此刻,多少文化经典之地却悄悄收敛了锋芒,将更加璀璨之光聚焦于舞阳县下辖的贾湖村,聚焦于考古发现的诸多新石器之"最"[6]和中国国务院公布的"全国重点文物保护单位"之地。

贾湖文化遗址,就有8项占据世界鳌头:它发现了世界上最早的7声音阶乐器;它发现了世界上最早的"酒";它发现了世界上最早的文字雏形之一的契刻符号;它还是世界上最早的原始宗教与卜筮起源地之一、世界上最早的稻作农业起源地之一、世界上最早的家畜驯养地之一、世界上最早的纺织业起源地之一和世界上最早的渔业人工养殖地。因贾湖文化遗址的光芒,我宁愿曲解"舞阳"地名之意而作别用。贾湖不就是一轮新生、耀眼的"舞阳"("跳舞的太阳"/the Dancing Sun)[7]而令人炫目的吗?

就说这乐器,迄今已出土30多支用鹤骨制成的骨笛,长度大约在17.3—24.6厘米之间,有2孔、5孔、6孔、7孔、8孔不等,是世界上出土个数最多、保存最完整、到今天仍能吹奏的最早乐器实物,豁然把人类音乐史推进到9 000年前,其研究成果发表在《Nature》杂志上,其考古成果则被镌刻在北京"中华世纪坛"[8]青铜甬道的显要位置。

再说这发酵饮品的"酒",研究报告就发表在《PNAS》杂志上[9]。美国 Dogfish Head-Chateau Jiahu 啤酒,就是依据贾湖"酒"提取物而研制的配方。10月5日在达拉斯得克萨斯大学(UTD)举办的第37次孔子沙龙[10] Wine and Chinese Culture 还认为,中国最早的造酒有6 000多年的历史,我便不无自豪地将其更新并推进了3 000来年的光阴[11]。

我虽不事考古,却乐意作文化体验之游。早就慕名贾湖,一直未能成行。适逢前几日"纪念贾湖遗址发掘30周年暨贾湖文化国际研讨会"在《说文解字》作者许慎的故里漯河市召开,我作为从故乡走出来的学者,应邀出席了此次盛会,分享了考古专家的发现和收获之喜。

研究会规格之高,自不必说;论题之广,超出了预期。最让我兴奋的是亲临考古现场。平生第一次亲临考古,看到考古专家小心翼翼地剥离文物,甚至还要筛出墓穴里的土壤,做各个学科的分析。每一具尸骨的头颈处都陪葬了一只烧制的陶壶,很难想象,人类竟是用情感和眼泪从远古一路传承,生生不息。

"瞧,那个墓穴里有笛子!"
"看,那具尸骨旁不是箭镞嘛!"
"唉,那副石碾肯定是那个古人碾稻谷用过的!"
…………

观者的指指点点、大惊小呼,却在各自心头化作了情感复杂的啧啧和唏嘘[12]。解读远古文明,最好亲临现场,好将厚重的历史一页页翻起[13]。

不过瘾,第二天我又陪父母亲身体验了一回。母亲问,这是谁家的祖先?他们的后辈在哪里?是呀,他们是一群什么样的人?又来自哪里?听专家介绍,这些古人身高都在170厘米和190厘米之间,这样的高度,对于远古的人类,实在匪夷所思。

贾湖文化遗址处于河南省纵贯南北的文化带上[14]。从南至北,就有南阳诸葛(三国诸葛亮)文化—舞阳贾湖文化—漯河许慎文化—郑州商城文化、少林文化—安阳殷墟文化等多处遗迹。体验这一文化带,若要尽兴,少则两日,多则三四日,尽可满载而归。倦了,泡泡舞阳新近开发的盐浴,更有别样滋味在心头。真可谓:

一轮舞阳照贾湖,舞阳贾湖耀四方[15]!

译文

Jiahu: Site of Shining Glory

Jiahu, Wuyang, Henan and China, a poetic array of place names, are now again showing up together in the limelight, along with the eighth archaeological excavation of the Jiahu site, a settlement occupied by ancient Jiahu people in the early Neolithic Period.

Jiahu is a village in Henan Province of central China. When it comes to this province, people of scholarly tastes can often mention with familiarity a cultural opulence it flaunts, for example, the ruins in Anyang City of the last capital of the Shang Dynasty (1600 BC – 1046 BC), where Chinese Oracle Bone and Tortoise Shell Inscriptions were unearthed, the White Horse Temple in Luoyang City that was constructed in the year of 68 in memory of the white horse of the Tang Dynasty (618 – 907) monk Xuanzang (602 – 664) after it carried the Buddhist Sutras to ancient Luoyang City, the remains in Kaifeng City of the ancient Kaifeng City Hall, once the *Yamen* where the upright judge Baozheng (999 – 1062) of the Song Dynasty (960 – 1279) heard cases, Mount Yuntai in Jiaozuo City, a retreat place for the "seven sages of the bamboo groove" living in the Three Kingdoms Period (220 – 280), i.e. the seven ancient Chinese scholars and poets who withdrew from the then political officialdom to a life of wine and literature in a secluded bamboo groove in Mount Yuntai.

Precisely speaking, Jiahu Village lies within the limits of Wuyang, a county in Henan Province with its name deriving from its location on the "Yang" side, i.e. the south side, of the Wushui River, meaning the side facing the "Yang", i.e. the sun. Wuyang County is a territory teeming with historical and cultural giants in Henan history. Did you ever hear of Fan Kuai (242 BC – 189 BC), a valiant military general who served Liu Bang (256 BC – 195 BC), first emperor of the Han Dynasty (206 BC – AD 220), and saved his life at the Hongmen banquet where Xiang Zhuang performed his sword art as the cover for his attempt on Liu Bang's life, Fan

Kuai was conferred the title "Marquis of Wuyang" in his life and was buried at his conferral place after his death. Do you happen to know that Sima Yi (179 – 251) of the Three Kingdoms period was also granted the title "Marquis of Wuyang"? And what about Wang Jian (847 – 918) and Di Qing? The former, emperor of the Former Shu (907 – 925) in the Five Dynasties and Ten Kingdoms period (907 – 960), was born in ancient Wuyang while the latter, King of Pingxi of the North Song Dynasty (960 – 1127), was buried there. It is no surprise that Wuyang County is reputed as a land of ancient imperial nobles.

Now at this moment when the Jiahu site is revealed to the world, classic cultural sites elsewhere seem to have quietly turned down their brilliance and given way to Jiahu Village of Wuyang County, where the Jiahu site lies shining with a brighter glory for the discoveries made there of the achievements by Neolithic Jiahu people and for its listing by the State Council of the PRC as an "important heritage site under state protection".

The Jiahu site yields evidence about Neolithic human achievements and outshines all others in as many as eight fields. They are the earliest musical instruments with a heptatonic scale, the earliest alcoholic beverage, one of the earliest forms of writing, i. e. the pictograms incised into tortoise shells, one of the birthplaces of primitive religion and divination, of rice cultivation, of animal domestication and of textile production, and finally the place of origin where aquaculture began its practice. For the cultural relics that the Jiahu site is resplendent with, I would like to twist the name Wuyang and interpret it as meaning "a dancing sun" ("wu" is "to dance" and "yang" "the sun" at the basic level of word meaning). In this reading of mine, isn't Jiahu village of Wuyang County gleaming like a bright, newly risen sun?

In terms of musical instruments, excavations have so far yielded more than thirty crane bone flutes measuring between 17.3 and 24.6 centimeters in length and carved with two, five, six, seven or eight holes. These flutes constitute the greatest number of the oldest instruments that have remained intact and still playable, and suggest a Chinese music tradition that dates as far back as 9,000 years ago. The scientific researches of these flutes were described and published in the journal *Nature* and their archaeological discovery was engraved in a prominent spot in the bronze path leading to the

China Millennium Monument in Beijing.

And the fermented alcoholic beverage was chemically examined through residue analysis and the results of the researches appeared in the journal *Proceedings of the National Academy of Sciences*. The American beer "Dogfish Head-Chateau Jiahu" had its brewing recipe formulated right on the basis of the residues extracted from the ancient Jiahu liquor. At the 37th session of Confucius salon on the theme "Wine and Chinese Culture", held on October 5, 2013 in the University of Texas at Dallas, the speaker claimed that Chinese people had a more than 6,000-year history of making liquor. I can now pronounce with pride that the Jiahu beverage predates the evidence for that history record by three millennia.

Though not an archaeologist, I was expectant of an exposure to the culture of the Jiahu site, which I had long been admiring but never had a chance to visit. It happened that the "Commemoration of the 30th Anniversary of Jiahu Site Excavation and International Seminar on Jiahu Culture" was held several days ago in Luohe City, Henan Province, the birthplace of Xu Shen (about 58 – 147), compiler of the East Han Dynasty (25 – 220) dictionary *Shuo Wen Jie Zi* (literally "Explaining Simple Characters and Analyzing Compound Characters"). As a scholar native to the host city, I attended the symposium by invitation and enjoyed knowing the happy discoveries made by archaeologists.

The symposium was of a high level and covered a wider range of topics than had been unexpected. The most thrilling experience was my visit to the excavation site, watching for the first time in my life the archaeologists removing cautiously the earth from around the excavated objects or sorting out samples of soil from the tombs for interdisciplinary analyses. Beside the head and neck of each body was entombed a pottery artifact, the burial object that embodies tears and emotion of the human population in their progression from one generation to the next.

"Look, there are flutes in that tomb."

"Hey, isn't it an arrow head beside the body?"

"Wow, that's a stone roller! The occupant must have used it to grind rice."

…

The spectators pointed and exclaimed, their multiple feelings articulated in the gasps and sighs coming out from the heart. For a better appreciation of a remote culture in its entirety, it would be advisable for one to be physically present at its excavation site so that he could dip into the richness of its tradition.

Not fully contented, I returned to the Jiahu site the next day together with my parents. Mother was curious as to who were those buried as ancestors, and where their descendants went. Yes, who were they and where were they from? According to the specialists, the ancients buried at the site, somewhere between 170 to 190 centimeters in height, were impressively tall for people living in the Neolithic period.

The Jiahu site sits in a longitudinal belt in Henan Province that is home to cultures originating from different historical periods. From south to north, these cultural relics include the sites in Nanyang City of Zhuge Liang (181-234), a statesman and strategist in the Three Kingdoms period, the Jiahu site in Wuyang County, the sites in Luohe City of Xu Shen, complier of *Shuo Wen Jie Zi*, as was mentioned above, the ruins in Zhengzhou City of an ancient Shang Dynasty City, the Shaolin Temple in Zhengzhou City, whose construction started in the year of 495, the ruins in Anyang City of the last capital of the Shang Dynasty, etc. Normally it will take at least two days, or preferably, three to four days to do full justice to such an abundance of historical and cultural heritages. To relieve the fatigue, if there is, from the tour, one can take a soak in the sea salt bath, a recent recreation available in Wuyang County, and it will sure add a special flavor to his experience.

The Jiahu site, the shining glory of Wuyang County, radiates upon the rest of the world by the richness of its cultural patrimony.

注释

[1]"舞阳"即河南省的舞阳县,是作者的故乡。"舞阳"中的"阳"本为"舞水河的阳面"的意思,作者按照其字面意义,将其别解为"跳舞的太阳",因此,有紧接的"照贾湖"一说。假如直译,并不能体现别解的"舞阳"和正解的地名之间的意义联系。因此,题目意译为"Jiahu:

Site of Shining Glory"。

［2］这是螺旋形表达的又一例，后一分句以前一分句结尾的词语开头，前后词语如链条一般重复出现，构成顶真句式，这是汉语尤其是文学作品中常见的表达方式，是增加文学色彩的修辞手段之一，而英语则很少采用类似的螺旋形表达方式，假如第一句直译成 Jiahu is in Wuyang, Wuyang is in Henan and Henan is in China，并不符合英语的表达习惯，可能无法向译语读者传递同等美感，可变通处理为 Jiahu, Wuyang, Henan and China, a poetic array of place names。此外，即使中国读者也不一定知道"贾湖""舞阳"等地名的行政级别，英语读者更是如此。所以，添加表示类别的名称是有必要的。考虑到第一句中的地名表达应以简洁为主，此处没有添加 village, county/city, province 等类属名词。下文再提及"贾湖""舞阳""河南"等地理名词时，可添加这些类属词语。

［3］"'贾湖'文化遗址"译为 the Jiahu site，并添加了 a settlement of ancient Jiahu people in the Neolithic Age 这个同位语，作为对中心语的信息补充。

［4］这个段落中的文化信息量非常庞大，有必要在译文中适当补充背景信息，翻译"殷墟""唐玄奘白马驮经处""'竹林七贤'隐居地"等几处时，都添加了必要的背景信息。这样，整个段落变得非常庞大，本段的最后一句，在语义上与上文的衔接就不是很紧密，因此，挪到了下一段。

［5］这个段落包含的文化信息也很多，翻译"舞水之阳""刘邦""项庄舞剑，意在沛公"等几处时，都添加了必要的信息。

［6］"诸多新石器之'最'"中的"最"是就目前为止的考古发现而言的，实际就是"新石器时代贾湖人的成就"的意思，可译为 the achievements by Neolithic Jiahu people。

［7］"跳舞的太阳"译为 a dancing sun，并在括号中补充动词"跳"和语素"舞"的意义，即"wu" is "to dance" and "yang" "the sun" at the basic level of word meaning，以便让译语读者明白为什么"舞阳"可理解为"跳舞的太阳"。

［8］"中华世纪坛"是一座艺术博物馆，位于北京市，英语名为 the China Millennium Monument。

［9］在"研究报告就发表在《PNAS》杂志上"这句的译文中补充了"研究"的手段，即 was chemically examined through residue analysis，使译文的语义更加连贯。

[10]"孔子沙龙"指孔子学院举办的沙龙活动,可译为 the Confucius salon。中国政府为加强世界对中国语言和文化的了解而设立"孔子学院",总部设在北京,在世界各地设立分支机构,绝大多数的分支机构与境外的大学合作。除了开设语言文化课程之外,境外的"孔子学院"还定期举办讲座等活动,传播中国的文化。

[11]"更新"和"推进"是创新表达法,意为"我可以自豪地说贾湖酒的历史比现有的考古记录早了 3 000 年",可译为:I can now pronounce with pride that the Jiahu beverage predates the evidence for that history record by three millennia.

[12]此处指参观者不时发出"啧啧"和"唏嘘"声,表达了不同的复杂情感,可译为 their multiple feelings articulated in the gasps and sighs coming out from the heart。

[13]比喻用法,意为"体会和感受厚重的历史",可译为 so that he could dip into the richness of its tradition。

[14]河南省纵贯南北文化带,文化沉淀来自不同的历史时期,因此译文中的 cultures 一词后面添加了修饰语 originating from different historical periods。

[15]原文的这两句结构对称,译文无法取得形式上的对等,为清楚表达语义,处理为:The Jiahu site, the shining glory of Wuyang County, radiates upon the rest of the world by the richness of its cultural patrimony. 译文保留了原文的大部分意思,并通过 by 引导的介词短语,补充了必要的信息。

原文

青 岛 纪 行

  3月下旬,我与另外两位同事出差奔赴青岛。希冀中,踏上发自上海经镇江直到青岛的火车。
  火车一路颠簸,走南京,过蚌埠,穿徐州,[1]从济南折转向东,横插青岛,出发前,已从网上查到有关火车运行的信息,意味着我们必须摇上18个小时才能到达目的地。火车铿锵之音并不悦耳,叮叮咚咚,吱吱呀呀[2]。下午3点40坐的火车,逢站还要伸头看看站牌,掐算离青岛的距离。盼了天黑,又望天亮,难耐中,却也到了青岛的土地。看看表,离到站时间还有半个小时,那就电话通知友人吧,20分钟后接站不迟。
  "大家做好准备,火车要提前进站!"
  列车员甩上这么一句不着边际的话,我们并不十分在意。他可能也疲惫了,想活跃一下车上的气氛。转脸看,列车员一脸的严肃。只见过火车晚点,哪有提前进站的道理!
  减速。刹车。火车戛然而止。[3]啊!竟提前足足20分钟。肯定诧异,诧异中传递着人们的惊喜。
  接站的友人还没到,我们在凉飕飕的海风中抖衣而立。前后左右,时不时传来旅客们向友人打电话祈望早接站,不曾想火车还有提前进站的话语。瞧,寡闻的不光是我们。这就是青岛,是青岛给了我们一个一生也不会忘记的惊喜。
  司机载着我们沿海滨大道飞驰。路有坡度,才上顶巅,又下谷底。马路洁净、宽敞,现代化的建筑鳞次栉比。早闻青岛的自然景观是"红瓦、绿树、碧海、蓝天",也闻青岛的人文旅游是"喝啤酒、吃海鲜、洗海澡、看崂山"[4]。这自然景观已然领略,不错,这就是梦中的青岛,和画上画的一般不二。惊羡之余,不由得发出一声叹息。不提防,司机回了一句:"镶着金边的抹布。"细究之,方知青岛沿海发展较快,远海处无法与之攀比。青岛房价太高,令人咋舌;外国人多,外来人多,消费一路见长……青岛人,没想到[5],抱怨迭起!
  初春时节,北方还裹着寒意。洗海澡,还不到季节;吃海鲜,可不能光顾自己。先买上一包,也让家人尝尝正宗的青岛海鲜。至于看崂山,那是青岛胜地,怎能有不看之理!

与青岛友人相聚,肯定少不了啤酒、海鲜。听友人点酒,就要"今天才出的啤酒"。我喝过多年的酒,可也不曾有过如此点酒的体验;上海鲜,硬是端上一些我叫不上名的。这也是知识,不懂就问呗,吃要吃出个名堂。一盘岩石状的物质,谁知就是书本中的牡蛎;一条扁头鱼,就是查查书,也未必知道它叫"摆甲"。不知道这鱼会不会也是人工养殖的,友人说:"哪能呢,这鱼离开海水就死。"

早提劲要爬崂山,只可惜时间太短。而且,同伴也都去过,我实在不情愿再劳动大家。那就等下次吧,等啤酒节,或别的更浪漫的时节。友人说,要读懂青岛,就要深入它的文化。

"再过几天等花儿开了再来,才好看呢!"从出租汽车司机的话里话外,我已然悟出青岛人对家乡的挚爱。爱与怨生,那可是人世间万物的运行之理。

短暂的一天半一闪即逝,当青岛的太阳爬上10层楼高之时[6],我的喜悦早已化作电话那端睡梦中家人的梦呓。

译文

A Trip to Qingdao

One late March day, I went with two colleagues on a business trip to Qingdao City. Expectantly, we boarded the train bound for our destination that departed from Shanghai via Zhengjiang.

The train chugged along, past Nanjing, Bengbu and Xuzhou all the way to Jinan, where it turned east and cut its way right into Qingdao. Prior to my departure, I had checked the train schedule on the Internet and learned that it would be an 18 hour bumpy journey. The train clanged unpleasantly along the tracks. We got on board at 3∶40 pm, and after that whenever it stopped along the way, I would always peer out of the window to see the station board, trying to figure out the amount of distance left to cover. The day passed and the night came. And it was the day again. At last, the train was running on the land of Qingdao. My watch told me there was still 30 minutes away from the scheduled arrival time. I might as well call our friend, telling him to meet us at the terminus in 20 minutes.

"Passengers, your attention, please! The train will be arriving at the terminus ahead of schedule. Please get yourselves ready."

This announcement of the attendant's we dismissed as a mere joke. Maybe he was bored himself and wished to lighten the atmosphere. We took another look at his face, which was serious, showing no sign of joking. A train was always known to arrive late, but how come it was earlier this time?

Slowing down, pulling into the station, the train screeched to a halt. Alas! It was ahead of schedule by 20 minutes. The passengers were happy, as happy as they were surprised.

We stood shivering in the chilly wind from the sea, waiting for the friend to meet us. Now and then, passengers were heard talking on the phone, telling the other end to meet them because the train had arrived earlier. You see, we were not the only ones that felt it was a fresh experience. It was Qingdao that gave us an unforgettable memory as soon as we set foot on it.

We sped along the seaside boulevard in a taxi. The vehicle lurched up and down on the wavy road. Coming into sight were clean, broad streets and a vast array of modern buildings. I heard long ago that the natural scenery of Qingdao is featured by its "red roofs, green trees, blue sea and azure sky", and that the must dos that give a taste of its culture and history are "drinking beer, eating seafood, swimming in the sea and climbing Mount Lao". The quick glimpse of the city's natural scenes along the way already convinced me that it was the very Qingdao I had dreamed of, which was as picturesque as a painting. Involuntarily I gasped in admiring awe. "A gilded dust cloth," blurted out the taxi driver. I inquired about the reason for his opinion, and learned that as a coastal city, Qingdao had been developing at a much faster speed than non-coastal areas, pushing the prices of commercial real-estate to increasingly high levels, and that with tourists swarming from home and abroad people's living expenses kept soaring up as well. These unforeseen issues invited complaints from Qingdao residents.

It was early spring and the north was still wrapped in cold. For a swim in the sea, it was not the best time. As for a tasting of seafood, I should not have it all to myself: I must get a package of seafood for my family and let them share the genuine flavor of the local seafood. When it came to Mount Lao, one of Qingdao's well-known tourist attractions, it was certainly a must go place.

Gathering with our Qingdao friends could not have gone without Qingdao's beer and seafood. The beer that the local friends ordered was the "beer freshly brewed on the same day". That was totally a brand new experience to me even though I had been an alcoholic drinker for years. The seafood served was something I never heard of. There was knowledge in eating; I could well ask if I did not know something. Eating was also an opportune moment to learn. A dish of stuff looking like rocks was actually oysters that were mentioned in books. The fish with a flat head was called "Baijia", and this information was nowhere to be found even in books. When I doubted that it could have been a farm-raised fish, one local friend replied definitely, "Impossible. This fish can't live out of seawater."

I was kept in high spirits by the idea of climbing Mount Lao, but had to give it up. For one thing, our stay was short; for another, both my colleagues had been there before and I just hated to bother them to keep me company. I would choose to wait until next time when it was a beer festival or some other more romantic occasion. One local friend told us that to have a better understanding of Qingdao was to know her culture.

"It will be more beautiful here in a couple of days. Flowers will be all blooming then," said the taxi driver. From his words I could perceive his earnest love for the city as a native resident. After all, love and grievance often go together, acting as the law of life that governs the operation of the human race.

A day and a half was a fleeting sojourn. When the morning sun was as high as the 10th storey of a building in Qingdao, my delight from the visit got across to my family on the phone and soaked into their morning dream.

注释

[1] 汉语是动词占优势的语言,几个站点名词各搭配一个动词,表达为"走南京,过蚌埠,穿徐州",显得平衡稳重,而英语用一个介词 past

就够了，译为 past Nanjing, Bengbu and Xuzhou。

［2］在汉语中，动作、声响效果等语义很少有单个的词语可表达，常用分析性的表达方式，如原文的"叮叮咚咚，吱吱呀呀"，而英语则相反，单纯词可融合动作、声响效果等含有一个以上的语义成分。因此，可用 clang 一词来表达火车的行进动作和发出的声响。

［3］这几个句子十分简短，动态感十足。其中"刹车"的动作执行者为火车司机，和上文的"减速"有语义重叠之处，可灵活处理，译为 pulling into the station，逻辑主语是 the train，和句子的主语保持了一致。

［4］原文的这两句在结构上很对称，但直译会令人费解。青岛的自然景观不仅仅是"红瓦""绿树""碧海""蓝天"，只是以这些为代表罢了，可译为 the natural scenery of Qingdao is featured by its "red roofs, green trees, blue sea and azure sky"。而所谓的"人文景观"，则指能让人感受到其人文气息的旅游景点或项目，可译为 the must dos that give a taste of its culture and history。

［5］上文描述青岛发展太快，带来不利因素，此处的"没想到"指青岛人没想到会有这些不利的因素，可译为 these unforeseen issues。

［6］"10层楼高"译为 the 10th storey of a building，而不是 a ten-storey building，前者为高楼的第10层楼，而后者则指只有10层楼的高楼。青岛为东部沿海城市，在3月份，太阳爬上10层楼高时，大约是早上7点之前。但此处不用补充额外的时间信息，译语读者能否明白这一层意思，无关紧要。

原文

汉墓健身之行

秋日里,我们应外国语学院工会之约[1],骑车到汉广陵王墓作健身之行[2]。

健身到汉墓,真是个理想的去处。除路途迢迢直接利于健身之外,沿途还可尽情领略秋之旖旎。天之淡,水之幽,蜀岗滴翠,烟浓望迷。[3]未及深秋,大地仍旧葱郁,万木依然峥嵘,与春相比,少了几分浮躁,多了些许深情[4]。此时凭吊历史[5],颇能抒发胸臆:或叹中华文化之精,或思墓主人生前之威仪;或哀逝者之悲,或喜偷生之愉;或惜时光之亘古,或怜人生之有日……纵观人生,心头不禁掠过一丝秋意。

丘垄依在,主人不存,留下的是那金丝楠木的棺椁[6],还有那价值连城的金缕玉衣[7]。汉广陵王颇具霸气,生做人王,死做鬼雄,墓中摆设,若其生之于世,待客处、沐浴室一应俱全[8]。斯人去矣,权却不及身后之事,财宝被盗,尸首被弃,这倒应了那句古语:生不带来,死不带去。

苍天精,统人生于须臾;大地能,拢万物于掌中。人啊,或许该少存贪念,直面人生! 大彻大悟乎,悲叹人生乎,声色犬马乎,及时行乐乎,[9]鄙人愚见,恐怕主要的是获致一分宁静的心境。

走出霭霭氛围,又闻翠岗清风。同睹一物,思想绝非相同。面对半瓶酒,积极者看到的一半是酒,消极者看到的一半是空。在过去中流连悲怆? 在今生寄希望来生? 不管怎样,面对作古之人,我们都庄严地在立志健身的横幅上签上了我们的大名[10]。

历史作证[11],我们善待今生。

王侯悠悠,令人唏嘘,天穹下,该会多一些健身者的足迹?[12]

> 译文

A Cycle Ride to the Mausoleum

One day in autumn, for fitness purposes we set off on a cycle ride, organized by the trade union of my Foreign Languages School, to the Mausoleum Museum of the first king of Guangling in Han Dynasty(206 BC – AD 220).

The distance to the Mausoleum made it an ideal finishing point for a cycling trip. Aside from the physical benefit from the substantial amount of exercise, the bountiful beauty of the season on show along the way was also a satisfying visual treat to the eyes. The sky was an opalescent white and the waters a tranquil sheen. The verdant luxury of the land filtered through a blurring gauze of haze. As autumn was still in its prime, the vegetation was thriving in luxuriance, hugging the earth in green. Autumn, as compared with spring, is tinged more with passion and less with restlessness, and a side tour of the historical place at this time of the year prompted a free outpouring of feelings: we marveled at the sophistication of ancient Chinese culture and imagined the augustness of the buried before his death; we mourned the perishing of life and took delight in being alive; we sighed in awe of the antiquity of time and grieved over the briefness of life. A panoramic view of life added a note of melancholy to the heart.

The king's mausoleum remained where it was; while his corpse had long decomposed in the sarcophagus of rare Nanmu wood underneath the precious jade burial suit. The imperial king extended his power from the human world to the underworld, and had his sepulcher constructed in resemblance to the residence he inhabited in his life, and accommodated with all amenities he was to use in his afterlife. Albeit such grandness, his reign ceased with his demise: the burial treasures were plundered and the skeletal frame deserted. The post mortal fate of the king well exemplifies an old saying that goes as "one takes away nothing at death just as he brings nothing at birth".

The supreme Heavens condemn the multitude to a short life, and the mighty Earth clutches the world in his iron grip. Given that, one should wisely proceed his life with less covetousness. It is also paramount to keep a peaceful mind no matter whether he understands life thoroughly, or views life negatively, thus drowning himself in sensual pleasures and living only for today.

Leaving the sepulchral gloominess, we were greeted again by the refreshing breeze in the air. Perception of even the same visual image can vary from one to another. In the case of a half-filled bottle, an optimist tends to view it as half full while a pessimist as half empty. Should one dwell on the past or yearn for a rebirth? In the presence of the soul of the deceased, we signed with solemnity our names on the participation banner, which act was to signify our commitment to adhering to a physical exercise routine.

As time is our witness, we will live in the present life with all of our power.

Ancient nobles faded pathetically into history. Life is preciously short, and as such will there be more physical exercise lovers?

注释

［1］国内大学里的各级工会都会定期组织一些娱乐活动,有兴趣的教工自愿报名参加。原文"应……之约"是美化的表达,实际就是"外国语学院的工会组织我们骑车到……",可译为 organized by the trade union of my Foreign Languages School。此行目的,即"作健身之行",译文通过 for fitness purposes 这个介词短语加以明确。

［2］"汉广陵王"译成 the first king of Guangling in Han Dynasty (206 BC - AD 220)。有几点需说明:(1)扬州的汉广陵王墓特指汉朝刘胥的陵墓,汉朝历史上有多任广陵王,他是第一任广陵王,因此,译文中添加 first 一词并非多此一举;(2)"汉广陵王"也可译成 the first Guangling king,但假如译语读者对"广陵"这个古地名比较陌生,可能会将 Guangling 误解为人名;(3)不少译文将"汉广陵王"按照汉语的语序译成 Han Guangling king,把 Han 作前置修饰语使用,可能会对译语读

者造成理解困难。

［3］这四个分句，两两相对，抑扬顿挫，整齐中有变化。译文可用完整的句子，也可用名词化的结构来表达，但应避免译文使用相同的句法结构，以免显得单调。此处假如译成 the white opalescence of the sky, the tranquil sheen of the waters, the verdant luxury of the land, the blurring gauze of haze, 四个名词（化）结构并列在一起，十分单调，而译成 the tranquil sheen of the waters surging against a white opalescent sky, the verdant luxury of the land filtering through a blurring gauze of haze, 则两个结构都很长，节奏上少了变化。这四个分句可译成：The sky was an opalescent white and the waters a tranquil sheen. The verdant luxury of the land filtered through a blurring gauze of haze. 译文在句法结构上长短交错，音韵节奏上稍胜一筹。

［4］"少了几分浮躁，多了些许深情"这两句可使用比较结构来翻译，即 Autumn is tinged more with passion and less with restlessness, 表达的是秋天和春天在两个特质方面量的比较。

［5］"此时凭吊历史"译成 a side tour of the historical place at this time of the year。参观汉墓不是这次骑车运动的主要目的，所以译文中添加 side 这个修饰语，表示入门参观是单程骑车锻炼结束后所做的顺带之事。

［6］"金丝楠木的棺椁"译成 the sarcophagus of rare Nanmu wood。Sarcophagus 原指用石头或大理石制作的雕刻精美的棺椁，但加上 wooden,（made）of wood/pottery 等修饰语，可表示制作的材料。金丝楠木为中国独产，英语中没有现成的表达方式，直接用音意合译法译成 Nanmu wood。不加 wood 这个类名词，一般的译语读者不知这是什么具体的材料。将"金丝"的意义省略，否则太烦琐。

［7］"价值连城的金缕玉衣"译成 the precious jade burial suit，这是英语中通行的表达方式，译语读者能明白其义。将"金缕"的意义省略，也是出于表达简洁的需要。

［8］很多文化都认为，人死之后会到另一个世界去继续生活，因此，对于"墓中摆设，若其生之于世，待客处、沐浴室一应俱全"几个小句，译文变通处理为：The imperial king … had his sepulcher constructed in resemblance to the residence he inhabited in his life and accommodated with all amenities he was supposed to use in his afterlife. 适当添加或删减了原文的一些信息。

［9］在这四个以"乎"结尾的句子中，第一个"乎"句可理解为表达

一种豁达的心态，因为"大彻大悟"一般都用作褒义词，后三个"乎"句表达的都是悲观的态度或行为，而且"悲叹人生"与"声色犬马""及时行乐"之间可理解为因果关系。积极和消极的两种态度或行为，用 no matter whether 来表达，并根据原文表达的语义关系，添加了 and/or 等衔接词。

［10］签名活动是组织者准备的，译文为了表意明确，将"横幅"表达为 participation banner，并通过 which act was to signify，明确"签名"行为的意图。

［11］"历史作证"可译成 As time is our witness 或 As time will tell。英语的 As ... is one's witness 表示"决心""预测""判断"等意思，大致与汉语的"作证"相当，例如 *Gone with the Wind* 中那句著名的 As God is my witness, I'll never be hungry again. 其他类似用法也有很多，例如 As the world is my witness, I will never trust again. As history is our witness, some of the most beautiful cars in the world have been failures.

［12］原文最后一段有两个语义片段，根据上下文添加了 Life is preciously short, and as such 以使语义更加连贯，符合英语的表达习惯。

原文

温馨时刻：文友[1]同游达拉斯

北得州文友社（North Texas Chinese Literary Society）是一个"以文会友"的社团。2013年1月19日，文友社举办了以"扬州"为主题的专题讲座，吴迪教授主讲"烟花三月下扬州——诗中扬州"，引经据典，娓娓道来；祖籍江苏的作家王晓兰女士特地从加州赶来，以其父亲生前魂牵梦萦的故乡情为主题，讲述了父亲60载回乡之路[2]的感人故事和她对故乡的热爱；我以"春风十里扬州路——人在扬州"为题，从一个外地人[3]的视角，讲述了扬州的人景、物景、风景和我的"心景"，分享了我的所感所知（见《达拉斯新闻》2013/1/25）。

次日，文友社陈社长、吴迪教授、简慈萱女士、孙淑芳女士，与汉湘夫妇一起，陪着王晓兰女士和我游览了达拉斯市区。

当日一大早，我们一行人到旅馆接上晓兰，直奔达拉斯市区。漫步于Reunion Tower及Hyatt Regency Hotel四周，摄影学会的慈萱会长与爱好摄影的晓兰、淑芳和汉湘互换心得，不断寻找最佳的取景角度。大家走一路，聊一路，照一路，歇脚于Hyatt Regency Hotel大厅[4]，再到顶楼瞭望市区全景。Reunion Tower仅隔咫尺，与刚才从地面仰视高楼的感觉迥然不同。此时阳光灿烂，冷暖适宜，蓝天白云，风景尤为亮丽。俯瞰大地，达拉斯就在脚下，交通四通八达，车辆川流不息。

一列火车，慢慢驶入视线，火车之长，惊心动魄！从未见过这么长的火车，有100多节车厢，待看到火车尾巴时，车头似乎已经跳出了视野，若非亲眼所见，只能视为天方夜谭。

我看到了著名的Trinity River。吴迪教授说，牛仔当年赶着牛群所跨越的正是这条河，走过的小径至今还在[5]；没有这条河，就没有达拉斯这座城，达拉斯是围绕这条河建设起来的。

待楼上之景看尽，一行人移步游览了市区。周日的达拉斯市区悠闲而静谧。我四处观望，众文友热心向我解释各著名建筑物的特色与来历。数John F. Kennedy总统遇刺印象最为深刻，公路上涂着的两个白色"×"，标出的是总统遇刺的着弹点。参观者比比画画，叙述着当年的骇人故事，边叙述还边唏嘘。

附近200码是John F. Kennedy Memorial Plaza[6]，方方正正，像一座无顶的房子，里面放着一块黑色的、有一张床大小的方石[7]。从事建筑工作的晓兰，认为这座看似"空"的建筑，却潜藏着"满"的寓意。在旁边的一块石碑上，设计者Philip Johnson先生说明了设计的理念：a place of quiet refuge, an enclosed place of thought and contemplation separated from the city around, but near the sky and earth[8]。

肯尼迪纪念碑碑文的结尾处写道：It is not a memorial to the pain and sorrow of death, but stands as a permanent tribute to the joy and excitement of one man's life. John F. Kennedy's life.

我们在返回的路上，品尝了正宗台湾小吃刈包及各式面点；免不了又听到了一些动人的故事。景观无数，见识各异。自然景观，连同人文景观，尽收眼底，又融汇心底。

回来路上，笑语串串，歌声不断。我陶醉于吴迪教授的深情曲调，钟情于慈萱女士吟唱的歌谣，沉思于玉琳社长讲述的师恩情怀……话筒忙着传递之际[9]，慈萱还不忘观察行路牌，指挥着汽车行走的路线。

他们本是这样一群生长于台湾的同胞，我来自中国内地，小的时候从不敢想，竟然能与这样的一群人团聚，而这样一群人，正以深厚的中华文化积淀，在海外传承和弘扬着中华文明。

孔子说："君子以文会友，以友辅仁。"（《论语·颜渊》）孔子还说："有朋自远方来，不亦乐乎？"（《论语·学而》）。我与众文友相聚达拉斯，正是对孔老夫子这两句经典的诠释。晓兰专程从加州来，我自中国内地来，和北得州文友社文友共同交流和学习，对文友社文友而言，我与晓兰是"有朋自远方来"，而我们相聚达拉斯，"不亦乐乎"，朋友之间交流，达到了"以友辅仁"、增进己身仁德的目的。

此次与文友相会之旅，真正是"文""友"兼济。

{ 译文 }

Happy Moments: A Tour of Dallas with Literary Friends

North Texas Chinese Literary Society, an organization set up for the purpose of "fostering friendship through literary activities", hosted on Jan. 19, 2013 a lecture series that featured Yangzhou, a Chinese city in Jiangsu Province. Professor Wu Di started with "The Misty and Flowery March: Yangzhou in poetry", a vivid and impressive speech peppered with quotations from classic poems. Ms Wang Xiaolan, a writer of Jiangsu descent, who traveled specifically for this activity from California of the US, recalled in her speech her late father's fervent nostalgia for his homeland Yangzhou, and recounted the moving story of her father's 60 years of periodical returns to it in his life and her own love for the native place as well. From my perspective as a non-native resident of Yangzhou, I gave in my speech entitled "The Glamorous Yangzhou: My Personal Experience" (published in *Dallas Chinese News*, Jan. 25, 2013) an account of the perceptions I had of the city concerning its people, objects and natural scenery as well as the picture of it I built up in my mind.

The following day Ms Wang Xiaolan and I went on a sightseeing tour of downtown Dallas in the company of Director Chen of the Society, Professor Wu Di, Ms Jian Cixuan, Ms Sun Shufang, and Mr and Mrs Han Xiang.

Early that morning we made our way directly to our destination after we picked up Xiaolan in her hotel. Cixuan, director of a photographic society, and Xiaolan, Shufang and Han Xiang, all amateur photographers, took pictures all the way while they were strolling around Reunion Tower and Hyatt Regency Hotel, and enthusiastically shared with each other opinions about the best angle for a picture. We just talked and photographed as we walked along. After a short rest of the feet at the lobby of Hyatt Regency Hotel, we continued our way to the top of the hotel for a panoramic view of the city. Reunion Tower now loomed close before the eyes, and a look at it from this point gave a completely different picture from that of an upward view from the ground. The sun was bright and the temperature agreeable, and white clouds were floating against the blue sky. The landscape was even more beautiful than ever. Viewed from atop the hotel, Dallas was down there, right beneath us, its extensive network of transportation carrying the busy traffic to all directions.

A train was moving slowly into sight. It was long, stunningly long. I never saw a train that could have as many as more than 100 carriages. When its tail was in sight, its head was almost gone from view. Had I not seen it for my own eyes, I would not have believed there could be such a long train.

I saw the well-known Trinity River, the very river which Professor Wu Di told me cowboys crossed in those days with their cattle. The trails they took were still kept intact there. The river was the backbone of Dallas, without which the city would not have taken shape into what it is today.

A complete appreciation of the scenes seen from the hotel top was followed by visits to more places in the city proper, which was immersed on Sunday in an atmosphere of leisure and peace. I enjoyed myself seeing around, and others gladly offered to explain to me the features of those prominent architectural structures and the stories lying behind them. Among them the most impressive was the site where President John F. Kennedy was assassinated. The two white X's on the road marked the two spots of the president's assassination. Visitors gesticulated and breathed sighs of lament as they talked about this historical event of terror.

About 200 yards away was the John F. Kennedy Memorial Plaza, where stood a memorial monument, a square structure looking like a roofless house. Inside it there was a black stone, square in shape and of the size of a queen-size bed. Xiaolan, an architectural professional, read into this "empty" structure an implication of "fullness". The stone tablet beside the square stone made clear the design philosophy of the designer Philip Johnson that this monument was intended to be "a place of quiet refuge, an enclosed place of thought and contemplation separated from the city around, but near the sky and earth".

The inscription for the memorial monument ended by saying "It is not a memorial to the pain and sorrow of death, but stands as a permanent tribute to the joy and excitement of one man's life. John F. Kennedy's life".

On our way back we stopped to have a taste of the authentic Taiwan style snack food "Yibao" and snacks of varied flavors, and shared more moving stories during our eating. The numerous scenes, natural or cultural, that we had seen during the day extended our learning and experience, and nourished both the eyes and the mind.

The return journey was one of laughter and singing. I was all charmed by Professor Wu Di's mellow melodies, Cixuan's singing of folk songs and Director Chen's narrative of her emotional attachment to her former teachers. Even between intervals of her singing, Cixuan still remembered to watch out for road signs and gave route directions to the driver.

They were Chinese growing up in Taiwan, China and I was Chinese brought up in Mainland China. It never occurred to me that I would have a chance to associate with people like them. And it was them who were actively engaged in an overseas role in inheriting and promoting Chinese culture with their rich reserves of cultural knowledge and learning.

Confucius said, "Noble people foster friendship through literary learning and enhance virtue through friendship." (*Confucian Analects: Yanyuan*) And Confucius also said, "It is a happy occasion gathering with friends coming from afar, isn't it?" (*Confucian Analects: Learning*) The two classic Confucian quotes could be well exemplified by the gathering of Xiaolan and me with these literary friends in Dallas. To the Literary Society, Xiaolan and I were "friends coming from afar", one from California, the other from Mainland China, to share and learn. And our gathering together in Dallas was "a happy occasion" when the mutual exchanges between friends brought about the happy end of "fostering virtue".

This tour of mine with literary friends was a real good experience of gaining both learning and friendship.

注释

[1]"文友"来自《论语》的"君子以文会友,以友辅仁",原指以文德结友,后指以诗文相交的朋友或有共同文学爱好和兴趣的朋友,可译为 literary friends。

[2]"60 载回乡之路"译为 60 years of periodical returns to it (Yangzhou),译文中添加 periodical 一词,是出于英语精确表达的需要。

[3]作者在扬州居住已有 16 年之久,是正宗的扬州居民,所谓"外地人",指非土生土长的扬州居民,可译为 a non-native resident。

[4]"大厅"指宾馆、公寓楼或其他大型建筑内的底层靠近入口的空间,相当于英语的 lobby。

[5]这一句译为 the very river which Professor Wu Di told me cowboys crossed in those days with their cattle。Professor Wu Di told me 这个主谓结构可放在关系词 which 和谓语部分之间,相当于一个插入语性质的成分,假如放在句首,可表达为 Professor Wu Di told me that cowboys crossed this river in those days with their cattle。

[6] Plaza 指城市中的露天广场或店铺聚集的广场。肯尼迪纪念广场上有一座纪念碑,是一个无顶的建筑物,整句可译为:About 200 yards away was the John F. Kennedy Memorial Plaza, where stood a memorial monument, a square structure looking like a roofless house. 其中增添 where stood a memorial monument,以明示原文隐含的信息。

[7]肯尼迪纪念碑中有块方石,有"一张床大小",根据实际情况,译为 of the size of a queen-size bed。

[8]为说明纪念碑的设计理念,原文引用了石碑上的一段文字,其中心语是 place,译文中添加 this monument was intended to be,以求文字表述符合英语的句法和语义逻辑。

[9]车上有话筒,可以一路欢歌笑语,但上文没有任何这方面的交代,假如照实把"话筒"翻译出来,读者可能费解,假如添加信息,则没有太大的必要,所以将"话筒忙着传递之际"变通表达为 Even between intervals of her singing。

原文

别了,得州

  默默收拾行囊,结束访学的180个日子[1],带着满心的收获:别了,得州!
  幸遇的友人、偶遇的路人,带着你们的关心和问候:别了,得州!
  …………
  有些不舍!才写了个《得州的云》(《达拉斯新闻》2013/1/4),还有念叨不完的风物、念叨不完的得州和达拉斯。自从去年8月来到得州,便有着一种期待:记录不完的语言、体验不完的文化,当然还有结交不完的朋友[2]。
  再走一走去年走过的路吧!初来达拉斯,我冒着酷暑步行体验本地的文化:裸露的皮肤晒脱了,树荫下歇歇脚,继续前行;口渴了,看不到超市,问问偶尔路过的行人、整理草坪的工人,他们便送水给我;迷路了,美国人热情有加,指点迷津。"处处留心皆学问"[3],学英语、学文化,处处是知识,哪怕一个字迹不清的标牌,也要努力辨识。
  再走一走半年来去过的商场吧!我住在McCallum,近的有Ross和Marshalls,远的有Macy和Outlets。我本不喜欢逛商场,特别是服装商场,然而在德国,也学着去尝试。我学会了寻找Coupon;学会了treasure hunt;认识了名牌服装,竟还能如数家珍:Calvin Klein, Izod, Columbia, Van Heusen, Tommy Hilfiger, Levis, Polo Ralph Lauren, Nike, Adidas, Clarks, Bass, Jones New York, Nine West, Ferry Ellis, Reebok。购物时,营业员既不会紧贴着你影响你的选择,也不会在你不购买时给你脸色[4],临末送上一句Have a great day,总让人暖在心里。
  看美国地理,得州在正南,是头,美国东西海岸风景带兼作两翼,得州似乎是"偏安一隅"[5],"安"就安了。如果把美国比作闹市,那么住在得州真有"结庐在人境,而无车马喧"之感。现代交通,特别是空中交通十分发达,而得州地广人稀,高速公路更是四通八达,对我这无车的外来客而言,搭乘公交车出游也十分便捷,那就外出看山、看水去。得州空气清新,经常是蓝天白云。得州人选择得州而居,真是明智之举。
  别了,得州!

{ 译文 }

Farewell, Texas

Packing quietly, with a reluctant mind and a heavy heart, I have to bid you farewell, Texas.

My six months' stay as a visiting scholar is about to end. With a rewarding experience, I have to bid you farewell, Texas.

With care from friends and hello from strangers, I have to bid you farewell, Texas.

...

How sad I am at the thought of having to leave! Other than what I had in my essay "Clouds in Texas" (published in *Dallas Chinese News*, Jan. 4, 2013), I have so much more to say about Texas and Dallas, and so much more to say about the natural scenes here. Ever since last August when I was here, I have been steeped in an inexplicable excitement for the real-life language data I wish I could all have recorded, for the cultural richness I wish I could all have experienced, and of course for the people I wish I could all have made friends with.

Let me retake those routes I took previously. As soon as I was here in Dallas, as I remember, I went out walking in the intense summer heat for a fresh taste of the local culture. When the exposed skin got red and peeled off, I stopped for a short rest under the tree shade and continued with my trip. When I was thirsty and asked passersby or lawn mowers for the location of the nearest supermarket, they were so ready to share with me their water. When I got lost, the people I asked for help always responded warmly and pointed to me the right direction. As people often say, "One can learn a lot if he is attentive enough." There is knowledge to learn in every aspect of English and its culture: even an illegible road sign would draw me closer to make it out.

Let me revisit those shopping centers I have been to. Ross and Marshalls are pretty close to McCallum, where I am living, while Macy and Outlets are a bit farther out. I used to hate shopping around, especially visiting those shopping centers. However, when I was here, I tried to learn about it. I learned how to look for coupons and how to do treasure hunts. I got familiar with a long list of clothing name brands and could mention a lot in one breath, for example, Calvin Klein, Izod, Columbia, Van Heusen, Tommy Hilfiger, Levis, Polo Ralph Lauren, Nike, Adidas, Clarks, Bass, Jones New York, Nine West, Ferry Ellis, Reebok, etc. When shopping, sales assistants never follow clients closely to push a deal through or put on a long face when clients buy nothing, and their closing "Have a great day" can always fill a heart with such warmth.

Geographically, Texas lies right in the middle of the Southern US and looks as if it were the head of the country. With the longitudinal scenic east and west coast of the country being two wings as it were, Texas seems to be lying in a secluded corner, however. In spite of that, for its residents it is "an oasis of serenity amid the hubbub of the outside world" if the whole country could be likened to a bustling cosmopolitan city. Modern means of transportation, especially of the aerial type, are conveniently accessible, and the highways in Texas, vast and sparsely populated, form a network emanating in all directions. To a visitor without an auto like me, the public transportation system is a handy option of getting access to natural scenery. So, why not make use of it? Fresh air and the frequent scene of white clouds floating in a blue sky are the appeal that Texas has for those who make the wise decision to reside in it.

Farewell, Texas!

注释

[1] 写作此文时,作者的访学还没有结束,因此,句子的谓语动词用将来时间表达方式,译为 My six months' stay as a visiting scholar is about to end。

[2] 这个段落中有五处"不完"的表达,为使译文表达多样化,前两处"不完"所在的句子用比较级的形式,译为: I have so much more to say about Texas and Dallas, and so much more to say about the natural scenes here. 后三

处"不完"所在的句子用虚拟语气,译为 the real-life language data I wish I could have recorded, for the cultural richness I wish I could have experienced, and of course for the people I wish I could have made friends with。

[3] "处处留心皆学问"这句话加上引号,说明是大家都熟悉的俗语,译文中添加 As people often say 这样的表述。

[4] "给你脸色"在英语中有很多形象的表达法,如 show a cold face, pull/wear a long face, make a face 等。

[5] "偏安一隅"是贬义词,意为"在残存的一片土地上苟且偷安"。原文将这个贬义词置于引号之中,其贬义色彩就减弱了,甚至消失了。这个小句的意思是"尽管地处美国南方正中,但有了热闹的东西海岸风景带,得州似乎反而成了一个角落",可译为 Texas seems to be lying in a secluded corner。

Ⅲ·散文英译专评

原文

石 榴 花[1]

　　大千世界,万紫千红;五彩奇花,争艳斗胜。名花有人攀附,野花招徕不屑。我在不经意间瞥见一树红彤彤的石榴花,竟让我对这名花与野花之间之花,生出了一番感慨[2]。或许她太过平常,童年至今,屡次相遇,竟不曾为其娇容所动。就是在这几日,爱怜却兀自生起。

　　六月初这几天,扬州的天气出奇地凉爽,颇有春暖乍寒之意。步行去学校,整整一个小时的路程,健身自不必说。路边的一草一木近在咫尺,多了亲密接触,而接触时还免不得产生些许思绪。随手捡一截干瘪的树枝,推着往前走[3],童年时学着拖拉机前进的突突声又在耳畔响起;张嘴衔一片树叶[4],蹩脚的口技[5]还能多多少少再现童年时弄叶的玩姿。

　　每次步行,都能瞥见路边稍远处长着一棵树,好似结着泛红的果实。前两天路过时就光是那么想象:难道是一棵枇杷树结着生涩的果实?难道是人家扬州人[6]司空见惯了所以看不上?难道是人们的文明水平[7]提高了,竟放纵这好果子自在生长?管不了那么多,童年爬树偷果子的情形一时占了上风[8],乡间野趣原来就在这里。

　　为饱口福,绕绕路,多走它几步。可走到树下,不免怅然所望。原来是一棵开着红花的石榴树,花太小,远看模糊。我说呢,要是结着一树的宝贝,怎躲得过那些个"早起的鸟儿"呢!

　　既来之,则安之。[9]我对着这满树的红花细细地打量。有的花,可谓怒放,绸缎般的"石榴裙"紧束在"细腰"之上;"细腰"之侧,总有那么几枚未及开放的花骨朵儿,似"红果"[10]头饰扎在小姑娘的头上。咦?小姑娘害羞了吧[11],俏模样藏在婆婆的树叶里,却掖不尽"榴月"(农历五月的古时雅称)里满身的"石榴红"。倏忽间,未及开放的花骨朵儿变成了二胡上的琴轸,"石榴裙"化作了唢呐,就连黄色的花蕊,也变作了小喇叭若隐若现的穗饰。满树"乐器",怎不闹春![12]

　　我对石榴花可谓真情所至。别人知其美却忽略其美[13],或因石榴花不像其他鲜花那么花香浓郁,或因石榴树是果树,石榴尚未结出,自然还未实现其最主要的价值。但不管是为着花香,还是为着未来的果实,说到底,都带着那么点功利。是功利之心,遮掩了对美的赏析。

石榴花虽不馥郁,却有着别样美丽,因不以花香媚俗,便不会招惹俗人折枝;石榴花是"红颜",不仅未遭"天妒",且总能颐养天年。

石榴花,你个小精灵,我可是读懂了你!

{译文}

Pomegranate Flowers

The world is a blazing brilliance of colors, a dazzling flourish of flowers vying for charm. While renowned flowers win sycophantic admiration, wild ones simply grow humbly unnoticed. Pomegranate flowers, not a prized species anymore, nor a wild type, evoked in me an unexpected sentiment of emotion after I, quite by accident, caught sight of a pomegranate tree glowing red with flowers. Ever since my childhood, I have had different encounters with pomegranate flowers, and perhaps because they are much too ordinary I should have failed to be touched, not even once, by their charm. It is not until recently that I began to generate an affectionate fondness towards them.

Early June of this year saw in Yangzhou an unusually cool temperature, giving one the illusion of a returning early spring. While I was walking to campus, the one-hour trip, which was definitely a good exercise, also brought closer contact with grass or trees adjacent to the roadside. As I was doing so, thoughts tended to arise involuntarily as well. I casually picked up a dry tree branch and walked it along as if I were maneuvering a tractor, its chugging tune that I once imitated as a child reverberating in my ears once more. With a tree leaf placed between the lips, I was still able to whistle it, in an awkward fashion, evidencing my remaining competence in this childhood game with tree leaves.

Every time I went along the same route, I could always glimpse a distance away from the roadside a particular tree, which seemed to be bearing reddish fruits. Two days ago, I passed by it again, doubts in mind. Was it a loquat bearing astringent fruits? Were the fruits so common that people had their nose turned up at them? Or, was it because people were better-nurtured now so that they pampered the free growth of the fruits? Whatever the reason, I would not care. Childhood experiences of stealing fruits in the tree were prompting me to have one more try. What a rustic delight in doing that!

To have a taste of the fruits, I changed my usual route, which only involved a little extra distance to cover. However, I approached only to see a pomegranate tree bearing red flowers, which let me down a little bit. Being small, the flowers were indistinguishable in the distance. No wonder. How could a fruit-bearing tree have kept away the "early birds"?

As the old Chinese saying goes, "Since I am here, let me stay and enjoy it". I started to observe the flowers intently. Some flowers, in their full blossoms, were silky "pomegranate skirts" as it were, going tight and slender in the waist. And the "slender waists" were normally accompanied to the side by a couple of flower buds, which looked just like "red hawthorn fruits" embellishing the hairstyle of a little girl. Why, are you shy little girls, blooming flowers? You were hiding your pretty faces among rustling leaves, but you were not able to conceal all the "pomegranate red" bursting for this "pomegranate month" (an elegant name in the ancient times for the fifth month of the Chinese lunar calendar). Then in a blinking moment, it was as if the flower buds turned into the pegs of urheens, the "pomegranate skirts" into the suona trumpets, and even the yellow stamens or pistils into the indistinct decorations of some hidden horns. With all these "musical instruments" in the tree, what a loud celebration it was for the arrival of the spring!

My passion for pomegranate flowers can well be described as true and genuine. Aware as other people are of their beauty, they tend to turn a blind eye to it, probably because pomegranate flowers are not so scented, or because pomegranate trees are fruit producers and can only prove their principal value when fruits are born. No matter whether for the scent or for the fruit, basically it is utilitarianism that cloaks people's appreciative eye for the beauty of the flowers.

Pomegranate flowers, though not smelling sweet, are special in their beauty. As they never please people by scent, they do not incur picking.

They are "beauties", and are able to grow elegantly and leisurely, free from "the jealousy of gods".

Pomegranate flowers, you adorable little spirits, it's me who knows you well!

注释

[1] 石榴花在中国已有两千多年的栽种历史,因花朵鲜艳,果实多籽,深得人们喜爱,经常是古代诗人和画家笔下描绘的对象,在中国文化中曾经是名花。但到了现代,石榴花已不再像古时那么受人崇拜。因此,原文把石榴花称为"名花与野花之间之花",即石榴花既不是名花,也不是野花,译为 not a prized species anymore, nor a wild type。因石榴花只是到了现代才渐失名花地位的,所以译文中添加 anymore 一词来表达这一隐含的背景信息。

[2] 在表达事件时,汉语倾向于严格按照时间顺序来描述,而英语则可打破时间顺序。"我在不经意间瞥见一树红彤彤的石榴花……,生出了一番感慨"这一句的译文在语序上做了大调整,事件的时间顺序与原文中的描述完全相反,是为了让表达更加符合英语的习惯。

[3] "推着往前走"隐含了一些信息,意为"模仿开拖拉机的样子,推着树枝往前走"。译文中额外添加 as if 引导的分句,即 walked it along as if I were maneuvering a tractor,以方便译语读者理解。

[4] "张嘴衔一片树叶"这个分句中描述两个动作,"张嘴"和"衔"。汉语动词表达的动作,在英语中很多都倾向于使用静态表达方式,例如名词化结构、介词短语等。这两个动作在译文中都可用非动词或静态动词来表达,译为 with a tree leaf placed between the lips。

[5] "蹩脚的口技"是名词性短语,在译文中处理为动词加修饰语的搭配,即(I was still able) to whistle it, in an awkward fashion。这样处理,是因为英语的句法要求句子的形式完备,并且表意明确,符合逻辑。原文的"张嘴衔一片树叶"和"蹩脚的口技"之间,在语义上略有跳跃,如照原文直译,可能会造成费解,译文应填补这个语义上的跳跃,将"蹩脚的口技还能多多少少再现童年时弄叶的玩姿"这一小句中的"物称主语"("蹩脚的口技")切换成"人称主语"(I),"口技"表达成动词形式的 whistle,并添加宾语 it,这样处理既传递了原文的意思,但又不拘泥于

原文的形式。

[6]"人家"是汉语中特殊的人称代词,表达说话者的多种感情色彩。在这个上下文中,作者使用"人家扬州人",调侃揶揄,似有若无。英语中没有和"人家"相当的词语,从结构上看,"人家扬州人"固然可译为 the Yangzhou people 这样的同位语结构,但英语中这样的结构使用频率很低,而且一般也不传递说话者的感情色彩。因此,译文做了简化处理,将"人家扬州人"仅译为 people,连 Yangzhou 都省却了。

[7]"文明水平"对应的英语表达方式是 level of civilization,主要指群体所达到的整体的物质或精神状态,而这句中的"文明水平"主要指个人的品行修养,其行为符合公共道德的水准,可用 better-nurtured, better-educated 等词语。

[8]这一小句的意思是"想到童年爬树偷果子的情形,顿觉乐趣倍增,想再偷一次果子"。"一时占了上风"就是"想再偷一次果子"的意思,可译为 were prompting me to have one more try,不应根据字面意义译为 gained the upper hand,否则会令人费解。

[9]"既来之,则安之"典出《论语》,已成为汉语书面表达中的习惯用语,可直译,但为了表明是习语,所以补充必要的信息,译为:As the old Chinese saying goes, "Since I am here, let me stay and enjoy it."

[10]"红果"是某些方言中的名称,即"山楂""山里红""酸楂",并不是"红颜色的果子",可译为 red hawthorn fruits。

[11]原文将石榴花拟人化为害羞的小姑娘,语气词"咦"描绘了惊讶的语气,同时又起着衔接上下文的作用,提示读者这是现实与想象之间的切换。对于"咦,小姑娘害羞了吧"这一句,译文也是采用了同样的拟人修辞手段,添加了 blooming flowers 这个直接呼语,同时使用了 why 这个语气词,传达惊讶的语气。

[12]这一段的很多词语包含了汉语文化独有的信息,例如"石榴裙""榴月""石榴红""二胡""琴轸""唢呐""闹春""红颜天妒"等。这些词语所传递的文化信息和联想,译语读者不一定都能产生和原语读者一样的共鸣,但这些词语描述的都是具体概念,译语读者不难理解,因此,译文都进行了直译。

[13]这个小句译为:Aware as other people are of their beauty, they tend to turn a blind eye to it. 译文的句子是一个倒装句,as 引导的分句表示让步、转折时必须用倒装的形式,正常语序为:Though other people are aware of their beauty, they tend to turn a blind eye to it. 此处用倒装的形式,可获得音韵节奏上的额外效果:头韵和停顿。虚词 as 不强调时

取弱读的形式/əz/，和句首的 aware 构成头韵修辞格；aware 前置，动词 are 应取强读的形式/ɑː/，而不是弱读的形式/ə/，而且后面应有一个短暂的停顿，以表示动词后原有句法成分的空缺。倒装的形式读起来抑扬顿挫，而正常语序的分句则在音韵节奏上略显平淡。

> 专评

汉语散文英译中的韵味再现原则

在文学作品中，散文是翻译难度较高的一种文体，它集众美于一体，译者须从美学的角度把握和操作。刘士聪（2002：2-4）将散文中的美感因素表述为"韵味"，主要体现在三个方面：一、声响和节奏，二、意境和氛围，三、个性化的话语方式。

一、关于声响和节奏

汉语是声调语言，音节的声调和声韵组合模式让汉语形成抑扬交替、有韵无韵交融的独特旋律。散文在韵律和节奏方面的要求并不是十分严格，但也"讲究句式的长短开阖，跌宕起伏，音节奇偶相间，轻重交错"（曹明伦，2004：90）。散文的节律"虽不规则，但惟其随意，惟其自然而妙不可言"（刘士聪，2002：2）。

《石榴花》（以下简称《石》）一文长短句子交替使用，音节数量参差，显得错落有致，比如"名花有人攀附，野花招徕不屑""或许她太过平常，童年至今，屡次相遇，竟不曾为其娇容所动""满树'乐器'，怎不闹春"等句子，旋律节奏既舒缓又简洁，体现了汉语的音韵节奏美感。

声响与节奏作为散文的一个重要美学因素，应该在译文中得到充分体现。英语既是拼音文字，又是语调语言，容易形成高低强弱、波浪起伏的音韵节奏。汉语和英语在类型学上存在差异，在声响和节奏方面的表达也不尽相同，但在英语译文中体现汉语原文的声响和节奏，并非没有可能。在《石》的译文中，译者主要采用语义修辞、语音修辞和必要的语法结构等手段，从整体上再现原文的声响和节奏。

语言中的同义反复（tautology）可起修辞的作用，指说话者有意重复意义相同或相近的不同词语，来构成冗余信息。英语行文忌重复，然而假如说话者有意重复表达，则可起到积极的修辞作用。《石》文中两两相对的词语或句子很多，整齐的结构产生节奏上的平稳感觉，因此，译文中使用的几处同义反复修辞格，也都是为了获得类似的听觉效果。

试比较：

[1] 竟让我……生出了一番感慨。

... evoked in me an unexpected *sentiment* of *emotion*.

[2] ……爱怜却兀自生起。

... generate an *affectionate fondness* towards them.

[3] 我对石榴花可谓真情所至。

My passion for pomegranate flowers can well be described as *true* and *genuine*.

在上述几个例子中,斜体的两个相邻词是同义的,对表情达意不起任何作用。但是,从修辞角度看,同义词并列,语义重复叠加,在节奏上获得了平稳流畅的美感效果。而且,三个结构的语法关系各不相同,分别是同位结构、定中结构和并列结构,因此,在整体上,同义反复的使用并未给表达带来单调重复的感觉。

语言首先诉诸听觉。但是,若语言的语音组合模式或规律相差甚远,在听觉上产生的效果往往大不相同。比如,汉语音节的声韵组合及声调的高低变化,赋予汉语清晰有力、抑扬顿挫的音乐节奏,而英语音节的音韵组合和强弱交替,以及语调的升降变化,则给人以舒缓流畅、波浪起伏的听觉效果。相对而言,英语在抑扬顿挫的节奏感方面可能不如汉语那么强烈或明显。为了增加或改变语言的音乐效果,说话者会从音韵节奏的角度有目的地对语言材料进行选择和调整,这是语音修辞行为。

一般而言,英语的单音节或双音节词多的句子比多音节词多的句子节奏要快,短元音和爆破辅音多会使节奏加快,而长元音、流辅音(l, r, m, n)等则会使节奏放慢。此外,语音修辞手段,比如头韵、谐音、尾韵、拟声、双关等,也能增添音乐效果。

在音韵节奏上,原文抑扬顿挫、简洁明快的音乐感十分明显。在整体上,译文也以音节数量少的简单词为主,以期获得和原文近似的听觉效果。在译文中,译者还有意识地使用了一定数量的头韵修辞格,制造特殊的声响和节奏。例如:

[4] ……多了亲密接触……

... brought *closer contact* with grass or trees...

[5] 别人知其美而忽略其美。

Aware as other people are of their beauty, they *tend to turn* a blind eye to it.

[6] 石榴花虽不馥郁……

Pomegranate flowers, though not *smelling sweet*...

英语中同义词很多,译文中词语的选择还考虑了音韵方面的要求。如例[4]中的"亲密"既可表达成 close,也可表达成 intimate。后者三个音节,语体略微正式一点,但如果使用比较级,还要使用限定词 more,结构复杂;而 close 则是单音节词,用了比较级之后,读音更是简短有力,与 contact 并列,构成头韵修辞。例[5]和例[6]是类似情形,不用 ignore 或 fragrant 等词语来表达原文的"忽略"或"馥郁",也是出于音韵节奏方面的考虑。

汉语以意合为主,英语则以形合为主。汉语中语义成分或语义关系的省略或隐含很常见,而英语中则一般都必须以显性的形式来表达,讲究的是句法结构上的完整和语义表达上的明了。汉语和英语之间的这些差异是显著的,英语译文因而难以完全体现汉语原文在音韵节奏上的特有美感。尽管如此,译者还是可采用适当的句法结构以及其他可能的语法手段(如长短句交替),进行声响节奏方面的调节。

原文长短句子交替出现,整散结构并用,在可能的情况下,译文宜变换使用复杂的长句和简洁的短句。例如:

[7] 步行去学校,整整一个小时的路程,健身自不必说。路边的一草一木近在咫尺,多了亲密接触,而接触时还免不得产生些许思绪。

While I was walking to campus, the one-hour trip, which was definitely a good exercise, also brought closer contact with grass or trees adjacent to the roadside. As I was doing so, thoughts tended to arise involuntarily as well.

在例[7]中,原文包含两个句子,六个小句,而译文也是两个句子,分句的数量几乎与原文相等,在节奏的停顿间歇上,也几乎与原文亦步亦趋,传递了原文舒张有弛的节奏感。

汉语的语法单位很容易构成工整对仗的结构,两两相对的整齐结构在《石》文中随处可见,译者应尽量体现原文在音韵节奏上的这个特征。例如:

[8] 大千世界,万紫千红;五彩奇花,争艳斗胜。

The world is *a blazing brilliance of colors*, *a dazzling flourish of flowers* vying for charm.

例[8]是原文的第一句,由四个小句组成,每个小句又由四字词语组成。译文也相应采用了尽量整齐对称的结构,而且两个名词性结构之间舍用并列连词,以避免造成拖沓;此外,在两个平行结构中使用头韵修辞格,以增加声响效果。在语义上,译文并没有完全传递原文的意义,比如"万紫千红""五彩""奇"等词语的意义,这是因为原文的这一句描绘的是春夏之交的明媚景色,除了提供文章的主题背景之外,还起烘托气氛、增加听觉美感的作用。因此,译文可做变通处理,在语义接近的前提下,着重译语听觉上的效果,而不必拘泥于原文的语义信息。

二、关于意境和氛围

诗歌追求意境,散文亦然。意境,简而言之,是作者的思想、情感和志趣与所写景物的交融。作者借描写客观的景物,抒发自己的内心,营造引人入胜的氛围,创造情与景交融的艺术境界。

《石》文取材于日常生活,但文章并没有直接给予石榴花很多的情感表示,而是主要通过一系列形象而生动的描述,在字里行间接表达的。总体上,《石》文的叙述口吻是冷静的、中性的,而当描述石榴花时,作者的语气变得欢快而热烈,借用不同的修辞手段,尽显浪漫想象,达到了情与景的交融。译者必须正确解读原文的意境,才能在译文中加以传递,使得译文具有和原文类似的审美趣味。例如:

[9] 有的花,可谓怒放,绸缎般的"石榴裙"紧束在"细腰"之上,"细腰"之侧,总有那么几枝未及开放的花骨朵儿,似"红果"头势扎饰扎在小姑娘的头上。咦?小姑娘害羞了吧,俏模样藏在婆娑的树叶里……倏忽间,未及开放的花骨朵儿变成了二胡上的琴轸……满树"乐器",怎不闹春!

Some flowers, in their full blossoms, were silky "pomegranate skirts" *as it were*, going tight and slender in the waist. And the "slender waists" were normally accompanied to the side by a couple of flower buds, which looked just like red hawthorn fruits embellishing the hairstyle of a little girl. Why, are you shy little girls, *blooming flowers*? You were hiding your pretty faces among rustling leaves … Then in a blinking moment, *it was as if* the flower buds turned into the pegs of urheens … With all these "musical instruments" in the tree, what a loud celebration it was for the arrival of the spring!

在例[9]中,作者使用了明喻、暗喻、拟人等修辞手段,来刻画石榴花的姿态和形象。在中国文化中,石榴的意象和寓意深入人心,读者对此心领神会。此外,汉语行文追求委婉,以含蓄为美。除了"红果"这个明喻修辞格外,其余都是暗喻修辞格,作者直接将花朵分别比作不同的事物,非但没有让汉语读者费解,相反还令文章意味深长,回味无穷。但是,对于英语读者来说,石榴花可能难以产生类似的感受,加之英语行文讲究直白明了,所以相应将原文中的暗喻转换成了明喻,添加了 as it were, blooming flowers, it was as if 等表达方式。

译文保留了原文中比喻、拟人的意象,而且对于"闹春"的翻译,也因添加了修饰语 loud 而再现了原文传达的声音效果。当然,和原文相比,译文损失了委婉含蓄,这也是为更好地传递意义而不得不采用的变通措施。又如:

[10] 石榴花,你<u>个</u>小精灵,我可是读懂了你!

Pomegranate flowers, you *adorable* little spirits, it's me who knows you well.

[11] 石榴花是"<u>红颜</u>",不仅未遭"<u>天妒</u>",且总能颐养天年。

They are "*beauties*", and are able to grow elegantly and leisurely, free from "*the jealousy of gods*".

例[10]单说的量词"个",带着几分嗔怪、俏皮和轻松。比如,我们经常说"你个小能豆儿""你个傻帽儿""请回个信",甚至公交车、地铁上播音员还经常说"请给需要帮助的乘客让个座儿",此时添加任何数词("让一个座儿")或表示数量的副词("让很多个座儿")都会破坏这样的情感氛围。为了体现这种情感,译文中特意添加了 adorable 一词,将原文的虚变通处理为译文的实。在例[11]中,"红颜天妒"一词中的"红颜"是转喻用法,在译文中只能意译成 beauties,但该词在英语中既可指人,也可指物,因此,将它置于引号之中,提示读者此处 beauties 的意义是非常规的,而"天妒"则直译成 the jealousy of gods,这在英语读者中是可以接受的既定用法。但即使没有这么巧合,照直翻译作者有意置于引号之中的表达,读者也一般会将其作为作者的有意识修辞而特别对待的。

三、关于个性化的话语方式

个性化的话语方式指的是,在特定的语境中,作者选择和使用某种语言表达手段而形成的个体风貌和格调,具体体现在作者选词造句、谋篇布局等较为客观的层面,又体现在作者思想情操与审美志趣等较为主观的层面(张保红,2010:31)。

细读《石》文,可以明显感受到简洁朴实和华丽典雅并存的风格特色。随着表现方式和内容的变化,作者在不同的风格之间进行着切换,同时也展示了作者的情感和志趣。当着重叙事和描写时,作者采用语体上正式程度稍低的话语方式,语言倾向于简单朴实和轻松活泼,比如使用"看不上""管不了那么多""多走它几步""我说呢""俏模样"等口语色彩浓郁的表达方式和自由灵活的句式。而当着重议论和抒情时,作者则采用语体正式的话语方式,比如使用"攀附""招徕""馥郁""屡次""可谓""尚未""自不必说"等典雅色彩浓郁的词语和"不曾为……所……""颇有……之意"等整齐对称的结构。这两种不同的话语风格,与描写的事物和展示的主题相辅相成、相得益彰。

翻译时,把握作者的个性化话语方式,对再现原文的艺术性和情感非常重要。译者应从原文的篇章结构、作者使用的表达方式,以及词语、句法等不同角度,对作者的个体话语风格进行深入细致的理解和把握,并在译文中加以恰当地体现,对作者的表现意图进行移植。一般来讲,原文用语简单的,译文不宜华丽,反之亦然。例如:

[12] 为饱口福,绕绕路,多走它几步。

To have a taste of the fruits, I *changed my usual route*, which *only involved a little extra distance to cover*.

[13] 前两天路过时就光是那么想象……

Two days ago, I *passed by* it again, *doubts in mind*…

[14] 名花有人攀附,野花招徕不屑。

While renowned flowers win *sycophantic admiration*, wild ones simply grow humbly unnoticed.

[15] 六月初这几天,扬州的天气出奇地凉爽,颇有春暖乍寒之意。

Early June of this year saw in Yangzhou an unusually cool temperature, giving one *the illusion of a returning early spring*.

例[12]和例[13]的口语色彩很浓厚,具体表现为动词"绕"的叠音用法,以及"它""光是""那么"等虚词的使用,使得话语风格更加家常。在译文中,为了契合原文的风格,译者也相应地使用了简单常用的小词和结构(斜体部分)。例[14]和例[15]中"攀附""招徕""春暖乍寒""颇有"等词语和两两相对结构的使用,则体现了华丽典雅的风格,而译文也相应使用了英语中的正式表达方式,比如大词(sycophantic)、名词化结构(admiration, illusion),以及英语文学作品常见的"无灵主语+有灵动词"的搭配(Early June of this year saw)等。

散文作为文学作品,要求译文对于原文内容和美感因素的求真度相当高。在原文和译文之间,译者应尽可能充分发挥译语的优势,贴近译语的习惯表达形式,最大限度地再现原文的韵味(关于汉语散文韵味在英译时的再现问题,可参阅:周领顺,2012)。

原文

节俭意识与道德行为[1]

　　节俭大约分为两类，一是人们为果腹度日而节俭，一是人们因衣食无忧而节俭。前者节俭迫于生活的压力，限于物质层面；后者节俭则为美德，已上升到了一种精神境界。[2]

　　人之初接受节俭的教育大多是从唐代李绅《悯农（其一）》诗开始的："锄禾日当午，汗滴禾下土。谁知盘中餐，粒粒皆辛苦。"[3]人们偏于做字面理解，并由此对孩子进行劝诫。教育者一般以"一粒粮食从种到收农民要付出多少辛勤的劳动"开场，以要求受教育者"一定要珍惜粮食"作结。显然，这主要是从物质层面上看问题的，其效果对于生活在城市的孩子而言，不但不会有深切的感受，而且还可能会从李绅《悯农（其二）》"春种一粒粟，秋收万颗子"感受到粮食从种到收所带来的魔幻般的惊喜！

　　从经济学的角度，所谓的"粒粒皆辛苦"早已发生了质的转变。粮食从种到收只是农民的事，城市人用自己的劳动所得——钱，购买农民的产品——粮食，粮食一旦进入购销渠道[4]，就意味着变成了可以用以交换的商品。对于消费者，"粒粒"不再是农民的粮食，而是自己所付出的劳动，这叫"等价交换"[5]，对于种田的农民或消费者，只是分工不同，各取所需。只看到表面现象就牢骚满腹者在诗歌中不乏其例，如宋代张俞《蚕妇》："昨日入城市，归来泪满巾。遍身罗绮者，不是养蚕人。"宋代梅尧臣《陶者》："陶尽门前土，屋上无片瓦。十指不沾泥，鳞鳞居大厦。"如今的现实生活中，"遍身罗绮者，不是养蚕人"的大有人在，"十指不沾泥，鳞鳞居大厦"的比比皆是，但并非说明他们是寄生虫，属于剥削阶层。诗歌所透射的无非是"四海无闲田，农夫犹饿死"［李绅《悯农（其二）》］和"屋上无片瓦"的残酷现实以及以剥削为主要特点的社会制度下贫苦劳动者的生活写照。

　　"粒粒皆辛苦"者，广义上讲应指所有劳动者[6]。但从现实来看，某些"大款"的劳动所得，是超过本身所付出的和所应得之外的"剩余价值"，比如歌星表演一首久唱不衰的老歌，就可轻易收入数万元；明星做广告就那么一颦一笑，所得足以令最基层的劳动者数辈人瞠目结舌[7]。"粒粒皆辛苦"吗？谬矣[8]！你不管怎样提高水电等生活消费品的价格，他照样有理由挥金如土："烧钱"一如既往，不觉毫发有损，怎能为之动容？！对于那些公款吃喝者，只能过之，并无不及：钱不从己出，何痛之有！

从珍惜粮食、节约水电等物质的层面倡导节俭可能对什么样的人群起到警示的作用呢？

首先，对于真正的"粒粒皆辛苦"者，这样的宣传收效不会太明显，因为节俭是他们赖以糊口和生存下去的有效方式之一，节俭出于必须；其次，对于那些"大款"，这样的宣传收效不会太明显，钱来得容易，根本用不着节俭；再次，对于公款吃喝者，这样的宣传收效不会太明显，他们没有节俭的理由，要节俭，就压根儿不要走近公款吃喝的餐桌前。而对于那些通过不正当手段而获得不义之财者，节俭如浮云，因为他们早已丧失做人的底线。

榜样的力量是无穷的。有权而从不行使"浪费"权利者，有钱而从不挥霍无度者，甚至将己之钱财献给公益事业者，时有所闻。[9]节俭与否，决定了一个人的精神风貌，特别对于全球资源日益匮乏的今天，节俭构成了一个人道德行为和完美人生的必有部分。

译文

On Frugality and Morality

The practice of frugality broadly falls into two categories. In one, it is observed by people who have to struggle for their physical survival, and in the other, by those who live free of worries about food or clothing. The former group does so as a daily necessity under the pressure of subsistence, suggesting a focus of their economy on material supplies, while the latter group does so as a virtuous trait, their conduct thus ascending to a moral altitude.

In Chinese culture, people gain their initial awareness of frugality mostly from their introduction to the poem "Sympathy for Farmers(No. 1)" by Li Shen of the Tang Dynasty (618 – 907), which goes like this: At noon they hoe up weeds/Their sweat drips on the soil/Who knows the rice that feeds/Is the fruit of hard toil? The poem tends to be interpreted literally and is employed as a vehicle for instilling in children a frugal philosophy. The adult begins by stressing the hard work farmers have to put in to reap a grain of rice and concludes with the exhortation that food is not to be wasted in any case. Evidently, such education emphasizes the physical aspects of farm work and might not imprint a deep impression upon urban children, who could even adversely feel a stupendous joy at the scenario of grain cultivation as described by "A seed is planted deep in spring / With myriad grains reaped in autumn", the two poetic lines in "Sympathy for Farmers (No. 2)" by the same poet.

From the economic perspective, the "fruit of hard toil" can undergo a significant change in nature. Grains, for example, are the product of farmers, who take exclusive charge of their growth from sowing to reaping. As the fruit of agricultural work, they are purchasable by urban people with the return for their work, i. e. money. Hence, grains become interchangeable commodities once they are in circulation in the market. From the consumers' point of view, this is an "exchange at equal value", in which grains, when transferred in ownership from farmers, are what is acquired as a result of their own work. Between farmers and other consumers, the difference lies in the division of labor, whereby each gets what he needs from others. Complaints arising from failure to see this point often find expression in poems as in "The Silkworm Woman" (i. e. I went yesterday to sell silk in town/I had my kerchief wet with tears when back/I found those people who are dressed in silk/Had never done a silkworm breeding task) by Zhang Yu of the Song Dynasty (960 – 1279), or "The Potter" (i. e. The potter used up clay around his hut/His own yet went without tiles on the roof/People who never soiled their hands with mud/All lived in mansions covered with dense tiles) by Mei Yaochen of the same period. In contemporary society, people who are dressed in silk or live in mansions are probably not silkworm breeders or construction workers. However, it does not follow that they are parasitic exploiters. What these poems actually profile is the abject reality for the impoverished farming population in an ancient exploiting society, who inhabited cottages absent of a tiled roof, or even starved to death though they were industrious, leaving no land uncultivated.

Broadly speaking, the industrious population as a term should denote the entire working class. However, in reality, some wealthy people often receive disproportionate shares of "surplus value", which far exceed the value of the work they put in, as in the case of singers who, by performing a classic song on the stage, can pocket as much as tens of thousands, or superstars who, by a single appearance in a commercial, can rake in a staggering amount that could stun the lowest strata of the working class. Is their remuneration justified by their work? Probably not. Given that, no matter how high the price is raised for daily necessities like water or electricity, they could be as profligate as ever, spending money like water. Why do they have to commit themselves to frugality when the quality of their life goes unaffected by a mere rise in price? And those who lavish public funds on banquets could be even more squandering. How could they get seized by heartache when they are not overspending their own money?

If frugality was to be advocated from the perspective of economizing food, water or electricity as material resources, how could it achieve a desirable educational purpose for the public?

For the really industrious population, such preaching would have little significance in that frugality as an effective means of sustaining a living is a protocol they have to follow. For those big money earners, it would not work, as they are able to make easy money and see no need for austerity. For those who go after wining and dining at public expenses, it would not have much effect, either, for they do not have an impetus for frugality, or otherwise they would have refrained from such sumptuous meals. And, finally, for those who have accumulated wealth by resort to ill-gotten means, their baseness knows no bounds, and the appeal for frugality would definitely fall on deaf ears.

Moral examples are shining models of behavior to follow. It is far from rare to hear about those who are in the position of power but never abused their convenient access to extravagance, or those who are in possession of affluence but always remain on guard against prodigality while being generous in charitable donations. Whether one eschews wastefulness embodies his moral state, especially in the present society that is being jeopardized by an increasing scarcity of global resources. Frugality should be an inseparable constituent of one's morality as well as of his or her ideal life experience.

注释

[1] 总体而言,原文在语言风格上直白朴实,但又不失华丽典雅,在语体上是非常正式的。译文尽量保持同样的风格,简单常用的词语和大词雅词交替使用,句子结构的安排采用非常正式的形式,如名词化结构(如 concludes with the exhortation, a single appearance 等)、"介词+名词化结构"的搭配(如 from their introduction to the poem 等)、"虚义动词+名词化结构"的搭配(如 undergo a significant change 等)及复杂的句法结构等。

[2] 原文的第一段在结构和语义方面整齐对称,译文在传递意义的同时,在形式上也尽量靠近原文。但英语表达一般忌简单的重复,原文采用重复之处,译文采用了省略、替代等不同的手段。"一是人们因衣食无忧而节俭"这一句的译文承上省略了主语和谓语动词,表达为 and in the other, by those who live free of worries about food or clothing。而下一句中的"前者节俭""后者节俭"的译文则采用了替代的方式。"前者节俭"译为 does so as a daily necessity,其中 as a daily necessity 是原文没有的信息,为额外添加,是为了和下文"后者节俭"的译文 does so as a virtuous trait 保持一致,获得结构上整齐对称的效果。

[3]《悯农(其一)》这首诗的译者是许渊冲,见《唐宋诗一百五十首(汉英对照)》,北京大学出版社,1995年版,第213页。

[4]"进入购销渠道"就是"进入市场的流通领域"或"所有权发生了改变"的意思,译为 (once) they are in circulation in the market 比较自然,大可不必直译成 they enter the channel of purchase-and-sale。

[5]"对于消费者……这叫'等价交换'"这几个小句,译文的语序和原文的语序完全相反。汉语一般先做铺垫性陈述,后说结论,这是一种逻辑上的先后关系;英语则可先说结论,后做铺垫性描述,这是一种违反逻辑顺序的语序。汉语缺乏或少用形式手段,因此,说话者往往按照事件实际发生的时间先后顺序或逻辑上的先后关系组织安排语言成分,而英语则可借助形式手段,既可按照也可违反时间上或逻辑上的先后顺序,来安排信息。

[6]"'粒粒皆辛苦'者"和"劳动者"的指称都是广义上的,包括体力劳动者和脑力劳动者。因此,译文分别用了 the industrious population 和 the entire working class 这样的表达方式,而不用指称体力劳动者的

laborers 等词语。

　　[7] 该小句应理解成明星一次的收入抵得上劳动者数辈人的收入或明星的收入让不同层次的工薪阶层瞠目结舌。因此，可变通译为（singers）can rake in a staggering amount that could stun the lowest strata of the working class，这样处理符合英语追求逻辑严密的表达习惯。

　　[8] 明星只凭广告里露一下脸，收入就不菲，也不能完全算没有付出辛苦的劳动，只是劳动没有直接付出在广告里。所以，在翻译"谬矣！"一句时，为了避免绝对，让话留有余地，译文添加 probably 一词，而不是用表达"绝对"之意的 definitely，absolutely 等词。

　　[9] "有权而从不行使'浪费'权利者……时有所闻"这几个小句的翻译有几个方面需要注意。(1) "浪费"不是人的权利，所以译文没有用看似对应的 right 等词语来翻译原文的"权利"，而是变通表达为 never abused their convenient access to extravagance，意为"从不滥用（权力带来的）挥霍便利"。原文之所以用"权利"，是为了更好地和动词"行使"构成搭配，翻译时应揣摩作者用词的意图。(2) "有钱而从不挥霍"和"将钱财捐给公益事业"，在行为上是矛盾的，因此，译文使用表示明显对照或对立的连接词 while，将两个看似对立的行为联系在了一起。(3) 汉语和英语在表达习惯方面，有很多不同的地方，不能死译、硬译，句中的"公益事业"其实就是"慈善事业"的意思，即 charitable donations，不能根据字面意思表达成 public career 之类。(4) 原文的结构比较工整，译文也尽量保持原文的风格。原文的"权"和"钱"押尾韵，译文中的 in the position of power 和 in possession of affluence 结构相似，position 和 possession 读音相似，语音上有一定的美感。此外，译文在整齐中也尽显变化，前一句中"从不行使"的否定意义通过否定词 never 的词汇意义来表达，后一句中的"从不挥霍"的否定意义通过介词 against 的词汇意义来表达。

> 专评

逻辑性与艺术性的统一

《节俭意识与道德行为》（以下简称《节》）一文属于杂文。杂文，或者说是议论性散文，是广义散文的一种。英语里常说的 essay，就包括了汉语写作体裁中的这一类，所以《鲁迅杂文集》译为 Selected Essays of Lu Xun，是合乎情理的。杂文是随感式的杂体文章，一般形式短小，语言犀利，内容无所不包，格式丰富多样，有杂感、杂谈、短评、随笔、札记等。总体上，杂文偏于议论，以议事论理为目的，属于议论类文体，以批判为其灵魂，所以译文的题目增加了表示"论"的 on。

杂文是一种直接、迅速反映社会事变或动向的文艺性论文，它执行的是"杂而有文"的原则。所谓"杂"，说的是事理之间的逻辑性，即通过一定的逻辑形式糅合贯通到一起。而杂文又是形象说理的，所以"杂文"之"文"，谈的是艺术性。它惯用各种修辞手法，或贬或讽，借以表达作者的观点和情感。我们讨论《节》文的翻译，便主要围绕杂文的逻辑性和艺术性及其在翻译中的再现策略而展开。

《节》文以"节俭"为主题展开议论，主要针砭的是社会上的浪费现象。作者将节俭意识与道德行为联系起来，把它作为行为的一个道德标准加以约束，认为达此才算拥有真正的美德，才算达至理想的精神境界。为了实现这一目标，作者调动了各种说理的手段，译者也应循此做出努力。

《节》文曾由笔者的研究生译为英语，收录于周领顺编著的《散文英译过程》（2012：248 – 257）一书，但外国朋友表示不能完全领会作者真意。原因是什么呢？该书提供的读后感给出了部分答案，比如认为"句子很长，且句子和句子之间没有明显的连词相连，缺少严谨的逻辑联系，致使读者读完后的印象是冗长庞杂而不甚明白句子要表达的含义"，"译者做到了忠实原文，可是一味地忠实原文（形式上），一味地采用直译的方法，丢失了原文的可读性，片面的直译忽略了原文的隐含意义"等。刊登于此的原文做了些许改动，但主体内容未变，而这里呈现的译文，是我们的全新之作。

评析此文，我们拟从杂文的两大特点（逻辑性和艺术性）入手，结合周领顺(2014a:76－77)"求真"(为实现务实目标,译者全部或部分求取原文语言所负载意义真相的行为)和"务实"(在对原文语言所负载的意义全部或部分求真的基础上,译者为满足务实性需要所采取的态度和方法)的一些思想,展开相关的翻译讨论。

一、杂文的逻辑性及其求真性翻译

众所周知,在语法和篇章层面,汉语的语言组织偏重意合,语法关系、语义成分常隐含或省略,而英语则不同,句法结构在形式上要求完整,语义表达上要求明确直白,不容含糊,篇章衔接也是偏重形合。因文体不同,在语言内部这个倾向在程度上也会略有差异。如,汉语的新闻、政论等文体中,使用句间形合手段的频率则要高于小说、散文等文体。上文所述,杂文偏于议论说理,重逻辑,因此《节》文也借助了不少句内和篇章衔接手段,如"但""因为""并""即使……也……""不但……而且……""显然"等,以使得语义逻辑的表达严谨,丝丝入扣,此与一般偏于"形散"的抒情散文不同,翻译时自然要使之得到相应的体现。仅举一例,以资比较:

[1] 节俭大约分为两类,<u>一是</u>人们为果腹度日而节俭,<u>一是</u>人们因衣食无忧而节俭。

The practice of frugality broadly falls into two categories. *In one*, it is observed by people who have to struggle for their physical survival, and *in the other*, by those who live free of worries about food or clothing.

《节》作为杂文,相比典型的文学文体,较多采用了一些形式手段,尽管如此,表达逻辑性或语义关系的成分,在上下文中省略或隐含的情形还是很多,体现了典型的汉语语言表达特征。汉语和英语之间在组织形式上存在差异,在翻译尤其是汉译英时应加以关注。译者常需要仔细揣摩原文的意思,根据上下文添加一些原文句子表层形式中没有表达出来的语义信息,有时甚至需要对原文的表层形式做较大的改变,不然就有可能让译语读者如坠云里雾中。《节》的译文中,必须添加语义成分或对原文形式做改变的情形并不少见。例如:

[2] 对于消费者,"<u>粒粒</u>"不再是农民的粮食,而是自己所付出的<u>劳动</u>,这叫"等价交换"。

From the consumers' point of view, this is an "exchange at equal value", in which grains, when transferred in ownership from farmers, are *what is acquired as a result of* their own work.

[3] 从珍惜粮食、节约水电等物质的层面倡导节俭<u>对于什么样的人群可能起到警示的作用呢</u>？

If frugality was to be advocated from the perspective of economizing food, water or electricity as material resources, *how could it achieve a desirable educational purpose for the public*?

例[2]中的"'粒粒'……而是自己所付出的劳动"一句，作者为了取得结构上比较整齐的效果而省略了一些语义成分。根据上下文，这一句实际要表达的意义为："'粒粒'……而是自己付出劳动之后换来的东西。"译者为完整地表达这一层意思，在译文中添加了 what is acquired as a result of，否则足令疑窦顿生：明明是农民所种的粮食，一旦消费者购买之后，怎么就变成了他们自己所付出的劳动了呢？而例[3]的原文，表面上看来是一般的疑问句，实际是用作反讽的，也是为了引导读者注意和思考，如不仔细品味，翻译不到位，就会给读者留下期待得到明确答案的言外之意。为了获得类似的效果，译者将其译为 how 引导的反问句，而未用和原文表面对应的 what 疑问词。这样处理，在形式上虽然和原文有一定的距离，但译语读者获得了相似的阅读效果。另外，也是为了使译文在上下文的语义连贯上更加显豁，便于译语读者的理解。

二、杂文的艺术性及其务实性处理

杂文具有较高的文学性。在翻译《节》文时，译者便尽量体现原文语言的文学特征和其他美学因素。例如，原文中整齐工整的结构比比皆是，译文也尽量亦步亦趋（例[1]）。又如，原文中点缀了不少古典色彩浓厚的用词和结构，译文便使用了一定数量的语体正式、带有文学色彩的大词或结构（如 ascending, exhortation, whereby, affluence, remuneration justified, prodigality, feel a stupendous joy at the scenario of grain cultivation as described by, jeopardized by an increasing scarcity of global resources 等）。在向原文靠近的同时，译者力求译文语言不露翻译时可能产生的穿凿之痕，尽可能达到自然顺畅的效果。以下主要讨论形象色彩词语和诗歌的翻译问题。

第一，形象色彩词语的翻译问题。

汉英民族在思维方式上存在差异，汉民族善形象思维，英民族则善抽象思维；在词汇和表达层面，汉语和英语之间的一个显著差异是，汉语倾向于使用形象生动的词语,而英语则倾向于使用简洁直白的词语。

语言之间在使用形象色彩浓厚词语上的差异,只是多少有别,不是本质上有无的对立。假如译语中有对应的形象表达,则未必非要另辟蹊径不可。例如,《节》文中的"大款""挥金如土"等词语,译文中使用了英语中类似的形象表达方式 big money earners 和 spend money like water。但在多数情况下,译文舍弃原文词语的形象性,是为了获得更加自然的效果。例如:

[4] 明星做广告就那么<u>一颦一笑</u>,所得足以令最基层的劳动者数辈人<u>瞠目结舌</u>。

... superstars who, by *a single appearance* in a commercial, can rake in a *staggering* amount that could *stun* the lowest strata of the working class.

[5] 而对于那些通过不正当手段而获得不义之财者,节俭如<u>浮云</u>……

For those who have accumulated wealth by resort to ill-gotten means... the appeal for frugality would definitely *fall on deaf ears*.

例[4]中的"一颦一笑""瞠目结舌"等词语描述的是面部表情,但在此语境中实际上前者表示"轻而易举",后者表示"难以置信"。假如译文能够形神兼备,当然是再好不过,否则以表达深意为主。例[5]中的"浮云"是近年来流行的网络词语,意为"虚无"或"不值一提",取云之"轻飘、无根基而不牢靠"之义。在文中,作者用"浮云"主要表达的是,对于节俭的倡导之于某些人而言,根本是多余的,他们回馈的是充耳不闻的态度。因此,译者改变原词语的形象,将其切换为 fall on deaf ears 这一英语中常用的形象表达,以收获自然的效果。

第二,诗歌的翻译问题。

说到艺术性,免不得要涉及文中诗歌的翻译。毕竟,诗歌是最具形式感的艺术形式。对于诗歌,一般情况下是从美的角度欣赏和进行翻译再现的(焦鹏帅、曹明伦,2012),但文中的几处诗歌,其功能是为加强说理之用的。对于说理性、批判性的杂文,逻辑性上的"求真"是首要的,艺术性上的"求美"在难以兼得的情况下,甚至可以做出牺牲。此时和许渊冲(2000)的指导思想发生了些许抵牾。他说:"求真是低标准,求美是高标准;真是必要条件,美是充分条件……如译得似的诗远不如原诗美,那牺牲美就是得不偿失;如果译得'失真'却可以和原诗比美,那倒可以说是以得补失;如果所得大于所失,那就是译诗胜过了原诗。"

文中引用了四首古诗,分别是《悯农(其一)》《悯农(其二)》《蚕妇》和《陶者》,除了《悯农(其一)》直接采用了许渊冲的译文外,其余的均由我们自己译出。其中的诗句作为修辞的手段,散落在整篇文章的各处。例如:

[6] 所谓的"粒粒皆辛苦"早已发生了质的转变。

[7] 如今的现实生活中,"遍身罗绮者,不是养蚕人"的大有人在,"十指不沾泥,鳞鳞居大厦"的比比皆是。

[8] "粒粒皆辛苦"吗?谬矣!

诗歌难译,举世公认,弗罗斯特(R. Frost)所谓"诗为译之失"(Poetry is what gets lost in translation),一语中的,但皆以意境美难以再现为前提。在该文中,这些古诗之美并非欲再现而后快,其重点在于求意义之真,以帮助说理,并处理好用作修辞手段的某些诗句。

汉语是单音节语言,语素之间的组合灵活自由,例如"粒粒皆辛苦""十指不沾泥,鳞鳞居大厦"等诗句后面增加一个"者"字或"的"字,就用来指称某一类人。对于汉语读者来说,这些古诗浅显易懂,耳熟能详,作者引用自然。但英语在句法形式上追求完整,在表达上崇尚直白简洁,假如直译,反而显得啰唆,如把"'粒粒皆辛苦'者"直译为 people who get fruit from hard toil,就不如意译成 the industrious population 来得简洁自然。除了例[6]中的"粒粒皆辛苦"采用直译之外,余者均采用了意译,即

[6] The *"fruit of hard toil"* can undergo a significant change in nature.

[7] People who are *dressed in silk* or *live in mansio*ns are probably not *silkworm breeders* or *construction workers*.

[8] *Is their remuneration justified by their work*? Probably not.

三、译 后 话

翻译讲究平衡,对讲究逻辑性与艺术性于一体的杂文翻译尤其如此。许钧(2002:87)说:"翻译是一种'平衡'的艺术,好的翻译家,就像是'踩钢丝'的行家,善于保持平衡,而不轻易偏向一方,失去重心。"(关于翻译平衡性的讨论,详见周领顺,2014b:218-223)

曹明伦(2002)说,学习翻译,就是学习如何处理"最接近"和"最自然"这一对矛盾。所谓"最接近",就是在语义、语气、情感、风格等方面尽可能地接近原文,而所谓"最自然",则指译文的语言要尽可能地通顺

自然。翻译的根本是要确保译文和原文如影随形,即达到"最接近"的效果。但在实际的翻译过程中,有时为了实现"最自然",也会出现偏离。

意志体的译者,是原语和译语的操纵者,要同时对作者和读者负责,努力维持平衡,是译者的着力用心之处。对于文学作品而言,靠近作者、向原文求真,是默认的译者之为,这是由文学作品作为表达型文本的性质所决定的,但求真的同时还要务实,使译文自然,提高可读性,满足读者的需求。

原文

得州云霞

云,是最最常见之物。满眼的素材,随便摘来一片,揉碎了,就是一段文字。因其平常,所以人人会写;因其普通,所以极难状述其美;因其飘忽,所以即使书写出来,也很难再觅芳踪。[1]

各地的云大同小异。然而,我却想写一写得州的云,因为这云更多的时候带有得州的特点。得州地广,抬眼可见成片的土地,零星几棵树,只是点缀于广袤,颇有戈壁之风光;得州地广,广到少见高楼多见平房。[2]因为地广,云才变得那样辽阔,那样接地连天;因为地广,才可以眺望到天边,无云的时候,天空一片碧蓝[3]。不管是白云满天,不管是乌云遮地,开着车往前直驰,竟是直跃云海一般。[4]

得州不仅地广,还因为没有污染而使天空变得澄明异常。晴空无边,纵横交错的喷气飞机滑过,像轮船犁起的道道白浪,分不清是天在海里,还是海在天上。暮色里,千万只硕大的黑鸟呼啸着落了又起,更能衬托天色的诡异。

云每天都有变幻,似难归纳出个一般的特点。但得州之云,就有它的个性:震撼。立体感、层次感和玻璃般的质感,要什么感就有什么感;水墨画、山水画,就连中国画,都一应俱全。[5]君不见[6],当道路的尽头被乌云罩作黑色,而身后却还是阳光灿烂。肯定是画,但分明又多了几分动感。

乘坐飞机,那才叫美,[7]四周裹的都是白云。白云,我看是山,因为成团的白云有山一样的巍峨;白云,我看是海,因为在机身下,我好像站立山头俯瞰;白云,我看是千堆雪,因为需要发动千军才能扫除;白云,我看是万朵棉,因为只有借助神力才能收获。[8]大量的白云岿然不动,但见远处的飞机掠过,强大的气流并不会令其有少许改变;少量的白云如烟,快速流泻,即使穿越静止的云团也并不歇脚。白云团团时,大有排山倒海之势;白云点点时,似乎是顽皮的仙女将杰作造就;白云串串时,列于青天碧海之间,若百舸争流于浩瀚;白云丝丝时,擦着舷窗,似乎伸手可揽……远处的白云白中泛黄,摆个城堡样让人有不尽的鬼魅遐想。常用的形容词都稍显干瘪,不妨借上几个量词:团团、列

Ⅲ. 散文英译专评

列、点点、朵朵、片片、丝丝、串串?

云不寻常,晚霞亦然。一次从波士顿飞往旧金山,从东到西,整整一夜,我就徜徉在晚霞里。追着晚霞飞,思绪游弋于泛红泛黄的机翼和远处天边那抹亮丽,浪漫就激荡在亢奋里。而得州晚霞,美在平日。

得州晚霞,变换次第。[9]云时若炭火,块状堆积,从黑到红,再从红色走向沉寂;云时若金凤,似画笔画出的丝丝缕缕,好像在眼前飘飞;云时若波光,粼粼碎金洒满天西。红云经常与蓝天共舞,恰似演绎着烈火与碧海的传奇。

夕阳将云撕裂一道缝隙,挤出来,刺向远处的一溜建筑,建筑似金带,幻化在余晖里,而头顶的天空却还如黑云压城[10]一般;远处镶着玻璃的建筑,平日里没什么稀奇,但在夕阳下,却似整块的赤金在原野伫立。当周围夜幕开始拉起,本是银色的飞机,黑暗中竟如通红的金鱼游过天际,有的还拖着个长长的红尾巴,反射着高空尚未消退的夕阳瑰丽。待繁星眨着蓝光初上,西边的地平线却还似晨曦微露,身后的大半个天空竟已沉沉睡去。

大自然美得神秘,收在眼里,却在心底升起。我寄情于得州云霞[11],竟时常为捕捉美妙瞬间而学夸父追日。

译文

Clouds and Sunsets in Texas

Clouds are the most common of all. They provide resourceful materials for literary creation, and any piece, pulled down from the sky, could be crumbled into words. As they look familiar, people all know how to write about them. As they appear ordinary, words are too weak to do justice to their beauty. As they go unstable, they will dissipate and vanish even though they can be depicted in writing.

Though clouds do not present much difference between places, I am inspired to write about those I saw in Texas, because they are characterized, for most of the time, by Texan features. Texas is extensive in that vast stretches of land are a prevalent sight, and trees grow there sparsely and scantily as the lone sign of life, attributing the landscape with a desert trait. Texas is extensive also in that one-storey houses far outnumber high-rise buildings. Because of this feature, clouds stretch out so far as to connect the sky and the earth. And because of this feature, vision extends as far as the horizon, and the sky is an uninterrupted vibrant blue when it is cloudless. On a day of overspreading clouds, be they white or dark, a speedy car ride is an experience as of sailing in a sea of clouds.

Apart from being vast, Texas is also a place without pollution, which gives rise to a piercingly clear sky. In the blue infinity, in the wake of jet aircrafts crisscrossing the sky undulating clouds build up like waves being churned up by the passage of ships. It is a sky in the sea or it is a sea in the sky. No difference between the two. In the dusk, flocks of huge black birds soar up and down the sky, adding an unearthly touch to the twilight aura.

As clouds never remain the same for every day, it is hard to generalize particular properties for them. However, those in Texas have a personality, marked by a stupefying magnificence. They are stereoscopic, multi-layered, translucent: they possess whatever quality one can think of. They are ink wash paintings, landscape paintings, Chinese paintings: they demonstrate whatever form there exists. It is often the case that one end of the road far ahead is enveloped by sable clouds while the other end is still bathing in the glaring sunshine. Such a scene is definitely a painting, but one endowed with a motion element.

An aerial view is even more spectacular, with clouds encompassing the plane on all sides. Clouds, I perceive them as mountains, because they are likewise majestic when assembling in clusters. Clouds, I take them as the sea, because in a flight over them, I can command a panoramic view of them as from the mountain top. Clouds, I feel them to be snow piles, which can only be scavenged with gigantic manpower. Clouds, I see them to be cotton blooms, which can only be picked with superhuman force. Clouds of colossal masses are steadfast, and remain stationary even at the powerful turbulence of a distant plane passing by while those of thin wisps disperse quickly like smokes, and do not pause even when they are scudding through immobile clouds. Gathering in clumps, clouds share the same throng as of avalanches cascading down. Floating in spots, they are the artistic works as if done by elfish fairies. Lining up in strands between the azure sky and sea, they look like sailboats racing in a blue vastness. Drifting in threads near airplane windows, they seem to be within easy and close reach. And rising up in lofty towers, distant white clouds, tinted with gold, swarm one with whimsical imaginations. If basic adjectives do not suffice in describing the beauty of clouds, perhaps quantifiers can do a better job. What about clumps, rows, spots, pieces, slices, treads, strands, for example?

Clouds in Texas are no ordinary sight and the same is true of sunsets there. I was once flying from Boston to San Francisco, and during the flight from east to west I was left for the whole night soaking in the sunset glow. Chasing the sunset on the flight, I just had my thoughts rambling well beyond the red and yellow tinged aircraft wing to the gleaming radiance at the rim of the sky, the romantic mood surging high in the swelling excitement. However, the beauty of the sunset in Texas is manifested more in its diurnal routine.

The sunset is capricious in Texas, with clouds appearing as multiple images. Sunset clouds look like charcoal fires stacking up in lumps, and change in color from dark into red and from that eventually into a complete fade-out. Or they resemble golden phoenixes, floating as if just before the eyes like brush paintings of wispy strands. Or they shine like ripples, their shimmering golden fragments besprinkling themselves across the western sky. Or they dance in red to the rhythm of a blue sky, as though they were fires set magically ablaze on an azure sea.

The setting sun breaks through a crack in the clouds and thrusts its rays at a row of faraway buildings. Showering in this afterglow, it stands out like a golden ribbon against a sky of a multitude of dark clouds. The glass buildings in the distance, an ordinary sight at normal times, tower imposingly in the open country as whole pieces of solid gold under the sunset. Beneath the deepening shroud of darkness over the landscape, aircrafts, originally silver in color, sail across the sky like flaming goldfish, some leaving behind them a long reddish tail that rebounds the lingering gleams of a sunset glory. At dusk when stars begin to creep up the sky blinking blue, the western horizon is still illuminated, however, as if by the dawn light, upon a background of a half sky in the opposite direction that is already departing into sound sleep.

Nature, mysteriously beautiful, is perceived in the eye and cherished in the heart. A lover of the natural spectacles in Texas, now and again I acted like the mythical sun chaser Kua Fu, and went enthusiastically after the wonderful moments of their fleeting beauty.

注释

［1］原文的词语重复比较多，有表达性的，也有修辞性的。对于前者，在很短的上下文中，译文应尽量避免同形词语的重复。而对于后者，则一概再现，但是在重复中，也尽量体现出一点变化。例如，针对"因其平常……因其普通……因其飘忽……"这几个排比句，译文也同样采用了排比句式，但谓语动词使用的是 look, appear, go 等不同的连系动词，以体现重复之中有变化。原文第五段中的"白云，我看是……"，第七段中的"云时若……"等排比句的翻译也采用了同样的策略。

［2］这个小句中的"高楼"译成 high-rise buildings，"平房"译成 one-storey houses。House 本来就是低矮房子的意思，添加修饰语 one-storey，是为了与 high-rise buildings 构成结构上的平衡和对称。另外，"广到少见高楼多见平房"这个小句看似可表达成英语的 so … that … 结构，但根据语义，它是"得州地广"的具体体现，而不是"得州地广"造成的结果，因此，译为 in that 引导的分句。

［3］"天空一片碧蓝"中的"一片"不是一般的数量词，应理解成表示强调意义的数量词，意即"一整片"，因此，译文中添加 uninterrupted 一词。

［4］"不管是白云满天……竟是直跃云海一般"这几个小句的翻译，需要注意以下几个方面。（1）"白云满天"和"乌云遮地"，两两相对，结构对称，译文将这两个结构做了合并处理，只将"白"和"乌"表达成对称的结构，即 be they white or dark，也能体现音韵节奏上的平衡感。（2）"开着车往前直驰"译成名词化结构 a speedy car ride，更符合英语书面语的表达习惯。（3）"竟是直跃云海一般"这个小句中的"一般"，是汉语明喻修辞格的标记之一，英语除了 seem, like, as if 等常用的词语之外，还有副词 as。这个小句译为 an experience as of sailing in a sea of clouds，相当于 an experience like one sailing in a sea of clouds，而 as 的这一用法偏向正式。

［5］"要什么感就有什么感"和"都一应俱全"都带有夸张的意味，

分别译为 they possess whatever quality one can think of 和 they demonstrate whatever form there exists，译文的语义与原文基本一致。原文的句子形式整齐对称，译文的句子也取得了相似的效果。

［6］"君不见"是话语标记语，后面的句子一般描述的都是常见的事实或现象。如将其直译成 Can't you see，显得呆滞，"君不见"可变通译为 It is often the case that，比较自然，但在色彩上略失原文的文学性。

［7］这两个小句之间隐含了一些信息，假如表达完整，应是"乘坐飞机往外看，那景色才叫美"，因此，可译为：An aerial view is even more spectacular.

［8］作者将白雪比喻为"千堆雪""万朵棉"，这是汉语中常见的夸张表达法，两个结构对称对仗，分别译为 snow piles, cotton blooms，译文在结构和语义上也整齐对称。但译文没有体现出"千""万"的意义，是为了获得简洁明快的效果，如将所在句子译成 Clouds, I feel them to be tons of snow piles. Clouds, I see them to be rows of cotton blooms 则略嫌拖沓。

［9］"晚霞"指日落时天空的色彩和云彩，上文将"晚霞"表达为 sunsets，而原文的这一段主要描述日落时分的云彩。因此，在翻译"得州晚霞，变换次第"这两个小句时，添加了 clouds 这个意象。将整个句子表达为 The sunset is capricious in Texas, with clouds appearing as multiple images，使语义更加连贯。

［10］汉语擅长形象思维，习惯于多用形象词语表达概念，其使用频率大大高于英语。翻译时，常需舍弃汉语原文的形象，例如，把这个句子中的"黑云压城"意译为 a sky of a multitude of dark clouds 即如此。

［11］"寄情于得州云霞"译为 A lover of the natural spectacles in Texas，译文中的 lover 是施事者名词。汉语通过动词表达的概念，英语常用非动词的形式来表达，施事者名词便是其中之一。例如，"他舞跳得很好""他抽烟抽得很厉害"等情形，都可使用英语的施事者名词，分别表达为 he is a good dancer 和 he is a heavy smoker。

> 专评

汉语描写文主观描写的英译再现

  《得州云霞》成稿于 2013 年,由发表于美国《达拉斯新闻》(*Dallas Chinese News*)的两篇短文《得州的云》(2013 年 1 月 4 日)和《得州晚霞》(2013 年 2 月 1 日)并合而成。两篇短文描写的都是美国得克萨斯州(得州)的气象,并合之后冠以《得州云霞》之名,竟也天衣无缝。在雾霾成为寻常的今天,重读这些内容,倍觉清新和亲切。
  这是一篇描写文(Description)。描写文是用生动的语言描写各种事物、环境及人物状态、表现等的文体,表现手法以描写、叙述为主,同时兼有必要的抒情、议论和说明,以使读者如见其人,如闻其声,如临其境。
  具体地说,原文是一篇描写景物的文字,但又不是单纯的写景,作者赋予了它思想、感情,渗透着作者的真情实感。而描写又分为主观描写和客观描写两类。主观描写重在表达一种气氛和人的情绪;客观描写重在准确和清楚地呈现客观的景象。两种描写并不是截然分开、互相排斥的,它们往往相辅相成。主观的描写必须以客观的细节为基础,在客观的描写里,细节的选择本身也必然会表达作者的态度和信念。
  原文偏于主观描写类,借助对得州气象(云和霞)的观察,抒发作者的主观感受,所以以下主要从语言的音韵、修辞、表达习惯等不同方面,讨论汉语描写文主观描写的处理策略。

一、描写文中的主观描写与理解

  一说到描写文,读者就想到可能会有一些夸张等修辞手法表达的文字。段连城(1992:27)引用过某市举办国际龙舟会的宣传文字及其译文:
  中华大地,江河纵横;华夏文化,源远流长……轻快的龙舟如银河流星,瑰丽的彩船似海市蜃楼,两岸那金碧辉煌的彩楼连成一片水晶宫,是仙境?是梦境?仰视彩鸽翩飞,低眸漂灯留霓,烟火怒放,火树银花,灯舞回旋,千姿百态,气垫船腾起一江春潮,射击手点破满天彩球,跳伞健儿绽空中花蕾,抢鸭勇士谱水上凯歌……啊,××城是不夜城,龙舟会是群英会!

The divine land of China has its rivers flowing across; the brilliant culture of China has its roots tracing back long ...

The light-some dragon-boats appear on the river as though the stars twinkle in the milky way. The richly decorated pleasure boats look like a scene of mirage. The splendent awnings in green and gold chain into a palace crystal. Is this a fairy-land or a mere dream? Looking above, you can see the beautiful doves flying about. Looking below, you can see the sailing lamps glittering. Cracking are the fireworks, which present you a picture of fiery trees and silver flowers. Circling are the lantern-dancers, who present you a variation of exquisite manner. Over there, the marksmen are shooting to their targets; thus colourful beads whirl around. Besides, the bird's chirping, the potted landscape's charm, the exhibition of arts and painting, all claim a strong appeal to you. Therefore, we should say: xxxx is a city of no night; its Dragon-Boat Festival a gathering of heroes.

Come on, Dear friends! Come on, Honourable guests!

段连城就译文请教了一位美国专家,对方的印象是"充满了极度夸张"。"充满了极度夸张"的言辞肯定是主观描写,但主观描写的言辞是否就一定不能被人理解呢?

事实上,在学者们讨论该译文时,对该文出现的场合有所忽略,而外国读者的评论也应主要是就它出现的场合而言的。英语的应用场合讲究语言使用原则,或者说汉英转换原则总体上是"宁朴毋巧"(周领顺,2014a:186),但也并非没有主观描写的容身之处。笔者就上述译文也请教了一位美国专家,她保留了大部分主观描写,只是把它改写得更具有美国味(American English)罢了。

偏于主观感受的描写文在英语中也十分常见,对于英语读者,并不存在阅读的障碍。请看下面这段描写夕阳的英语文字:

It was now the sweetest hour of the twenty-four: —"Day its fervid fires had wasted," and dew fell cool on panting plain and scorched summit. Where the sun had gone down in simple state—pure of the pomp of clouds—spread a solemn purple, burning with the light of red jewel and furnace flame at one point, on one hill-peak, and extending high and wide, soft and still softer, over half heaven. The east had its own charm of fine deep blue, and its own modest gem, a rising and solitary star: soon it would boast the moon; but she was yet beneath the horizon. (*Jane Eyre*)

　　此刻是一天二十四小时中最可爱的时刻——"白昼已耗尽了它炽热的烈火",露水清凉地洒落在正喘息的平原和被烤焦的山顶上。在夕阳朴素地沉落的地方,不见华丽的彩云,却铺展着一片庄重的紫红,在一座小山的山峰上,仿佛有一小块地方在燃烧,闪现出红宝石和熔炉烈焰似的光辉。那片紫红伸展着,愈来愈高,愈来愈远,愈来愈柔和,终于铺满了半个天空。东方有它自己湛蓝得令人悦目的魅力,有它自己质朴的宝石——一颗正在独自升起的星。很快它就将拥有一轮可以自豪的明月,不过这明月此刻却还在地平线下面。(贾卫国,2000:775)

　　在描写文中,主观描写经常出现,而现实生活中的人们并不会因此而引起误解。文学的宗旨是要打动人的,汉英皆然,正如王国维在《人间词话》中所说的:"文学之事,其内足以摅己而外足以感人者,意与境二者而已。上焉者意与境浑,其次或以境胜,或以意胜。苟缺其一,不足以言文学。"从这一点讲,忠实于汉语原文的翻译,仍然是翻译的首要原则。毕竟,描写文属于典型的表达型文本,以再现原文的风格特征为主要目标。

二、感官在原文主观描写中的运用

　　在主观描写的语境中,作者为了向读者传递由己推人的感受,往往会借助形象化的表现手法,来描摹客观的事物,使之具体化,以获得表情达意的最佳效果。形象化的表现手法就包括对于感觉官能的运用。

　　通过视觉、听觉、触觉、嗅觉、味觉、动觉等感官的运用,可以促使读者直接感受到外界的事物。因此,在文学作品中,作者常从细节入手,抓住事物的主要特征,借助一定的语言表现形式和手段,生动形象地再现客观事物的面貌和特征,从而激活读者的感官,让读者感受到作品所创造的艺术氛围。

　　客观世界中的自然现象,如风、雨、雪、雷、云、霞等,都具有不同的动静特点。雷有声而无形,雪则相反,而风有动感,但无声无色又无形,如此等等。原文描写的是作者在美国得克萨斯州感受到的云和霞,它们具有形状、大小、层次、色彩等静态特征,又具有运动、变化等动态特征。既然是自然现象,各地的云和霞都应大同小异,但得州的地貌异于别处,因此,得州的云和霞就有了得州的特征。作者观察细致,想象丰富,把得州的云和霞描写得波澜壮阔,气势恢宏。

　　原文的文学艺术性强。作者运用了大量生动形象的词语、结构,以及比喻、拟人、夸张、排比、对偶等多种修辞格,从静态到动态,从视觉到触觉,再到动觉,从全景到细节,从虚到实,虚实交织,切换变化,将得州的云和霞描写得淋漓尽致,栩栩如生。例如:

[1] 白云,我看是<u>山</u>,因为成团的白云有山一样的巍峨;白云,我看是<u>海</u>,因为在机身下,我好像站立山头俯瞰;白云,我看是<u>千堆雪</u>,因为需要发动千军才能扫除;白云,我看是<u>万朵棉</u>,因为只有借助神力才能收获。(形状)

[2] 远处镶着玻璃的建筑,平日里没什么稀罕,但在夕阳下,却似<u>整块的赤金</u>在原野伫立。(色彩)

[3] 夕阳将云<u>撕裂</u>一道缝隙,<u>挤</u>出来,<u>刺向</u>远处的一溜建筑……(动感)

原文从云霞及其周围物体的形色、动感等方面的特征描写出发,运用多种语言手段,创造出不同的视觉意象和动觉意象。例[1]是原文中诸多排比结构之一,结合比喻和夸张的修辞格,描写了从飞机上观看云时的视觉意象,观察的角度是全景、远景,因此所描写的云的形状都是壮观景象,即云像"山""海""千堆雪""万朵棉"。例[2]描写的是晚霞中的建筑景色,将夕阳中的玻璃建筑比作整块的赤金,烘托了晚霞瑰丽的视觉色彩。而例[3]描写的物其实是静态的,但运用了动态的描写手法,通过"撕裂""挤出来""刺向"等一系列动态动词或短语,将原本静态的物象描写成了动态景象,可说是"动态虚景",使形象性大增。

同一个物体有时同时具备多个特征,因此,原文多处同时描写了云霞的视觉、动觉等多重意象。例如:

[4] 远处的白云<u>白中泛黄</u>,摆个<u>城堡</u>样让人有不尽的鬼魅遐想。(色彩+形状)

[5] 白云<u>团团</u>时,大有<u>排山倒海</u>之势;白云点点时,似乎是顽皮的仙女将杰作造就;白云串串时,列于青天碧海之间,若百舸争流于浩瀚;白云丝丝时,擦着舷窗,似乎<u>伸手可揽</u>……(形状+动感+触觉)

例[4]和例[5]分别从不同的感觉入手,刻画了云霞的多重姿态。例[4]描写了白云的颜色("白中泛黄")和形状("城堡样"),而例[5]这个排比句则主要描写的是白云的形状("团团"),除此之外,还分别描写了白云的动感("排山倒海")和触觉("伸手可揽")。当然,还有一些融各种感觉于一体的感性表达,例如:

[6] 立体感、层次感和玻璃般的质感,要什么感就有什么感;<u>水墨画</u>、<u>山水画</u>,就连中国画,都一应俱全。

上文的举例和分析显示,原文语言平实、质朴,并没有堆砌辞藻,但主观描写中大量使用的感官意象,给文章增添了浓厚的文学色彩。因此,在翻译时,译者也应致力于再现原文所描写的美感,好让译文读者也产生身临其境之感。

三、描写文主观描写中的意象英译策略

不同文化之间在官能的感觉方面具有相通之处,因此,在翻译语言表达的感官意象时,在译文中再现或替换原语意象也就成为可能。例如,汉语文化和英语文化都将愉悦的听觉感受和甘甜的味觉感受联系在一起,在各自的语言中都有"甜美的话语"、sweet-tongued 等相似的表达方式。但有时在表达上又存在差异。例如,汉语文化和英语文化背景中的人们,都能感觉到寒冷给皮肤带来的痛感,但在汉语中,这种痛感被描写为尖尖的物体带来的感觉,如"寒风刺骨",而在英语中,这种痛感则被描写为人被咬时的感觉,即 biting cold。也就是说,对于相同的触觉感受,汉语和英语是通过不同的意象来表达的。

"描写语句本质上是对意象的翻译,如果人的思维机理相同,则语言表达模式就会相同。字面意义与意象文化联想意义一致时,可直接转换成目的语文字"(金杰,2005:90)。原文是对自然现象的描写,不管描写的是实是虚,大量使用的意象中牵涉文化因素的情形不是很多,对于绝大多数的意象,译文可直接加以再现,而对于少数意象,则要变通处理。

第一,直接再现策略。

原文使用视觉、色彩、触觉、动觉等不同的动静意象来描写得州云霞,对这些意象的感知和解读在不同文化之间都是相通的,可直接移植到译文中。试比较上文例[2]、例[4]及其译文例[2]′、例[4]′:

[2]′ The glass buildings in the distance, an ordinary sight at normal times, tower imposingly in the open country as *whole pieces of solid gold* under the sunset.

[4]′ And rising up *in lofty towers*, *distant white clouds*, *tinted with gold*, swarm one with whimsical imaginations.

绝大多数文化背景中的人们对于"金""城堡""白中泛黄"等形状、颜色等意象有直接的感知,原文用这些比喻性意象来描写云霞的视觉特征,译语读者对此并不陌生,译文也因此完全给予了再现。

文学作品往往既带有原语的总体风格,又有作者的个人风格。一

般而言,在翻译时,译文也应该同时体现这两种风格,尤其是作者的个人风格,更应该在译文中加以再现。就主观描写而言,原文还使用了一些带有个性的超常比喻性意象,在翻译时应尽量加以保留。试比较:

[7] 满眼的素材,随便摘来一片,揉碎了,就是一段文字。

They provide resourceful materials for literary creation, and *any piece*, *pulled down from the sky*, *could be crumbled into words*.

天上的云实际由水滴聚集而成,但在例[7]中,通过动词"摘"的使用,将其视觉形状隐喻为有形的实体,且可被"揉碎"后变为文字,新鲜而有趣。译文几乎是直译的,pull down 的使用,crumble 和 words 的截搭,有助于保留原文绝大部分的形象色彩。原文的动补结构"揉碎"意为"以手搓的方式碾碎",考虑到该短语的语义重心在于表示结果的"碎",为求简洁,译文使用了 crumble 一词,只表达了"碎"这个结果,舍弃了"碎"的方式。例[7]是比喻性的用法,译文使用了表示虚拟语气的 could,以体现译语的语义表达对于句法方面的精确要求。

第二,变通处理策略。

考虑到汉语和英语之间的差异,译者应同时采用变通处理的方法,对于原文使用的动静意象,或舍弃,或替换。概括地说,译文中采用的变通处理方法,主要是针对汉语和英语在音韵节奏、修辞、表达习惯等层面存在差异之处。在翻译时,这些需要变通处理的地方尤其值得译者注意。

在音韵节奏方面,汉语具有独有的特征。汉语是单音节为主的语言,音节的自由度很高,现代汉语的双音化倾向明显,因此,一些双音节词所传达的语义是否在译文中加以体现,就必须由上下文而定。例如,原文的第五段描写作者对于云的不同形态的视觉感受,情感丰富,比喻、夸张、排比等修辞手段交替出现。在这个段落中,"云"就都成了"白云",这个"白"字描写的是云的视觉效果,但主要为了起平衡音韵节奏的作用,客观上也增加了文学性,所以并不显得累赘多余。假如不用"白"这个修饰语,"云团团时""云点点时""大量的云岿然不动"等描写,要么不能言之成理,要么缺少了文学色彩。而在英语中,并不需要为了词或短语的音韵节奏而添加赘词。因此,在翻译时,除了上文例[4]中的"白云"译成 white clouds 之外,这个段落中的"白云"一概简化处理为 clouds,其视觉意象不再现,反而能获得表达简洁的效果。

在修辞方面,译文尽量再现原文的辞格。原文使用了各种修辞手段,例如比喻、拟人、夸张、排比、对偶等,将得州云霞的动静特征,以意象化的方式形象地传递给了读者。对于原文读者和译文读者共有的感知,译文一概给予保留,如上文例[1]中将白云意象化为"山""海""雪""棉"等的比喻就是。但是,原语中独特的修辞手法,假如不是出于传递文化信息的需要,以舍弃或替换为妥。试比较上文的例[1]及其译文例[1]′:

> [1]′ Clouds, I perceive them as mountains, because they are likewise majestic when assembling in clusters. Clouds, I take them as the sea, because in a flight over them, I can command a panoramic view of them as from the mountain top. Clouds, I feel them to be *snow piles*, which can only be scavenged with *gigantic manpower*. Clouds, I see them to be *cotton blooms*, which can only be picked with superhuman force.

例[1]中的"千堆雪""千军""万朵棉"是夸张表达方式。汉语常用"百""千""万"等数词来夸张地表达数量多的意思,而英语则鲜有这样的修辞用法。除此之外,单音节的"千"和"万"还可起到平衡音节的作用,例如"千堆雪"和"万朵棉"语义对称,结构对仗,两两相对,独具汉语音韵节奏的美感。译文舍弃了例[1]中数量夸张表达法,仅将"千军"表达为 gigantic manpower,而将"千堆雪""万朵棉"表达为复数概念的 snow piles, cotton blooms,也不失对称。这种变通,顺应了译语的修辞和表达习惯。类似的情形还有上文例[5]中的"百舸",出于同样的原因,在译文中也简化为 sailboats。

为体现语言之间在修辞手法方面的差异,译者还可通过更换意象的方式来实现。例如,上文例[5]中的"排山倒海"这个成语意为"推开山岳,翻倒大海",形容来势凶猛,声势浩大。英语中有大量的形容词来表达这个汉语成语的意思,但在例[5]的译文里就不适合使用单个的词语,因为下文都是结合具体化的事件来描写云的形状和气势的。因此,译者更换"排山倒海"中的"山"和"海"的意象,代之以 avalanches(雪崩)这个译语读者更为熟悉的意象。试比较上文例[5]及其译文例[5]′:

> [5]′ Gathering in clumps, clouds share *the same throng as of avalanches cascading down*. Floating in spots, they are the artistic works as if done by elfish fairies. Lining up in strands between the azure sky and sea, they look like sailboats racing in a blue vastness. Drifting in threads near airplane windows, they seem to be within easy and close reach.

有时,译文中保留了原文的意象,但在具体的表述方面,应以阐释原文的语义为主。试比较：

[8] 红云经常与蓝天共舞,恰似演绎着烈火与碧海的传奇。

Or they dance in red to the rhythm of a blue sky, as though they were fires set magically ablaze on an azure sea.

例[8]描绘了云和天的视觉与动觉形象,使用了拟人、比喻等修辞手法,但这两种辞格层层嵌套,要比较清晰地传达原文的语义,颇费脑筋。译者不能囿于原文的形式,而是需要透彻理解原文的意思,然后将语义灵活地表达出来。例[8]直白地说就是,"红云在蓝天里飘浮,和蓝天跳舞,看上去就像火燃烧在海面上一样",译文按照这个意思来表达,既突破了原文的形式,又再现了原文的所有意象,清晰又不失形象。

在表达习惯方面,译文也有多处微调整。原文使用了大量的排比修辞,译文完全可以再现。但英语的用词和结构等注重变化,因此,在原文使用排比结构的地方,译文在保留原文修辞手法的基础上,都尽量在细微之处给予再现英语的这一表达习惯。例如,在例[1]这个排比句中,"白云,我看是……因为……"结构描写白云的形状特征和气势,重复了四次,译文在再现原文的这一排比结构形式的同时,在重复中体现了变化:用了不同的动词来表达"看",即 perceive, take, see, feel 等同义词,用了不同的从属词来表达"因为",即两次使用 because 引导的分句,两次使用 which 引导的分句。又如,在翻译例[5]的"白云……时"排比句时,也是采取相同的"整齐+变化"原则。在例[5]中,"团团""点点""串串""丝丝"等都是量词的重叠形式,用来描绘白云的视觉形状,可以单独作谓语。在译文中,clumps, spots, strands, threads 等对应词前分别添加了-ing 分词,如 gathering, floating, lining up, drifting 等,这一方面体现了变化,另一方面在表达上也接近了原文的气势。这些-ing 分词形式中的动词,属于动静跨类动词,既可描述动态的动作,又可描述由该动作产生的结果性静止状态,例如,在孤立的语境中,They gathered around him 既可理解为"他们向他围拢了过来",也可理解为"他们围在他身边",前者描述动作,后者描述状态。在例[5]的译文中,这些动词的-ing 形式都表示状态,在语义上,与原文中"团团"等词语描绘白云的静态形状特征的用法相一致。

汉语是以动词为主的语言,大量使用动词来表达事件,传递了一种较强的动态感,而英语除了动词之外,还可使用名词化结构、介词等形式,比较而言,英语动词的使用频率可能低于汉语。上文例[3]中一系列动词描写的动觉意象,需要在译文中适当加以变换表达形式。试比较例[3]及其译文例[3]′:

[3]′ The setting sun *breaks through* a crack in the clouds and *thrusts its rays* at a row of faraway buildings.

例[3]中使用了三个动词或短语,"撕裂""挤出来""刺向",按照时间先后顺序,描写了夕阳的动态虚景。译文同样使用了动态动词,但原文中的"挤出来"在译文中体现为介词 through,更加符合英语的表达习惯。

[原文]

姜太公钓鱼

翻译课上,学生们竟围着我书桌上的一尊"姜太公钓鱼"铜像[1]争吵得沸沸扬扬,这与上课要讨论的内容可没有一分钱的关系。

说起我这尊"姜太公钓鱼",可是有来历的[2]。

四月下旬,朋友陪我去看温州的楠溪江。江边有一个古村落叫丽水街,说它古,古到连时间都放缓了脚步,任凭时光在蹲坐闲聊的老人们中间流泻,听任寂寞在择菜的女人中间蔓延[3]。

村前有一溜长廊,贩卖山货[4]的小摊,鳞次栉比。长廊的入口处,并排放着几个叫卖古董的摊位,被灰尘罩上的"古朴"外衣,反倒与古董的色调和谐一致。我向来对旅游景点兜售的这类"古董"不屑一顾,多半有假,而我也不擅长砍价。正待匆匆前行,我回头一瞥,瞄见角落里放着一尊貌不惊人、难登大雅的渔翁[5]钓鱼铜像。渔翁神态煞是可爱,特别是那份闲情,不禁让我为之动容。

铜像也就巴掌那么大。渔翁盘腿坐在三根竹子捆绑而成的竹筏上,背靠一只硕大的鱼篓,悠然作垂钓状。筏子的宽度刚好能容下渔翁的身子,猜得出,老人家定是划船、撑筏、潜水的高手。老者头戴竹编圆帽,身穿雕花长袄,光脚卷着裤腿,一幅做水中活计的打扮。[6]右手闲散地搭在腿上,左手握成拳头,中间有孔,上下见光,应是手握鱼竿之处。鱼竿不见踪影,或原为一节细竹,抑或一截木棍,因年久腐朽不见了踪迹。当然,也可能是金属棒,被人抽去。[7]

好个讨价还价。我刚接货在手,耳畔就传来一声女子细声细气的呵护。

"你买这个'姜太公钓鱼'买值了。"

啊,这是"姜太公钓鱼"?我若在交易前得知"姜太公"在此,料必难掩窃喜。这可是大名鼎鼎、人尽皆知、能令"诸神退位"的姜太公啊。一旦喜形于色,砍价断不会底气十足。看得出,她与卖主同村,却不像个"托儿",毕竟我们已成交在先。她的一句"买值了",实在所言非虚;单就告知"姜太公钓鱼",已使我深以为喜。

放在书桌上,围着"姜太公钓鱼"的故事浮想联翩;把玩于手中,每一个细节都能荡起情感的涟漪。今天再次端详,不经意间竟发现鱼篓里画有鱼的图案。随着学生们鱼贯而入,争论便随之蔓延开去。

"有三条鱼。"一声惊呼,凑过来几个脑袋。

"是四条,里面还夹着一条小鱼。"又是一阵骚动。

"不对,是五条,你数数鱼的眼睛!"果然如此,方法决定结果。

"也不对,'竹篮子打水一场空',竹篓怎能盛水?几条鱼怎可能一直摆放[8]到鱼篓的口沿呢?"我自以为是,一下子甩出个现实问题。

"肯定是鱼太多,堆到了口沿。"学生对渔翁的高超技艺赞美有加。

"可鱼是活的,鱼篓又没盖子,怎可能不跳出来呢?"我再次甩出个现实问题,甩出的是生活阅历。"姜还是老的辣"嘛。

…………

争论戛然而止,倏忽间却飘升到了更高层次,从物质层面转战精神领域[9]。

"艺术嘛,讲究的就是写实和写意的结合。"

"画的那几条鱼就是象征性的[10],不然鱼怎可能都是平躺的呢?"

"姜太公是神,对于神,一切皆有可能。"

"或者,这是不是姜太公还说不定。如果不是,这就是一个伪命题。"

一语爆出,振聋发聩。认识在升级,答案在颠覆。

这不是姜太公吗?

我从网上找到了好几幅网友拍的实物照,和我手里这尊极其神似。[11]虽然缺少关键证据[12],但我愿将其理解为"姜太公钓鱼"[13],皆因对"愿者上钩"意义的解读而让我获得的无限释怀之感。姜太公明着钓的是鱼,实际钓的是人;这人,历史上是周文王,而今却是人的心态。"愿者上钩"不一定都意味着上当,还意味着积极心态者的主动进取,虽蕴含着冒险和投机,但与"我愿意"的心态并行不悖。学生们和我争论的升级,证明了认识的提升和境界达到的层次。

"姜太公钓'鱼'",却把我"钓"上了,人家买的是古董,而我买的却是百读不厌的人生大哲理!

译文

Jiang Taigong in Fishing*

In my translation class, students once fell into a heated argument over a bronze sculpture on my desk of "Jiang Taigong in fishing", and this did not even have the slightest relevance to the contents of my class.

This sculpture of mine has a story to tell about itself.

In late April this year, I went with the company of friends on a sightseeing trip to the Nanxi River in Wenzhou. Bordering on this river is an ancient village by the name of Lishuijie. It is old, and time seems to have decelerated, moving in slow motion for old people who sit or squat around chatting idly and for women who gather together trimming vegetables in creeping loneliness.

The village boasts a long corridor, lined up by booths selling dried mountain produce. Right at its entrance, placed in juxtaposition with each other, were several antique stalls, which, dust-coated, had a tonal congruence with the archaic items they were trading. I used to turn a cold shoulder to "antiques" for sale at scenic resorts. For one thing, they were mostly fakes; for another, I was a poor bargainer. As I was about to move on, I glanced back and spotted at a corner an uncomely and humble sculpture of bronze, carved in the image of an old angler in fishing. I was allured, however, by the endearing air and especially the light mood the angler was putting on.

---

* Jiang Taigong was an old man of insight and talent living in the late Shang Dynasty (1600 BC – 1046 BC). As he detested the dark reign of his emperor, he resided in seclusion by the Weishui River, waiting for his chance to actualize his political aspiration. He used to fish at the north side of the river in an unusual style, i. e. casting above the water a fishing line with a straight "hook" going baitless. While passersby all laughed at his stupidity, Jiang replied gravely, "Fish will rise and bite my 'hook' when they are voluntary." Later, King Wen of the Zhou Tribe went hunting by the same river and assigned Jiang as his prime minister after having had congenial conversations with him. Jiang assisted the king in the overturn of the Shang Dynasty. Jiang Taigong's fishing tale is the source for the Chinese idiom "bite the hook of one's own accord", which denotes metaphorically "fall voluntarily into a possible trap".

The sculpture was a miniature about the size of a human palm. His back against a bulky bamboo basket, the angler was fishing in a leisurely manner, sitting cross-legged on a raft, which was made of three bamboo poles secured together, making a perfect width for his body. I figured that he was a good performer of skills in rowing, rafting and diving. He was dressed in a style suitable for aquatic work, wearing a bamboo hat and an embroidered coat, going bare-footed with his trousers rolled up to the knees. His right hand was casually placed on the lower thigh while his left was curled into a hollow fist, with light going through it. So it should be where a fishing pole had been. The pole was gone now, and it might have been a piece of bamboo or wood, which should have perished with age, or a metal bar, which could have been snitched away.

I negotiated a bargain. Just as I took the sculpture from the vendor, a soft female voice came into my ears.

"It's worth the price, I mean this 'Jiang Taigong in fishing' you got."

What? Was it? Had I known it before the deal I would have failed to conceal my delight. Jiang Taigong was such a well-known figure! He was even fictionalized as a master deity, so mighty as could scare off all other lesser deities. With visible delight I would have placed myself in an unfavorable position in the bargain. I could tell that she was a fellow villager of the vendor but was not acting as his shill for sure, as she showed up after our deal was closed. She could not have been more right in her it's-worth-the-price comment. And she pleased me more than anything else by her mere mention of "Jiang Taigong", the name itself.

The figurine stands on my desk, and the legend about Jiang Taigong's fishing sparks my imagination now and then. I hold it in my hands, and every detail of it sets off ripples in my heart. Today when my eyes rested upon it again, I noticed by accident carvings of fish in the basket. And arguments sprang up as students walked into my office.

"I see three fish." At this, more heads came closer.

"It's four. There's a smaller one between them." Another stir arose.

"No, it's five. Count their eyes!" So it was. The right method had the say about the result.

"Impossible. A bamboo basket doesn't hold water, see? How is it several fish can pile up to the brim of a basket?" I tossed out a real-life question, self-contentedly.

"There must be a lot more inside." This remark was also a compliment to the angler's superb fishing skill.

"They are live fish, and the basket has no cover. How come they don't jump out?" I popped up another real-life question upon life experience. Just as "an older ginger is hotter", so an older person is more experienced.

…

The argument ground to an abrupt halt and resumed instantly at a higher level from concrete to abstract.

"Art is art. It's a clever mixture of realism and the freehand style."

"Those fish are art images only. Otherwise, why are they all lying flat?"

"Jiang Taigong was a deity. For him, nothing was impossible."

"Or, it might be someone else in fishing. If so, we are arguing on a false track."

The words burst out and provoked thought. As understanding deepened, answers were ruled out one by one.

Was the angler not Jiang Taigong at all?

I found on the Internet pictures taken of the "Jiang Taigong in fishing" that might belong to the photographers and recognized a close resemblance between theirs and mine. Even without crucial evidence for a definite conclusion, I would still opt to believe mine was a Jiang Taigong, just for the ease of mind I had from my reading of the idiom that derives from Jiang Taigong's fishing tale, "bite the hook of one's own accord". Jiang cast a fishing line with a straight "hook" for fish when his real intent was to "hook" King Wen of the Zhou Tribe. The king got himself "on the hook", as had been expected, by assigning Jiang as his prime minister. Thus the idiom now applies to a mental outlook, i.e. a willingness to take a chance. Though it implies venture and risk-taking, the idiom does not necessarily mean an outcome of being entrapped. On the contrary, it can suggest an affirmative mental outlook as I understand it, connoting an active aggressiveness that represents an I'm-willing-to attitude and characterizes people with a positive mindset. The escalating argument between students and me attested to an improved understanding and an elevated level in the spiritual plane.

Jiang Taigong was hooking "fish", and had me "hooked" as well. While other people may take the sculpture as an antique, I got to read into my purchase a wisdom of life that will never cease to intrigue me.

注释

［1］"我书桌上的一尊'姜太公钓鱼'铜像"译为 a bronze sculpture on my desk of "Jiang Taigong in fishing"。On my desk 是修饰语,位置提前,放在中心语 a bronze sculpture 和 of "Jiang Taigong in fishing"之间,是为了保持结构上的平衡。若按照正常语序表达成 a bronze sculpture of "Jiang Taigong in fishing" on my desk,则显得头重脚轻。英语中的"尾重原则"在短语和分句等不同的句法层面都起作用。

［2］"可是有来历的"译为 has a story to tell about itself。To have a story to tell 是英语的一个类习语结构,主语既可以是有灵的,也可以是无灵的,例如,We all have a story to tell about? our first days in this new country.（有灵主语）Almost every Florida town has a story to tell about those who served in a war.（无灵主语）在无灵主语句的用法中,to tell 相当于 to be told,但习惯用不定式的主动形式。

［3］"任凭……流泻""听任……蔓延"这两个小句要译好并不容易,假如按照字面形式翻译,很可能成为硬译的死穴。原文将时间拟人化,译文用了两个 for 引导的结构,即 for old people who … 和 for women who … 来表达这两个"任凭""听任"结构,也是考虑到原文的拟人修辞格,除了"流泻"一词没译出外,基本上传递了原文的意义。此外,原文的这两个小句整齐对称,译文的结构也获得了类似的效果。

［4］汉语中的"山货"指"山区的一般土产,如山楂、榛子、栗子、胡桃等",或"竹子、木头、陶土等制成的日用器物,如扫帚、簸箕、麻绳、砂锅、瓦盆等"［《现代汉语词典（第 6 版）》,商务印书馆,2012：1130］。作者在小摊前看到的"山货"是前者,所以译为 dried mountain produce。作为土产的"山货"一般为非人工种植,而且是干货,而英语中的 produce 一般指农产品,而且是新鲜的。因此,译文中添加 dried,mountain 等修饰语,以减少"山货"和 produce 之间的语义差异。假如用 mountain product 这个词语来翻译"山货",则主要与"山货"的第二个义项对应。

［5］"渔翁"译为 angler，指用鱼钩垂钓者，而英语的 fisherman 一词则指以捕鱼为业或以垂钓为娱乐的人，不适合原文的"渔翁"一词。

［6］这几个小句描述渔翁的外貌，先说细节，后概括，即"老者头戴……身穿……光脚……一幅……打扮"，而译文的语序则完全相反，先概括，后说细节，即 He was dressed in a style … wearing … going barefooted with his trousers … 这样转换符合英语的思维方式和表达习惯。

［7］同注释［4］，这几个小句表达的也是作者对过去状态或事件的判断或推测，可用情态助动词和动词完成体的搭配来表达，即 it might have been, should have perished with age, could have been snitched away。

［8］这个小句中的"摆放"译成不及物用法的 pile up 为妥，当说话者不强调动作的施事者时，不必使用英语的被动形式，又如：On the floor of the boat the fish piled up, gasping their last breaths. The junk could pile up to the ceiling.

［9］"从物质层面转战精神领域"指的是，争论从围绕具体问题发展到围绕抽象问题而展开，可译为 resumed instantly at a higher level from concrete to abstract。

［10］"象征性的"指把鱼画到竹篓的口沿，就代表鱼篓里装满了鱼，可意译为：Those fish are art images only.

［11］假如信息表达完整，这两个小句表达的意思是："我从网上找到了好几幅网友拍的实物照，照片中的姜太公钓鱼和我手里这尊极其神似。"汉语在表达时常常隐含或省略一些信息，以至于看上去不合逻辑，只要不造成理解困难即可。而英语的表达习惯则讲究语言的形式和语义逻辑高度一致，不留模糊之处。因此，翻译这两个小句时，就必须添加必要的成分，补充信息，可译为：I found on the Internet pictures taken of the "Jiang Taigong in fishing" that might belong to the photographers and recognized a close resemblance between theirs and mine.

［12］这个小句中的"关键证据"（crucial evidence）指姜太公钓鱼所用的"直钩"，译文中是否补充"直钩"的信息都可接受，不影响理解。

［13］这个小句中的"姜太公钓鱼"实际指"姜太公钓鱼的雕像"，用雕像表现的主题指代物体本身，是"借代"修辞法，为的是表达简洁，译为 believe mine was a Jiang Taigong，译文中的 a Jiang Taigong 是英语中的转喻修辞用法，意为 a sculpture of Jiang Taigong。英语中的专有名词可用于单数或复数的形式，用来指称以该专有名词命名的人或物、艺术家的作品等。例如，a Mary 意为 someone whose name is Mary，a Monet 指代 a painting painted by Monet。

> 专评

文化联想与讲好中国故事

习近平主席所倡导的"讲好中国故事",并不限于翻译,而从翻译上看问题时,我们关注的重点应该是对翻译讲好中国故事这一形式及其效果的关注。《姜太公钓鱼》一文中的"姜太公钓鱼"本身就是一则故事,其中的中国文化历史信息,特别是借"姜太公钓鱼——愿者上钩"这一歇后语所表达的中国文化历史信息非常丰厚,所以无疑是"中国故事"的一部分。

"讲好中国故事"包括两个侧重点:一是"讲好"中的"讲","讲"即翻译方式;二是"讲好"中的"好","好"即翻译效果。作为一名译者,应首先在翻译过程中,克服"讲"所可能面对的问题,之后才能在效果上让异域文化背景下的读者实现对于原文意义的上下贯通,从而提高参与度,增强理解力。如何让异域读者自然产生相应的文化联想,是我们需要面对的首要问题。作者是针对原文文化背景下的读者而创作的,而译者是针对译文文化背景下的读者而翻译的。因此,消除文化之隔,既是传播文化的需求,又是强化读者文化联想的必需。

《姜太公钓鱼》一文是游记,却又有着夹叙夹议的风格特征,融记叙文、议论文等文体于一体,处于文体的"中间状态"。

一、歇后语与文化联想

原文的标题《姜太公钓鱼》,隐含着"姜太公钓鱼——愿者上钩"这样一个歇后语。在汉民族文化背景的讲话者和读者看来,这是不言而喻的常识,是司空见惯的日常表达。

说它是歇后语,是因为当仅仅说出前半截"姜太公钓鱼"时,就可以"歇"(停止)去后余的部分("愿者上钩"),而仍能保持意义自明,使读者心领神会。《现代汉语词典(第6版)》对"歇后语"是这样解释的:

由两个部分组成的一句话,前一部分像谜面,后一部分像谜底,通常只说前一部分,而本意在后一部分。如"泥菩萨过江——自身难保""外甥点灯笼——照旧(舅)"。

或者可以这样说,歇后语的前一部分起"引子"的作用,后一部分起"后衬"的作用,在一定的语境中,通常说出前半截,"歇"去后半截,就可以让听众领会和猜想出它的本义。比如"姜太公钓鱼——愿者上钩",在汉文化背景里,前半截"姜太公钓鱼"说出来后,读者会自然产生对于后半截"愿者上钩"的联想,至于讲话者是不是需要明说出来,要看他的使用目的。后半截不明示,可以让交际的双方产生更多心照不宣的效果,简洁而省力;明示后半截,则可产生繁复而生动的交际效果。"歇后语"中的"歇后"对于歇后语本身来说如此,对于借翻译讲述中国故事来说也是一样的道理,让异域读者产生自然联想,也是翻译的意义所在。

"歇后"就是自然联想,译文读者能够自然联想,就是译文具有可读性和中国文化对外传播所希冀达到的"好"效果的体现,但因语言和文化有隔,所以就翻译"信达雅"三字箴言而言,"信"较易,"雅"也未必太难,唯独"达"的实现却非易事。不能"达",跨文化交际便无以为继;不能"达",就意味着未能再现原文的意义,甚或说根本未经翻译。所以,"翻译"定义虽然繁多,但只有满足了两个条件,即语码转换和意义再现,才构成翻译之为翻译的根本,而意义是否得以再现,要看是否传达给了读者。比如歇后语,如果不能让读者产生"歇"后语义的自然联想,就等于没有让原文的意义得到很好的贯通。所以,本文说的"歇后",不仅不限于歇后语本身,还涉及联想意义再现的其他表达。

汉语歇后语既然只有在汉文化背景里,在"歇"去后半截时令读者对余后的意义产生联想,那么在异域文化中并没有"姜太公钓鱼"这样一个故事,为什么不在译文的题目里把"姜太公钓鱼"的信息完整表达为 Jiang Taigong in Fishing: Fish Will Rise and Bite the Hook When They Are Voluntary 呢?这是因为,以故事的形式引入,更能轻易博取读者的注意。另外,原文题目的表面不见得潜藏着后半截的信息,也未必一定表明是以讲述该歇后语为主要目的的,而对于异域的读者而言,他们能够在读完故事后产生对于缺省语义的联想,也就等于实现了阅读和文化传播的目的。

传播文化,是翻译的主要目标之一。在这种情况下,要再现原文的深厚文化,实现上下语义的自然贯通,更多的时候要采取"厚译"(Thick Translation)的做法。"厚译"是应对丰厚文化底蕴信息再现和传播的一剂良方。

二、"厚译"与文化联想

"厚译",或曰"增量翻译""厚重翻译""深度翻译"等,包括"注释""按语""副文本""跋"等几种。"厚译"在以文化传播为主导的翻译中,发挥着关键的作用。

根据常见的"厚译"类型看,增补原文文字字面结构信息的信息形式,就会显得厚重起来。但"厚"的程度并不均匀,当增添了原文字面不存在的信息时,就已经进入了"厚"的范畴。以注释为例。注释的厚度,可大约分为知识性注释和研究性注释两类,前者较"薄",后者较"厚"。说前者较薄,是因为知识性的信息是背景信息,是共有的,属于常识;说后者较厚,是因为研究性的信息是译者自己的、独创的,属于无中生有。后者是常谓的学者型译者之为,他们身兼翻译家和学者双重身份,其翻译活动与学术研究是分不开的。按照王秉钦(2004:212)的话说,这类译者是"翻译什么,研究什么;研究什么,翻译什么"。因《姜太公钓鱼》译文所补充的信息是共有的、常识性的,所以均属于较薄的信息,这里着重加以说明。(有关"厚译"的更多讨论,见于周领顺、强卉,2016)

对文化之隔进行知识性信息的增补在翻译实践上屡见不鲜。虽然这些做法在翻译教科书中并没有专门以"厚译"命名,但译者出于方便读者或者其他目的而增补的超出原文文字结构信息的信息形式是多种多样的,"增益"或"增词译法"(徐莉娜,2014:201-268)等方法实际就是"厚译"的原始表现形式之一,是"最为常用的翻译技巧之一"。比如 Bill Clinton visited China a month ago 这一句,如果译为"克林顿一月前访问了中国",原文的字面结构信息并非不完整,但如果翻译为"<u>美国前总统</u>克林顿一月前访问了中国",画线部分显然超出了原文文字的结构信息,但并不能因此说,超出的这部分不存在于原文的字里行间。按照"增词译法"的规定,"不是指随意增加可能改变原文意义的词语,而是指根据译入语的语法、语篇规则或语言习惯在不改变原文意义和逻辑关系的前提下适当增词以保证译文语言通顺流畅的翻译方法"(徐莉娜,2014:201),即增词不增意,所以属于知识性的背景信息无疑。

"薄"信息也仍然可以再进一步划分为不同的层次。比如采用脚注时,量一般较大,所以较"厚";行内化解时,量一般较小,所以较"薄"。在译文中,较"厚"的"厚译"做法用到了"姜太公钓鱼"故事的注释上,毕竟该故事贯穿全文的始终,需要多费些笔墨,尽量交代清楚,所以处理为：

  Jiang Taigong was an old man of insight and talent living in the late Shang Dynasty (1600 BC – 1046 BC). As he detested the dark reign of his emperor, he resided in seclusion by the Weishui River, waiting for his chance to actualize his political aspiration. He used to fish at the north side of the river in an unusual style, i.e. casting above the water a fishing line with a straight "hook" going baitless. While passersby all laughed at his stupidity, Jiang replied gravely, "Fish will rise and bite my 'hook' when they are voluntary." Later, King Wen of the Zhou Tribe went hunting by the same river and assigned Jiang as his prime minister after having had congenial conversations with him. Jiang assisted King Wen in the overturn of the Shang Dynasty. Jiang Taigong's fishing tale is the source for the Chinese idiom "bite the hook of one's own accord", which denotes metaphorically "fall voluntarily into a possible trap".

  这个较"厚"注释的添加有益于译文读者的理解。原文的重点在于对"姜太公钓鱼——愿者上钩"这个成语的重新解读。对于汉语读者来说，"姜太公钓鱼"的故事耳熟能详，而对于译文读者来说，相关信息则完全空缺。"姜太公钓鱼"的故事细节繁杂，非脚注不能为。

  除此之外，译文中更多的情形则是采用行内"薄"式化解的方式。例如：

[1] 我再次甩出个现实问题，甩出的是生活阅历。"<u>姜还是老的辣</u>"嘛。

  I popped up another real-life question upon life experience. *Just as "an older ginger is hotter", so an older person is more experienced.*

[2] 姜太公明着钓的是鱼，实际钓的是人；这人，历史上是周文王，而今却是<u>人的心态</u>。

  Jiang cast a fishing line with a straight "hook" for fish when his real intent was to "hook" King Wen of the Zhou Tribe. *The king got himself "on the hook"*, as had been expected, *by assigning Jiang as his prime minister. Thus the idiom now applies to* a mental outlook, i.e. *a willingness to take a chance.*

  在汉文化里，"姜还是老的辣"用来比喻年长者经验多、办法多、手段高明，而在英语文化中则无此隐喻，译文读者不一定能产生自然联想。因此，译文应以补出原文隐含的信息为妥。例[1]的译文使用英语中表达两样事物类比的 just as … , so … 结构,意为"正如……一样……""……也……",来体现原文明示的喻体("姜还是老的辣")和隐含的本体("年长者经验多"), just as 分句表达前者, so 分句表达后者。此外, an older ginger is hotter 置于引号之中,加之这是一个英语的类比结构,译文读者自然能够推测这可能是原文中的熟语表达。

例[2]是作者对"姜太公钓鱼——愿者上钩"这个成语的解读,后半部分是关键。关于"姜太公钓鱼"的背景信息,上文已经给了详细的注释,但译文中还是添加了斜体部分的文字,作为补充。在理解例[2]时,汉语读者会自动从记忆库中提取相关的背景信息,来填补原文的信息空缺,而译文读者则不具备这样的信息储备,因此,译文中画龙点睛地明确了周文王"愿者上钩"的具体表现,即 The king got himself "on the hook"… by assigning Jiang as his prime minister. 此外,原文为了增加修辞效果,获得结构与语义上的对称和平衡,将"钓"分别与"鱼"和"人"搭配,并进而将"人"解读为历史上的"周文王"和现今"人的心态"。如果按照英语语法来分析这个原文,例[2]有不合逻辑之处:"这人"怎么是"人的心态"呢？英语表达讲究直白、明确,句子的语法和语义都必须符合规则和逻辑,否则就是错的,但在汉语中,这样的表达不但可以接受,而且很普遍。因此,例[2]的译文舍弃原文对称的形式,添加 Thus the idiom now applies to 这样的字眼,将隐含的意义填补完整,使得形式表达的语义符合逻辑。同时,添加 a willingness to take a chance,进一步说明了"人的心态"的确切所指。

有的文化信息未必不"厚",但是否一定要加以体现呢？不能一概而论。例如:

[3] "也不对,'竹篮子打水一场空',竹篓怎能盛水？"

"Impossible. A *bamboo basket doesn't hold water*, see?"

例[3]中的"竹篮子打水一场空"对于各个民族而言都不难理解,它是全人类共有体验的一部分,正如"下坡容易上坡难"一样,中外皆然。但这个成语在原文中传递的只是其本义,与下一句的"竹篓怎能盛水"在语义上有重叠,说话者使用这个成语主要用来增强话语的生动性,是出于修辞的考虑。一般认为,习语在英语中属于"陈词滥调"(cliche),使用频率要低于汉语,尤其在口语中。因此,译文对于例[3]中重叠的语义进行了简化,有意省略原文的"竹篮子打水一场空"这个形式。

三、专有名词与文化联想

"姜太公钓鱼"中的"姜太公"是原文中最关键的专有名词。"姜太公"中的"太公"字面意义是"曾祖"(great grandfather)。关于它的来历有过不同的说法,委实难以定论。从网上检索发现,人们多用汉语拼音直接把"姜太公"处理为 Jiang Taigong,但也有译成 Grand Duke Jiang 的。Duke 一词不十分恰当,因为它带有浓厚的英文化色彩,与"姜太公"中的"太公"一语所指相差甚远,而且用 duke 来描述姜太公的职位也不相配。

"姜太公"作为一个称谓,在中国家喻户晓,如果上下文中没有分解其各个部分的含义,翻译时就可忽略不计。事实上,如果翻译时都要讲究中国人名的含义,就很难将翻译进行下去。从这一点讲,将翻译看作有选择性的行为是正确的。以拼音出现的 Jiang Taigong 在世界华人圈里无人不知,类似的情况如"老子"。"老子"也是尊称,翻译时从未见过深度的阐释,拼音的 Laotsz 一语通行中外,如果拼写为本名的 Li Er(李耳),难保不会徒增理解的困难。

文化信息有浓、淡两类,或者说有实有虚(周领顺,2014b:68)。实指时为实,当用作比喻意义时便是虚指。在原文中,与专有名词"姜太公"密切相关的是他能够令"诸神退位"的神力。是实是虚,要看是不是故事的一部分。试比较:

[4] 这可是大名鼎鼎、尽人皆知、能令"诸神退位"的姜太公啊。
Jiang Taigong was such a well-known figure! *He was even fictionalized as a master deity*, so mighty as could scare off all other lesser deities.

在汉文化中,"诸神退位"有两个意思:一是在《封神演义》中,姜太公被描写为神,被赐打神鞭,他一出现,其他诸神害怕挨打,纷纷逃离;二是民间利用"姜太公退神"的故事,把写有"姜太公在此,诸神退位"的字幅贴在门上,以镇宅辟邪,图个吉利。对于这两个意思,即使汉文化中的读者也未必完全了解,而在原文中"诸神退位"无非表示的是"姜太公"这一符号所拥有的神力,是作者将故事本身姜太公所拥有的神力与其在作者还价时可能产生的震撼力混为一体,说到底还是它的比喻用法,属于虚指。作者夸张表述了姜太公能让"诸神退位"的神力,并由此想象,如果在还价前了解雕像的身份,也会被"吓得"倒退而放弃在价格上的坚持。例[4]中的"诸神退位"的虚指用法假如照实体现,而不加信息的增补或进行所指的虚实转换,说不定译文读者会如坠云里雾里,与原文中"姜太公钓鱼"的信息相混淆。因此,译者考虑到文化因素的差异,舍弃例[4]中的虚指用法,将能令"诸神退位"的"姜太公"还原为实指,在译文中添加 He was even fictionalized as a master deity 这样的表述,以方便译文读者对原文文化的联想。

四、修辞与文化联想

原文的语言生动活泼,而隐喻、轭式搭配、反复等修辞格的多次妙用更为文章增添色彩。语言之间修辞格的使用既有共性,又有差异。通常情况下,原文和译文之间如有对应关系最好,否则就需要变通处理。例如:

[5] 姜太公明着钓的是鱼,实际钓的是人。

Jiang *cast his straight hook for fish* when his real intent was *to* "*hook*" King Wen of the ancient Zhou Tribe.

[6] "姜太公钓'鱼'",却把我"钓"上了。

Jiang Taigong *was hooking* "*fish*", and had me "*hooked*" as well.

在汉语中,动词"钓"能表达隐喻意义,意为"用手段猎取(名利)",它与指人的名词搭配时,表示"让人上当或把人吸引住",比如:"电话诈骗手段翻新,'教育退费'专钓学生家长""教你如何钓到一个钻石王老五"等。在英语中,hook 所表达的隐喻意义及其用法和汉语类似。动词 hook 意为 to succeed in making someone interested in something or attracted to something,比如 cigarette ads designed to *hook young people*(online *Longman Dictionary of Contemporary English*)。因此,在例[5]和例[6]的译文中,译者都直接使用了 hook 这个词形,以尽量再现原文的修辞效果。

如果能将原文的修辞效果移植到译文中最好,否则应灵活处理。比如下文例[7]和例[8]的译文都舍弃了原文的用词形象,在结构上也不如原文整齐、对称,是为了获得译文表达的习惯性和流畅性。试比较:

[7] 我再次甩出个现实问题,甩出的是生活阅历。

I *popped up* another real-life question *upon* life experience.

[8] 人家买的是古董,而我买的却是百读不厌的人生大哲理!

> While other people may *take* the sculpture *as* an antique, I got to *read into my purchase* a wisdom of life that will never ceases to intrigue me.

例[7]中的"甩"重复使用,和"问题""生活阅历"搭配,前者是常式,后者是变式,但语境提供了足够的上下连贯的信息,使得"甩出的是生活阅历"的用法自然、贴切。人体动作动词,比如汉语的"扔""甩""投",英语的 cast, hurl, pitch, pop, throw, toss 等,都有很多隐喻用法,且语言之间有不少相同之处。汉语和英语的这些动作动词都可以和"问题""困难""眼神"等抽象名词搭配,传递生动形象的修辞效果。但汉语和英语在句法、表达习惯等方面存在差异,如将例[7]表达为 I popped up another real-life question *and what I popped up* was life experience,则显啰唆,缺乏美感。译文对原文做了变通处理,选用 popped up another real-life question 和 upon life experience 来表达原文的意义,在形象色彩上,pop 和原文的"甩"类似,在音响效果上,up, upon 和原文重复使用的"甩"有些许接近。因此,译文部分保留了原文在修辞色彩上的美学因素。

例[8]和例[7]类似,句中的"买"分别与具体名称和抽象名词搭配,表达具体意义和隐喻意义。两个"买"隐含地表达了不同的认识和态度,别人买"姜太公钓鱼"只是做个表面文章,或为收藏或为观赏,而作者买"姜太公钓鱼",则从中品味出了新的人生哲理。也是因为汉语和英语在句法和表达习惯方面的差异,译文对原文的用词形象做了变通处理,将第一个"买"译为 take,既可表示"要""买"的意思(如 I'll take this one as a gift for my mom),又可表示"看待""对待"的意思(如 I take him as a friend),与原文一语双关的"买"有相通之处。第二个"买"主要通过 my purchase 来表达。另外,汉语把"人生哲理"比作书,可"百读不厌",英语似无此隐喻,译文舍弃了原文的这个形象,但使用了 read 这个动词,来表示"从雕像中读出了人生哲理",在形象和语义上接近了原文"百读不厌"的隐喻用法。

五、结束语

在"讲好中国故事"的过程中,总有这样那样的文化障碍问题,需要我们采取各种各样的方法来应对。我们暂且不去挑剔国外汉学家译者为了务实于自己的目标市场在翻译时应该有多大的自由度,但对于"中国译者"的"中国选择"而言,坚持对于原文意义的求真,是贯彻"讲好中国故事"、增强文化传播有效性的必需。从长远看,中国译者的求真译作,必然能够吸引那些真正有志于求取中国'真经'的西方学者的目光。(许钧、周领顺,2015)

> 原文

春风十里扬州路：人在扬州

"春风十里扬州路：人在扬州"，一是述说扬州城之美，二是述说人在扬州的真实感受，而"人"自然就是作者我自己。或者说，其一是诗人笔下充满诗意的扬州，其二是世俗里俗我体会到的扬州。

"卷上珠帘总不如"——人景

歌颂扬州之美的古诗数不胜数，著名的就有本文题目所示的杜牧这首"娉娉袅袅十三余，豆蔻梢头二月初。春风十里扬州路，卷上珠帘总不如"[1]一诗。诗无达诂，就"春风十里扬州路"及其下句"卷上珠帘总不如"而言[2]，具体描摹的当然是诗人意中女子之美。但既然是"卷上珠帘总不如"，到底是说诗人"情人眼里出西施[3]"呢，还是说春风十里的扬州路上真正的美女确实如凤毛麟角呢[4]？这就牵出一个话题："自古扬州出美女"。

"扬州美女"样子若何？该诗是诗人在离开扬州之际，赠他所结识的一名扬州歌妓的。扬州繁华自不用说，因历史上主要靠水路运输，而途经扬州的京杭大运河自然承担起了这一重任：有了运输，便有了商贾，有了商贾，便有了财富，而有了财富，便有了美女。所以，诠释"自古扬州出美女"之精妙，还在于另解的"扬州美女产外地[5]"之说呢。

"二十四桥明月夜"——物景

杜牧有"青山隐隐水迢迢，秋尽江南草未凋。二十四桥明月夜，玉人何处教吹箫"一诗，久唱不衰。对诗中景物的争论，自从该诗问世之日，就不曾停息。

扬州可在"江南"？扬州地处江北，按照官方的解释[6]，长江以北的都是北方。但扬州人可不愿与北方为伍。毕竟，扬州和镇江、南京仅一江之隔，接近南方，却叫北方，那才叫憋屈。勉为其难叫个"苏中"，意味着江苏中部，但在同纬度的其他省份，并不见这样的称呼。扬州历史上是个服务型城市，以"三把刀"（厨刀、修脚刀、理发刀）闻名。历史上，江浙富庶，但主要指的是浙江全境和江苏的苏南地区，以苏（州）、（无）锡、常（州）为最。

扬州可有"青山"？扬州地处平原。扬州城北部有一风景带，远看有岭,称为蜀岗,有鉴真和尚修行和欧阳修居住过的大明寺,是扬州的龙头[7]。扬州有水无山,实是一憾。

扬州可见"二十四桥"? 现在的瘦西湖确实建造了一座"二十四桥"[8],长度、宽度、栏柱、台阶,处处和"二十四"对应。不过,杜牧的数字诗大多是不靠谱的,也说明诗歌属于浪漫主义与现实主义兼而有之的一种文艺形式。

"烟花三月下扬州"——风景

最脍炙人口并让扬州赚得满钵金的是李白那篇活广告:"故人西辞黄鹤楼,烟花三月下扬州。孤帆远影碧空尽,唯见长江天际流。"[9]"烟花三月"似乎完全等同于"扬州",变成了扬州的代名词。

阳历的四月大约等同于阴历的三月[10],此时繁花似锦,桃红柳绿,莺歌燕舞,游人如织。历史上的扬州曾经美不胜收,这是毋庸置疑的。但从李白《送孟浩然之广陵》一诗本身看,"烟花三月"交代的是与人分别的时间,诗中的"黄鹤楼"是分别的地点,前两句写实,后两句写意。李白并未着意描画扬州之美,他的《江夏行》有句佐证[11],"去年下扬州,相送黄鹤楼。眼看帆去远,心逐江水流",且带着"谁知嫁商贾,令人却愁苦。自从为夫妻,何曾在乡土"的心情[12],并未着意提及后人传唱的"烟花三月"这看似浪漫的一语,说明"烟花三月"只是个轻描淡写的时间概念或季节概念。若专写扬州之美景,则需对主题"烟花"做进一步的说明。比如,我将后两行续写为:

绿柳笼纱罩长堤,
红桃弄姿映水流。

"烟"指"春烟",以柳树为代表(如"草长莺飞二月天,拂堤杨柳醉春烟");"花"以桃花为最,所谓"桃红柳绿"是也[13]。王维有"桃红复含宿雨,柳绿更带春烟[14]"诗句,正是对"烟花"的进一步描摹。"烟花三月"有美景,分手地"黄鹤楼"所在的武汉也莫不如此。

"天下三分明月夜"——"心景"

令人咀嚼的扬州必定是历史风韵犹存的扬州,这就涉及扬州城的开发和建设问题。扬州懂得发掘利用,比如历史上有过"扬州十日"屠城,连城墙也不复存在,然扬州人硬是将城墙根基上建起的民居拆除,把裸露的城墙根罩上个大棚子,使之成为一景;把早已建成民居的东关街居民迁出,仿古建成了一个集特色工艺、地方小吃和小件购物为一体的步行街;除了拓展早已闻名遐迩的景点外,尽可能开发扬州其他可看之景,让外地人一天之内打不得道,回不得府。

历史遗存无处不在。在瘦西湖的游船里,依旧能听见船娘土得掉渣的小调儿;扬州八怪[15]的真迹,在纪念馆里还能一睹芳容;隋炀帝观赏过的琼花,时节赶好了,在公园里随处可见;与鲁菜、川菜、粤菜并称为中国四大菜系的淮扬菜[16],更见今日刀工;朋友谈心的最佳去处,还是琳琅满目的茶肆;传统工艺:玉雕、漆器、剪纸,间杂于民居之中;泡脚、修脚、捶背,一溜几家,有的红火有的冷清。"早上皮包水,晚上水包皮。"新扬州还继承着老扬州的某些遗风。

唐代徐凝有名句:"天下三分明月夜,二分无赖是扬州。"回眸历史看今朝,试问:

明月如今再三分,

能送几分与广陵?

译文

The Glamorous Yangzhou: My Personal Experience

  This essay, as the title suggests, aims at an account of Yangzhou from two perspectives: the beauty of the city and my first-hand experience of it as a resident; or, in other words, the poetic Yangzhou as portrayed by poets and my mundane perception of it through my own eyes.

  "Pearly screen uprolled, none's so fair": the people scene

  There are numerous classical poems featuring the beauty of Yangzhou. Among them the poem by the Tang Dynasty (618 –907) poet Du Mu(803 –852) has gained lasting popularity. It goes as follows: "Not yet fourteen, she's fair and slender/Like early budding flower tender/Though Yangzhou Road's beyond compare/Pearly screen uprolled, none's so fair." The last two lines sketch the beauty of the girl who captured the poet's heart. Poetic language tends to allow for open interpretation. When the poet claimed that "Pearly screen uprolled, none's so fair", does it mean that the girl was incomparably "fair" only in the eye of the poet himself as the perceiver, or that the girl excelled all others in beauty in the sense that real beauties were actually rarely seen in ancient Yangzhou? The reading of these two lines naturally brings forth the topic of Yangzhou's reputation for having been "the birthplace of beauties since ancient times".

What did ancient Yangzhou beauties look like? The poem quoted above was composed, when the poet was ready to depart Yangzhou, in dedication to a sing-song girl he met during his stay there. Yangzhou enjoyed great prosperity in ancient times as an important port situated on the Beijing-Hangzhou Canal, which served as a major means of transportation. Owing to a convenient access to water transportation, the city thrived in trade and commerce, accumulating great wealth, which in turn could have magnetized beautiful women to it. Thus the secret of Yangzhou's reputation for being home to beauties could have lied in the possibility that its beauties might have been non-natives, swarming to it from elsewhere.

"When the moon shines on the Twenty-Four Bridge bright": the object scene

The poet Du Mu had another immortal poem about Yangzhou: "The hills loom up green, the waters flowing long/In late autumn River South grass is not yet gone/When the moon shines on the Twenty-Four Bridge bright/Are you somewhere teaching the flute in the moon light?" Ever since the poem came out, there have been disagreements over the scenes and objects depicted in it.

First of all, does Yangzhou sit on the south side of the Yangtze River? No, it borders its north bank. According to the official demarcation of regional boundaries, a region that is north of the Yangtze River is classified as the north. Be that as it may, Yangzhou people always reject the idea of their city standing on the same ground with the north. After all, separated by the Yangtze River from southern cities like Nanjing, Zhenjiang, Yangzhou is geographically a mere river's breadth from the south. However, it has to appear as a northern city. How disheartening this could be! It could do with the name "Centre of Su", meaning its location in the centre of Jiangsu Province. However, cities at the same latitude in other provinces have never been referred to this way. Yangzhou once was and still is a service-oriented city, renowned for its industries dependent on the "three knives", i. e. cuisine knife, pedicure knife and haircut knife. Of the two reputedly affluent provinces, Zhejiang and Jiangsu, the former has wealth that is distributed relatively evenly across it, while the later has richness that is accumulated mainly in its southern region, especially in the cities of Suzhou, Wuxi and Changzhou.

Another question is, does Yangzhou have "green hills"? The answer is "no" again, for Yangzhou rests on a plain. In a scenic zone in the north of Yangzhou, a leading tourist attraction of the city, there rises, when seen from afar, something of a hilly ridge named Shugang, where Daming Temple is nestled. The temple is, by the way, the place once occupied by the Tang Dynasty Buddhist monk Jianzhen (688 – 763) to study his sutras, and later by the North Song Dynasty litterateur and statesman Ouyang Xiu (1007 – 1072) as his residence. The truth is that Yangzhou is abundant in water, not hills. That really is a pity!

And finally, did Yangzhou ever have the Twenty-Four Bridge, the one mentioned in Du Mu's poem? There is now a bridge, named "Twenty-Four Bridge", going across a stretch of the Slender West Lake in the city. It was constructed not long ago and designed to match the numerical value "24" in every aspect, in length, breadth, and number of columns and steps. However, the numerals in Du Mu's poetry may not make much realistic sense. Furthermore, poetry is an artistic form of realism and romanticism.

"In misty and flowery March he sails down to Yangzhou": the nature scene

The poem that is the most favored and has brought huge economic benefits to Yangzhou is "Seeing Meng Haoran off to Guangling" (an ancient name for Yangzhou) by the Tang Dynasty poet Li Bai (701 – 762): "Leaving Yellow Crane Tower, east my old friend will go/In misty and flowery March he sails down to Yangzhou/The lonely boat dims and is lost at the end of blue sky/And all I can see is the Yangtze River's seaward flow." "Misty and flowery March" (in the lunar calendar) and "Yangzhou", occurring in the same line in the poem, are so closely bound up together that a mention of one always leads to the thought of the other.

March in the lunar calendar, approximate to April in the solar calendar, is a time when flowers and trees get their color back and bloom in full glory, infusing into every pore of a scenic place the hustle and bustle of tourists. It goes without saying that ancient Yangzhou was amazingly beautiful. Yet, as the above poem shows, "misty and flowery March" specifies the time of departure and Yellow Crane Tower the place of departure. The first two lines describe the scene and the last two the feelings of the poet. The poet did not pen the beauty of Yangzhou at all in the above poem, nor did he in his another poem "A Song of Jiangxia": "When you went southward yesteryear to Yangzhou/At Yellow Crane Tower I bade you adieu/As I watched your sail till it vanished afar/My heart went after you with the river flow". The "misty and flowery March", appreciated as romantic by later readers, was not even touched upon in this poem, for the poet had the theme centering on sympathy over a woman married to a merchant, who was doing business in Yangzhou: "Wedding a merchant, I've never known/Could be a bitter feel taken alone/Ever since we became man and wife/You've not ever been with me at home". So it is evident that "misty and flowery March", denotative of a temporal notion, is not specific to Yangzhou and bears no significant meaning. If the poem "Seeing Meng Haoran off to Guangling" were to have focused on the beauty of Yangzhou, it ought to have given more details about the "misty and flowery March" scene there. Its last two lines could have been like this:

Willow twigs shade over the long bank like a green veil,

Peach blooms of red shower their grace in the water flow.

"Misty" describes the hazy visual effect in the spring air, and is often associated with the image of willow trees in poems, as in "February warblers fly among the grass high above the ground/Bent willows 'gainst the river bank, they wave in the spring haze drowned". Of flowers, those of peach trees are the most charming, especially when they go in contrast with green willows, as the Tang Dynasty poet Wang Wei (701 – 761) had it, "Peaches look rosier, bearing dew from the night rain/Willows appear grassier, swaying in the spring haze". These poetic lines are further examples of the flowery spring scene. With the onset of the "misty and flowery March", beautiful scenes unfold before the eyes everywhere, including in Wuhan, the location of the Yellow Crane Tower, the place of departure in Li Bai's poem.

"Of all the moonlit nights on earth when people part": the mind scene

What makes people most reminiscent is the Yangzhou that gives a real flavor of its history and culture. An issue arises concerning how to preserve and construct the rich heritage of the city. Fortunately the Yangzhou municipality is wise and knows how to do it. For example, the 10-day massacre that happened in Yangzhou in the Qing Dynasty (1616 – 1911), did not leave much trace in the modern city. For the historical site of the event to be restored, the residences there were pulled down and made way for a huge wall to be constructed over the remains of the ancient city walls. Dongguan Street, previously occupied by residents, were evacuated and turned into an ancient style pedestrian street lined with businesses on both sides specializing in specialty art crafts, Yangzhou-flavored delicacies and souvenirs. In addition to the exploitation of the already well-known scenic sites, new spots were developed and added onto the tourism list to keep tourists glued to the city and stay more than one day.

Yangzhou boasts a lot that can represent its claims to antiquity. In the touring boats sailing on the Slender West Lake, female oar rollers can be heard singing old-fashioned popular tunes. The authentic masterpieces by the "Eight Yangzhou Eccentrics", the eight native painters and calligraphers living in the mid-Qing Dynasty, are housed in their memorial museums for public display. In the blooming season, Qionghua flowers that Emperor Yang(569 – 618) of the Sui Dynasty (581 – 618) was rumored to have viewed in Yangzhou are a prevalent sight in parks. The Huaiyang style cuisine, which originates from Jiangsu Province and is as reputed as the other three styles originating respectively from Shandong, Sichuan and Guangdong Province, is more refined today than it was in its knife skills. Tea houses offer a diversity of customer options and may be one of the nicest environments for gathering with friends. Traditional art crafts like jade wares, paint wares, paper cuttings are objects of collection that even find their way into local residences. Businesses set up in close vicinity to each other provide services of foot soaking, pedicure or back tapotement: some are hot and some are not. A morning tea in a teahouse and an evening bath in a bathhouse is part of a traditional lifestyle that Yangzhou people have enjoyed through the ages. All this highlights the historical legacy Yangzhou has inherited from its past.

As the Tang Dynasty poet Xu Ning wrote, "Of all the moonlight shed upon the earth/Yangzhou is deserving of the two-thirds". Looking from past to present, I have this question:

Of all three shares of moonlight for today,

How much Yangzhou would deserve do you say?

注释

[1] 杜牧这首诗的译者是许渊冲,见谢真元主编,《一生必读唐诗三百首鉴赏》(汉英对照),中国对外翻译出版公司,2006 年版,第 381 页。

[2] 原文此处重复了所引杜牧诗歌的最后两句,译文不必如此重复,概括地表示为 the last two lines 即可。

[3] "情人眼里出西施"是汉语成语,在孤立的语境里,译为现成的 Beauty is in the eyes of the beholder 完全可以。但根据原文,不可完全照搬现成的译文,可译为 incomparably "fair" only in the eye of the poet himself as the perceiver,既充分表达了原文的意思,又获得了译文语义上更加连贯的效果。

[4] 这一小句表达的言下之意是,假如古扬州城里的美女如凤毛麟角,那么诗人中意的女子的美就是相对的了,可译为 or that the girl excelled all others in beauty in the sense that real beauties were actually rarely seen in ancient Yangzhou。

[5] 翻译"扬州美女产外地"这一说法,需要转换思维方式,不必拘泥于原文的字面意思,可译为 its beauties might have been non-natives, swarming to it from elsewhere,即"扬州美女非土生土长"之意。

[6] "按照官方的解释"应理解为"按照官方对于行政区域的划分",可译为 According to the official demarcation of regional boundaries。

[7] "龙头"的上文有"扬州北部的风景带""蜀岗""大明寺"等,这句中的"龙头"实指扬州北部的风景带。

[8] 根据上下文,这个小句子中的"建造了"意为"因建造而存在"。译文用 there-be 句型表达这种结果性的"存在",而将"建造"这个动作表达为一个过去事件。在汉语中,动态动词后跟体态助词"了",表示一种由动词所表示的动作造成的结果,因此,"动词+了"可与表示时段的时间词语搭配。例如,在"房子买了两年,早已过了交房日期,开发商却迟迟不交房"这个情形中,"买了两年"并不是指"买"这个动作本身持续了两年,而是"买"之后的结果持续了两年。

[9] 李白这首诗的译者是陈君朴(陈君朴编译,《汉英对照唐诗绝

句150首》,上海大学出版社,2005年版,第50页)。

[10] 上一段提到 misty and flowery March (in the lunar calendar),在这一段中,译文对首句的语序做了调整,译为 March in the lunar calendar, approximate to April in the solar calendar,以 March in the lunar calendar 开头,与译文的上文在语义上更加连贯。

[11] "佐证"什么?佐证《江夏行》中的"扬州"只是一个行程的目的地,诗人并没有刻意描绘扬州的美景。译文应体现这个隐含的意思,将这两个小句变通处理为:The poet did not pen the beauty of Yangzhou at all in the above poem, nor did he in his another poem "A Song of Jiangxia"。

[12] 在这个小句中,"心情"前的修饰语是李白《江夏行》一诗中的四句诗,这四句诗描绘了诗中女主人的悲愁心情,抒发的是诗人对平民小人物的同情,可译为 the poet had the theme centering on sympathy over a woman married to a merchant, who was doing business in Yangzhou。译文对女主人公的背景略做了介绍,并以 sympathy 一词点明了这四句诗的实际含义。

[13] 桃花在绿柳的映衬下更显妖娆美丽,"所谓'桃红柳绿'是也"这个小句译为 especially when they (peach flowers) go in contrast with green willows。

[14] 这两句诗出自王维的《田园乐》一诗,全诗为:"桃红复含宿雨,柳绿更带春烟。花落家童未扫,莺啼山客犹眠。"这是一首六言绝句,平仄相对,工整对仗,偶句入韵。所引两句诗译为:Peaches look rosier, bearing dew from the night rain/Willows appear grassier, swaying in the spring haze. 除了传递原诗句的语义外,译文在形式上也尽量贴近原诗,peaches 和 willows 相对,look 和 appear 相对,rosier 和 grassier 相对,bearing 和 swaying 引导的两个分词短语在外部形式上一致,但内部结构上有差异,前者为动宾结构,后者为动词和修饰性成分的搭配。

[15] "扬州八怪"直译为 the "Eight Yangzhou Eccentrics",并以同位语的形式补充必要的信息,即 the eight native painters and calligraphers living in the mid-Qing Dynasty。

[16] "淮扬菜"指发源并流行于江苏省淮安、扬州、镇江及其附近地区的菜肴,译文以关系分句的形式,即 which originates from Jiangsu Province,补充了必要的信息。上文提到扬州位于江苏省,此处仅简单地将"淮扬菜"的发源地表述为"江苏省",以获得简洁的表达效果。

> 专评

文学翻译的忠实度和文化传播的有效性

扬州城久负盛名,一句"烟花三月下扬州",招揽了数不胜数的观光客。扬州在世界华人圈里经久传唱,该事实也构成了本文汉英翻译实践和评析的基础。原文便是基于笔者(周领顺)应邀在美国"北得州文友社"(North Texas Chinese Literary Society)所做的同题演讲而写就的,全文刊登于2013年1月25日的《达拉斯新闻》上,因篇幅所限,这里提供的原文有所删节。

传承和传播中国文化,在当今中国文学、文化"走出去"的战略背景下更具意义。因此,评析也将从中国文学(原文的文风)和中国文化(地域文化)有效传播的角度出发,阐发翻译应有的行为和翻译预期的意义。前者涉及文学翻译的忠实度问题,后者涉及地域文化传播的有效性问题。前后相辅相成,地域文化正是借助文学载体得以传播的。关于地域文化,周作人说:"我相信强烈的地方趣味也正是世界的文学的一个重大成分。"(丁帆,2007:12)就是说,越是地域的,越要走向世界,与习近平倡导的"讲好中国故事""阐释好中国特色"的理念并行不悖。

一、文学翻译的忠实度

文学翻译的忠实性在翻译的现实中演变为"忠实度"(周领顺,2014a:125)。忠实之时,难免需要不同程度的变通。这是翻译界老生常谈的一个话题。为了更好地与实践相结合,以下将从原文的题目和翻译、原文的风格和翻译、原文的诗歌和翻译等三个方面讨论文风的翻译问题。

第一,原文的题目和翻译。

原文是从两个方面入手的,即诗歌中的扬州和作者体会到的扬州。文章题目和分节题目也由两个部分组成,即古诗句和概括性的表述,它既是文章的内容,又是文章的题眼,因此,在理论上,题目的形式应在翻译时加以保留。

文章题目的前半部分"春风十里扬州路"引自杜牧的《赠别(其一)》,受过一定教育的原语读者必定了然于心,但译语读者则比较陌生。因此,译文舍弃了表面的形象性,译为 The Glamorous Yangzhou 只取了该诗句表达的内在意义。全诗的译文出现于正文中,译语读者自然能理解通透,但用作题目,首先要做到一目了然,才能立刻引起译语读者的阅读兴趣。

文章题目的后半部分"人在扬州"呈现的是"×在××"结构,该结构常见于文章的题目,比如"吃在广州""穿在上海""车在美国"等,一般直译便可。但"人在扬州"不宜直译,因为汉语中"人"的指称意义外延很广,和英语的 person, people, man, woman 等词均不对应,表达为 People in Yangzhou 虽然自然,但题目中的"人"实际仅指作者一人,并非泛称,若说成 the person in Yangzhou,显得不伦不类;若说成 the writer in Yangzhou,又欠自然。因此,"人在扬州"意译为 My Personal Experience,显得直白而简洁。

分节题目中前后两个部分叠加的形式却在翻译中得到了保留,如将"'卷上珠帘总不如'——人景"直译为"Pearly Screen Uprolled, None's so Fair": The People Scene。分节题目中的诗句所在的古诗在正文中皆有引用,且相距不远,不会让读者产生阅读和理解上的距离感,保留形象是恰当的。分节题目中的概括性表述在英语中也有对应的表达,直译是可行的。

第二,原文的风格和翻译。

原文使用的某些语言表达方式,若非出于特殊的修辞目的,都相应切换为英语习惯的表达风格。例如:

[1] "春风十里扬州路:人在扬州",一是述说……二是述说……
This essay, as the title suggests, aims at an account of Yangzhou from two perspectives …

[2] 其二是述说人在扬州的真实感受,而"人"自然就是作者我自己。
… and my first-hand experience of it as a resident …

[3] 有了运输,便有了商贾,有了商贾,便有了财富,而有了财富,便有了招之即来的美女。
Owing to a convenient access to water transportation, the city thrived in trade and commerce, accumulating great wealth, which in turn could have magnetized beautiful women to it.

例[1]是原文的首句,不厌其烦地重复了文章的题目。这种行文风格符合汉语的表达习惯,和"他什么都学他哥哥,他哥哥吃饭,他吃饭,他哥哥吃面,他也吃面"等表达方式中的词语重复如出一辙,而英语一般不擅此道。

例[2]是典型的汉语式表达,若照直翻译,大致可以说成 the first-hand experience of it by someone living in Yangzhou, that is, by me the writer of this essay,语法和语义虽然没有问题,但英语中很少有这种汉语常见的螺旋形(周领顺、周怡珂,2014:59)讲话方式。题目中的"人在扬州"难以直译,而例[2]中的"而'人'自然就是作者我自己"这一解释性的句子,自然就没有翻译的必要了,使用人称限定词 my,译语读者自然明白其意。此外,例[2]增添了 as a resident,体现了"人在扬州"的深层意义。

例[3]也是一种螺旋形表达,前后词语如链条一般重复出现,构成顶真句式,这样的行文方式在汉语中司空见惯,英语则不然,因此,译文做了相应调整。

在篇章衔接风格方面,汉语倾向于隐,英语则倾向于明。原文的"'二十四桥明月夜'——物景"一节有三处设问,分别引导三个段落,没有使用任何衔接手段。译文添加了衔接性成分,使语义的连贯显性化。试比较:

[4] 扬州可在"江南"?……扬州可有"青山"?……扬州可见"二十四桥"?

First of all, does Yangzhou sit on the south side of the Yangtze River? … *Another question is*, does Yangzhou have "green hills"? … *And finally*, did Yangzhou ever have the Twenty-Four Bridge?

另外,原文的某些风格源自汉语本身的结构特点。例如,作者有意将"打道回府"这一成语拆解成两两相对的并列结构,即"让外地人一天之内打不得道,回不得府",使汉语的灵活性得到了彰显。这类结构如同汉语的"离合词"(如"考了一个试"),实难在英语中尽显其貌。"打道回府"色彩丰富,为了在译文中尽可能减少损失,译文使用了形象性稍强的 glue 一词,将整句译为 to keep tourists glued to the city and stay more than one day,也算是对语言差异造成的损失做了少许的弥补吧。

第三,原文的诗歌和翻译。

原文引用了多首古诗,这些古诗一般都有现成的译文,若非迫不得已,一般不另起炉灶,如杜牧的"娉娉袅袅十三余,豆蔻梢头二月初。春风十里扬州路,卷上珠帘总不如"和李白的"故人西辞黄鹤楼,烟花三月下扬州。孤帆远影碧空尽,唯见长江天际流"就分别采用了许渊冲(谢真元,2006:381)和陈君朴(2005:50)的译文。

但我们也常根据语境的需要而变通。比如,原文结尾处引用徐凝的"天下三分明月夜,二分无赖是扬州"两句诗,许渊冲(谢真元,2006:379)译为:Of all the moonlit nights on earth when people part/Two-thirds shed sad light on Yangzhou with broken heart. 将惆怅的心境表现得淋漓尽致,再现了原诗的意境。但在这里,作者只是借用了表面上描写扬州美好的两句话,所以我们直译为:Of all the moonlight shed upon the earth/Yangzhou is deserving of the two-thirds.

原文中有两处作者续写的诗句,一处是对"故人西辞黄鹤楼,烟花三月下扬州"两句的续写,另一处是对"天下三分明月夜,二分无赖是扬州"两句的续写,如例[5]、例[6]所示:

[5] 故人西辞黄鹤楼,烟花三月下扬州。
<u>绿柳笼纱罩长堤,红桃弄姿映水流。</u>

[6] 天下三分明月夜,二分无赖是扬州。
<u>明月如今再三分,能送几分与广陵?</u>

原文引用的古诗为五言、六言或七言绝句,除了王维的"桃红复含宿雨,柳绿更带春烟",其余的并不追求平仄协调或对仗工整,但都讲究韵律。汉语古诗的韵律可以是 abcb 或 aaba 式,翻译时还可以处理为 abab 或 aabb 式。对于作者续写的诗歌,译文也尽量和原诗的韵律保持一致,必要时为此而进行变通处理。试比较例[5]和例[6]及其译文:

[5]′ Leaving Yellow Crane Tower, east my old friend will go;
 In misty and flowery March he sails down to Yangzhou.
 Willow twigs shade over the long bank like a green veil,
 Peach blooms of red shower their grace in the water flow.

[6]′ Of all the moonlight shed upon the earth,
 Yangzhou is deserving of the two-thirds.
 Of all three shares of moonlight for today,
 How much Yangzhou would deserve do you say?

例[5]译文的韵律和原文保持了一致,都是 aaba 式。例[6]原诗为"萧娘脸薄难胜泪,桃叶眉长易觉愁。天下三分明月夜,二分无赖是扬州",韵律为 abcb 式,而续写后的诗句则有所失,作为弥补,译文采用了 aabb 的韵式,当然其中的 aa 并不是严格的韵脚一致,earth 和 thirds 只是元音相同罢了。

二、文化传播的有效性

文化传播的有效性也是翻译界老生常谈的一个话题。扬州是一座文化古城，有关扬州的文字里，少不了具体的文化意象。下文将从地域信息的翻译、历史信息的翻译、时令信息的翻译和生活信息的翻译等方面，讨论文化传播的有效性，并主要从译者的角度，认定译者行为的合理性。

第一，地域信息的翻译。

原文有争议的地域信息主要是"江南"，按照字面意义，"江南"指长江中下游平原的南岸地区，包括江苏省、安徽省长江以南的部分，以及上海市和浙江省钱塘江以北的区域。

自古以来，江南是历代文人骚客经常描绘的对象，带有浓厚的传统文化色彩。杜牧的"青山隐隐水迢迢，秋尽江南草未凋"一诗有不同的译本，大多将"江南"译为 south 或 the South（如郭著章等，2010：195；陈君朴，2005：238），也有人译为 south of the Yangtze River（如唐一鹤，2005：230）。而英语的 South 是一个非常笼统的概念，根据 The American Heritage Dictionary of the English Language（3rd edition），它指的是 the southern part of a region or country。原文引用杜牧的这首诗歌，主要是为了引出扬州究竟属于江南还是江北的问题，因此，"江南"不能简单地译为 south 或 the South。综合各种因素考虑，我们译为 River South，将 River 作修饰语，以限定 South 的范围，且大写，特指"长江"。当然，译语读者不一定即刻明白 River 之所指，但下文紧接的描述提及长江作为地理分界的标志，想必读者会有自然联想，从而明白 River 之所指。

历史上，扬州别名"广陵"。译语读者不一定熟悉此信息，因此，译文不仅补充了李白诗歌的题目，还对题目中的"广陵"增加了说明，即"Seeing Meng Haoran off to Guangling"（an ancient name for Yangzhou）。在例[6]中，作者也用了"广陵"来指称扬州，一是因为原语读者大多熟悉背景信息，二是因为这两句诗是对徐凝诗句的续写，用"广陵"可避免与"二分无赖是扬州"句尾词形重复。我们将此"广陵"仍旧处理为 Yangzhou，主要考虑到此处距离上文的补充信息比较遥远，有可能会增添译语读者阅读的障碍（关于"扬州""广陵"的翻译，更多讨论见周领顺，2014a：111–112）。

第二,历史信息的翻译。

"歌妓"指旧时以卖唱为生的女子。英语中有一个借自日语的词语 geisha(歌伎),其所指和旧时的"歌妓"十分接近,但这个词日文化色彩太浓。而英语的 singer 意为"歌手",和"歌妓"的意义差别甚大。英语中有 sing-song girl 一说,根据维基百科,为 19 世纪初英语人士杜撰,指中国近代的"歌女",与古时"歌妓"的性质较为相似。

关于历史人物。一般而言,对于人物,增加一些基本信息即可,例如我们将"鉴真和尚"和"欧阳修"分别处理为 the Tang Dynasty Buddhist monk Jianzhen (688 – 763) 和 the North Song Dynasty litterateur and statesman Ouyang Xiu (1007 – 1072)。

关于"琼花"。传说隋炀帝开凿大运河正是为到扬州观赏琼花之用的,不过隋炀帝下扬州看琼花的故事未见记载于正史。因此,"隋炀帝观赏过的琼花"的译文 Qionghua flowers that Emperor Yang(569 – 618) of the Sui Dynasty(581 – 618) was rumored to have viewed in Yangzhou 增加的 was rumored to,就是为了说明隋炀帝观赏琼花不一定属实。

第三,时令信息的翻译。

关于"烟花三月"。"烟花三月"在公历的四月或五月,陈君朴(2005:50)化繁为简,将其直译为 misty and flowery March,未必切合实际。为准确起见,当原文再次提及"烟花三月"时,我们在括号中补充了 in the lunar calendar 的信息。

"烟花三月"和"扬州"出现在同一个句子里时,起着互为联想的作用。因此,原文有"'烟花三月'似乎完全等同于'扬州',变成了扬州的代名词"的表述。但"烟花三月"是时间概念,而"扬州"是地理概念,不宜直译,所以意译为"Misty and flowery March" (in the lunar calendar) and "Yangzhou", occurring in the same line in the poem, are so closely bound up together that a mention of one always leads to the thought of the other。

关于"春烟"。"春烟"泛指春天的云烟岚气,或春天水泽、草木间蒸发的雾气。它是汉语诗歌中经常出现的意象,且常与柳树并提。因此,原文中的"'烟'指'春烟',以柳树为代表"一句,应理解为"'烟'指'春烟',诗歌中经常与春烟并提的意象是柳树",可译为"Misty" describes the hazy visual effect in the spring air, and is often associated with the image of willow trees in poems。

第四,生活信息的翻译。

关于"捶背"。"捶"可对应英语的 beat, pound, tap 等词。捶背的技法多种多样,上述几个英语词均无力涵盖。在北美等西方国家,服务行当中的"捶"是 tapotement,来自法语,属于按摩方式中的一种。tapotement 采用的技法和中国的"捶背"类似,但该词在语体方面与"捶背"是有差异的:"捶背"几乎人人皆知,而 tapotement 一般大众比较陌生。所以,此处主要侧重的是语义对等。

关于"早上皮包水,晚上水包皮"。在扬州,"皮包水"指喝早茶,"水包皮"指泡澡,是当地茶文化和沐浴文化的一种表现,假如直译为:In the morning people have water put into their skin, and in the evening they have their skin put into water. 其中 skin 的使用不免让人感到恐怖,或让人不知所云;假如添加 a traditional lifestyle in which Yangzhou people enjoy a tea in the morning and a bath in the evening 之类的注释,又不免啰唆。所以,我们将这一形象的话语意译为 A morning tea in a teahouse and an evening bath in a bathhouse,概括体现了扬州的文化,所不足的是造成了原文形象的一些缺失。

原文

喝茶与品茶

"喝茶"与"品茶"有稍许不同,尽管在口语中并没有严格的区分。从古到今,有数不胜数的品茶美文,而将品茶的感受写成文字者,自然是文人雅士[1]之为。不曾见过有关喝茶的文字,就大体反映了"喝茶"与"品茶"的差异。

"品茶",表面上品的是茶,实际品的是艺术,是文人雅士闲适的艺术享受。君可闻,明代杨慎就有"君作茶歌如作史,不独品茶兼品士"[2]的诗句。"喝茶"是对于粗犷之人,特别是体力劳动者而言的。喝茶要大口,大口才过瘾,喝茶者所求的是茶叶的实用功能,比如其"生津止渴""养生保健"之功。显然,"喝茶"属于物质层面,"品茶"属于精神层面。或者说,"喝茶"重在解渴,"品茶"旨在怡情,而我在以往最多只能算是"喝茶"者,甚至连"喝茶"者也算不上,只能算作"喝水"的吧。

我出生于中原农村。小时候家长让喝的"茶",实际就是白开水,长大了才意识到,我们那里从来就不成茶树,大多没见过茶叶,听说药铺里有,是专给人治病用的。城里人说的"喝茶"和农村人说的"喝茶"是不同的,农村人说的"喝茶"即城里人说的"喝水",喝的是白开水,而"喝水"在农村又具体化为"喝凉水""喝井水"等不同的说法。现在有了茶叶,也就有了"喝茶叶茶"和"喝白茶"(喝白开水)的区别了。

我从"喝水"到"喝茶"再到现在的"品茶"[3],也基本上走向了文人雅士[4],但远没有达到那种为了艺术而讲究茶艺的地步,每当端起茶艺小盏[5],"不过瘾[6]"之意还会涌上心头。

品茶有几个步骤:"尝茶""闻香""观汤""品味",对于我,能经常达到"观汤"和"品味"就算不错了。"观汤"就是观看茶水的颜色,当有了视觉上的享受之后,才会有切实的"品味"。

中国有六大茶类之分,即绿茶、红茶、黄茶、白茶、青茶和黑茶,表面上是按照茶的颜色分类的。茶的不同颜色,实际代表的是不同的制作方法。绿茶属于不发酵的茶,红茶属于全发酵的茶,青茶属于半发酵的茶,黄茶属于微发酵的茶,黑茶属于后发酵的茶,白茶属于轻微发酵的茶。茶叶的颜色对于内行人来讲,是另一番讲究[7],比如安吉白茶实属绿茶一类。

不管茶的种类是不是都是按照颜色划分的,但肯定有颜色的因素在里面。为了增加直观的"观汤"之感,我特意购买了一个玻璃杯子,凝视茶叶在茶杯里旋转,静观颜色在旋转时展现。常见的茶汤颜色有黄绿色、深红色和古铜色等几类。黄绿色荡漾着青春朝气,深红色沉淀着高贵典雅,古铜色反射着老到厚重。喜欢茶的颜色,是激起味觉享受的第一步,而茶汤和茶叶,共同构成了茶的原生态[8]。英美等西方国家习惯把茶叶制成碎末,置于一个白色纸袋中,一起放在杯子里冲泡,虽然凸显了茶叶的实用功能,但或许部分抑制了人们对于茶叶的艺术享受。在中国,也只有低档宾馆提供的劣质茶叶才如此包装,因而难免让人产生错觉[9]。

从"喝茶"过渡到"品茶",提高的是精神追求。"喝茶"和"品茶"两种说法虽然有稍许差异,但目前已经逐渐趋同。不管口头上邀人"喝茶"抑或"品茶",本质上并没有什么不同,都是把茶作为媒介而交友或谈事罢了。以茶为媒介[10],高雅如是,而人似也高雅如是也。

译文

Tea Drinking vs. Tea Sipping

"Tea drinking" and "tea sipping" slightly differ from each other, though they are perceived almost as the same in speech. Tea sipping, from past to present, has been a source of inspiration for numerous essays or poems written by literary scholars, who are in the mood to capture in words their tea sipping experience. By contrast, tea drinking has never been written about in literary creations. And this is enough evidence for the difference between "tea drinking" and "tea sipping".

Tea sipping, concerned less with tea than with the art involved in it, is an artistic luxury that the Chinese literati favor for their leisure. The trend for tea sipping can be seen from the two lines of a poem written by the poet Yang Shen (1488 – 1559) of the Ming Dynasty (1368 – 1644), which goes as "In a lyric ode to tea you wrote to the full/Tea was sipped for flavor and for spirit too". People of rough character, those doing physical work for instance, drink tea for its practical function of quenching thirst or promoting health. For such a purpose, tea drinking can only be satiating when the liquor is quaffed down. Obviously, tea drinking nurtures the body and tea sipping the mind. Or in other words, the former serves for physical content and the latter for mental delight. In terms of the level that tea enjoyers get to, I could be ranked at the most as a "tea" drinker previously, or even as less of a "tea" drinker than a water drinker.

In rural central China, where I was born, the so-called "tea" that I used to drink when I was small was actually plain boiled water. Not until I was grown up did I come to realize that my native land was never suitable for tea tree growth, and that local people had no access to tea leaves elsewhere except in pharmacies of Chinese herbal medicine, where tea leaves were available only for medical treatments. To rural people the concept "drinking tea", which was not the same as that referred to by urban people, simply meant drinking water, i. e. drinking plain boiled water. And in rural areas "drinking water" was further specified into "drinking cold water" "drinking well water", etc. When tea leaves were brought to the market in my native place, a new distinction was made between "drinking tea with tea leaves in it" and "drinking tea white", the latter actually meaning "drinking water without any tea leaves brewed in it".

Initially I drank water, later I also drank tea, and now I sip tea. It could well be said that I am now among people of refined taste. That being said, I do not practice tea art for art's sake, for I always wish I could take gulps rather than sips whenever I enjoy tea from a tiny cup, part of a set specially made to serve tea.

There are steps to follow in tea sipping: taking sips, sensing the aroma, observing the color and tasting the flavor. As for me, I would be more than happy if I could go as far as the final two steps in most cases. Observing the color means observing the color of tea liquor. The purpose of doing that is to experience a more genuine taste with a pleasant visual perception.

Chinese tea is classified by color into six major varieties, namely green tea, black tea, yellow tea, white tea, blue tea and dark tea. This classification also represents a distinction in the degree of fermentation in the tea manufacturing process. Green tea is non-fermented, black tea fully-fermented, blue tea semi-fermented, yellow tea lightly-fermented, dark tea post-fermented, and white tea very lightly-fermented. The color of tea leaves, as connoisseurs know it, has a lot more to say than meets the eye. For example, Anji white tea is actually a green tea by nature, produced in Anji County of Zhejiang Province.

Color definitely contributes to the classification of tea though it is not an exclusive element for it. To better observe the color that tea leaves give to the liquor, I specially bought a transparent glass, and began to appreciate better the sight of tea leaves unfolding and releasing color as they steep and swirl in the vessel. The common types of color that tea liquor takes on include yellowish green, dark red, dark amber, etc. The color of tea liquor exudes sensations: the yellowish green vigor and vitality, the dark red nobleness and elegance, and the dark amber diplomacy and profoundness. The color of tea liquor is an initial stimulation that induces the gustatory sense. The tea liquor and leaves are the two primitive components of tea that have a visual effect. Western countries like the UK or the US tend to have tea leaves processed into tiny leaf bits and packaged in small paper bags to be brewed in the cup. Such a practice, when it gives prominence to the practical function of tea, more or less lessens the drinker's aesthetic enjoyment of tea leaves. In mainland China, only those low quality tea leaves are so processed and mainly supplied to low-end hotels. Inevitably wrong impressions often arise about the packaged tea sold on the western market.

Transition from tea drinking to tea sipping is an elevation in the spiritual realm. Nowadays the two, however, are not strictly differentiated, though they do differ slightly. When one invites people to tea, it basically makes no much difference whether he phrases it as "to tea drinking" or "to tea sipping", for tea only serves on such an occasion as a vehicle for social interaction. Used as a social beverage, tea is an indicator of good taste, and its consumers are thus also presenting themselves as having good taste, or so it appears.

> 注释

　　[1]"文人雅士"中的"雅士"几乎总是与"文人"共现,构成一个四音节的短语,没有多少实际的意义,译出"文人"的意思即可,即 literary scholars。

　　[2]这两句诗引自杨慎的《和章水部沙坪茶歌》,诗中提到了陆羽和卢仝。二者分别被后人誉为"茶圣"和"茶仙",后者写过一首茶歌,非常有名,名叫《七碗茶歌》,是其《走笔谢孟谏议寄新茶》一诗中的一部分,道出了诗人喝了友人赠送的新茶之后体验到的美妙感受。杨慎的这两句诗写的应该是卢仝和他的茶歌,可理解为"你(指卢仝)写茶歌就像书写历史那样全面,才学兼备,你品茶不单品味茶道,还同时品味和修养身心",我们试译为:In a lyric ode to tea you wrote to the full/ Tea was sipped for flavor and for spirit too.

　　[3]这个小句译为:Initially I drank water, later I also drank tea, and now I sip tea. 而没有按照表层结构译成 From drinking water to drinking tea and to sipping tea. 前者表意更加明确,添加的 also 表明是在喝水的基础上增加了喝茶、品茶的习惯和爱好,而后者似乎更侧重表达"从喝水改为喝茶、品茶"的意思。

　　[4]"也基本上走向了文人雅士"意为"达到了文人雅士的境界或品位",可译为:It could well be said that I am now among people of refined taste. 这个小句中的"文人雅士"指品位不俗的人,译为 people of refined taste 为妥。

　　[5]除了将"茶艺小盏"译成 a tiny cup 外,还通过同位语的形式(part of a set specially made to serve tea)补充信息,说明"茶艺小盏"为茶道的一部分。

　　[6]"不过瘾"是"希望大口大口地喝"的意思,转换思维方式,可译为:I always wish I could take gulps rather than sips.

　　[7]"另一番讲究"不是指内行讲究茶的颜色,而是指茶的颜色里深藏奥妙的意思,而这只有内行才知晓。译文用了一个形象色彩比较浓厚的英语习语 has a lot more to say than meets the eye,字面意义为"比眼睛看到的还要多"。

　　[8]"原生态"是近年来很流行的词语,原指"没有经过人为修饰与处理的、原汁原味的状态"。这个小句的上文说的是茶的颜色和视觉

享受之间的关系,因此此处的"原生态"可理解为"能激起视觉享受的最基本的因素",可译为 the two primitive components of tea that have a visual effect,使上下文的语义连贯。

[9]"错觉",指"让人误解西方市场上出售的纸包装茶叶"的意思,简单地说就是"误解",可译为 wrong impressions。

[10]"媒介"可直译为 medium,也可译为 a social beverage,表意更加明确。

> 专评

中国茶文化的翻译与传播

　　文化是一个民族最具个性的东西,可以移植和传播,也可以通过翻译进行阐释,但决不会因另一种语言的阐释而变成别的民族的文化。所以,"爱屋及乌"和"Love me, love my dog"分属汉语民族和英语民族两种不同的文化,其蕴含的文化意义截然不同,二者之间是"对应"(周领顺,2014b:75)的关系。二者在表达功能上相似,所以常被误认为是翻译。可以类推,在功能上,英语习语"Kill two birds with one stone"和汉语习语"一箭双雕"相似,但后者也仅仅是前者的对应之物,并非翻译的结果。但是,假如将汉语的"爱屋及乌"转换为"Love me, love the crows perching on the roof of my house",将英语的"Kill two birds with one stone"转换为"一石二鸟"时,便是对于原文语言的转换和意义的再现,属于翻译的范畴,是对汉、英语民族文化的阐释。翻译是一种常见的文化阐释方式,习近平所倡导的"阐释好中国特色"中的"阐释",就必定包括翻译这一手段,而"中国特色"中自然包括了中国茶文化的内容。因此,讨论中国茶文化的翻译与传播,契合中国文化"走出去"的国家战略需求。至于是不是阐释得好,关键在于对原文的理解和表达。

　　茶作为一种饮品,自古以来为中国社会各阶层人士所推崇,制茶、饮茶、品茶的历史源远流长,形成了中国特有的茶文化,不但体现了物质文化的层次,还反映了精神文化的高度。中国文化中的茶文化是值得大书特书的。中国的茶文化(包括茶道)博大精深,而翻译是中国向世界传播茶文化的重要手段之一。

　　《喝茶与品茶》一文作者受自身经历的启发而写成。文章提出了"喝茶""品茶"说,并辨析了二者之间的差异,介绍了"品茶"的不同步骤;回忆了中原农村在当代不同时期的茶文化、对于"茶"的不同称谓、不同"茶"的不同所指等;记述了作者本人从喝白开水到喝茶再到品茶的变化过程,这一过程也是作者从物质层面到精神层面提升的过程。

　　本专评主要从静态信息(原文涉及的与中国茶文化有关的背景信息)和动态信息(原文描绘的人们饮茶过程中的文化特征)两个角度着手,讨论原文中茶文化的翻译问题。

一、静态信息及其翻译

第一,茶的分类。

中国是茶的发源地,至今已有几千年的历史。中国茶的种植、栽培、制作技术享誉世界,创造和开发了各种各样的茶。据统计,中国的茶叶达 6 000 多个品种。其中,最广为接受的是六大茶类的分法,即绿茶、红茶、黄茶、白茶、青茶和黑茶,依据的是茶叶或茶汤的直观颜色。例如,茶叶和茶汤的色泽以绿色为主调的是绿茶,在制作过程中保留了茶叶背面白茸毛的茶为白茶,而制作时茶叶的色泽由绿色变成黑褐色的茶为黑茶,等等。这个分类其实代表了不同的发酵程度,但以颜色命名,如例[1]所示。

[1] 中国有六大茶类之分,即<u>绿茶、红茶、黄茶、白茶、青茶和黑茶</u>,表面上是按照茶的颜色分类的。

Chinese tea is classified by color into six major varieties, namely *green tea*, *black tea*, *yellow tea*, *white tea*, *blue tea* and *dark tea*.

译文当然应保留原文的颜色意象,这是因为下文提到"表面上是按照茶的颜色分类的"这样的表述,只有保留颜色意象,才可保持上下文语义连贯。

颜色词描绘的是人们对客观世界中颜色的感知,不同的语言有不同的颜色词数目,反映了人们对于颜色范畴的不同划分。因此,语言之间颜色词的指称范围在很多情况下是不对应的,即使是描绘颜色范畴中比较典型的黑、白、红、绿等颜色的基本颜色词,其指称意义也有很多交叉重叠之处。例如,汉语的"黑"可对应英语的 black,dark,英语的 red 可对应汉语的"红""赤"。甚至同一事物在不同的语言中通过不同的颜色词来指称,这是观察事物的视角存在差异的缘故。

在六大茶类中,"绿茶""红茶""黄茶""白茶"可分别译为 green tea,black tea,yellow tea 和 white tea,需要费思量的是"青茶"和"黑茶"的翻译。

"绿茶"在英语中的名称是 green tea,"青茶"就不能同时命名为 green tea,否则定会产生误解。汉语中的"青"在不同的语境里可对应英语中的 green,blue,black 等,例如"青山:green mountain""青天:blue sky""青丝:black hair"等。在英语中,"红茶"约定俗成的名称是 black tea。因此,"青"字仅剩 blue 一词可用。在例[1]中,将"青茶"译为 blue tea 是可行的。K. C. Wilson 和 M. N. Clifford(1992:747)在其主

编的 *Tea: Cultivation to Consumption* 一书中,将"青茶"直接表达为拼音的 Qing-cha,还注明是乌龙茶的别名(the Chinese name for Oolong tea),并且将"青茶"的字面意义表达为 blue tea。"青茶"是一种半发酵的茶,干茶的颜色呈青褐色,而茶汤的颜色则因青茶的种类和品质的不同而呈现不同的色泽,从黄绿色、橙黄色到浅褐色、深褐色不等。因此,无论是从干茶的颜色,还是从茶汤的色泽,"青茶"和 blue 所指称的颜色之间,可说没有一丝的关联。假如以干茶的颜色来命名,"青茶"译为 dark green tea 或 brownish green tea 也算贴切,但名称中保留 green 一词,可能会使得译语读者将青茶误解为绿茶的一种,而且从表达的角度看,dark green,brownish green 等复合型修饰语也使得名称不够简洁。

同样,"红茶"的英语名称是 black tea,例[1]中的"黑茶"就不能再以 black 来命名,可表达为 dark tea。在汉语中,"红茶"的命名理据取自茶汤的颜色,而在英语中,black tea 的命名理据取自茶叶氧化后的颜色。"红茶"本应直译为 red tea,但因被南非红叶茶树(rooibos)产的"红茶""先占"(pre-emption),所以以 black 命名,这样不致产生混淆。也因"红茶"被 black tea"先占",所以不得已将"黑茶"译为 dark tea。当然,尽管 dark 可以表示颜色,但 dark 并不是真正意义上的颜色词。根据 *Longman Dictionary of American English* (4th edition),dark 意为 closer to black than to white in color,说明 dark 描绘的不是单一的颜色,而是靠近黑色的一种梯度。Dark 也常和其他颜色词搭配,表达一种较深的色度。当 dark 和 tea 直接搭配时,dark 所表达的颜色意义近似于 black。

有学者从顾客心理的角度论证,dark tea 的名称不利于黑茶在国际市场的推广,一方面,因为英语的 dark 与汉语的"暗"同义,dark tea 可隐含粗制滥造、质量不精之意,因此,建议用 heicha 这个拼音形式取而代之。考虑市场因素是对的,但我们这里主要讨论如何保留颜色意象的问题,忽略 dark 的内涵意义,是为了让上下文语义更加连贯。另一方面,"黑茶"命名为 dark tea,是否真的会产生不好的联想还有待考证。就像汉语的"黑"和英语的 black 在内涵意义方面都带有贬的色彩,但"黑茶"在中国市场上并未因名称而受冷落,"红茶"被命名为 black tea 之后,在西方文化中也被广为接受了。

第二,茶的功效。

茶源自中国,中国茶叶传到世界各地,成为最受人们欢迎的保健饮品之一。根据现有的研究,茶叶中含有茶多糖、茶多酚、氨基酸、维生素、微量元素等多种活性成分。中国传统医学认为,茶有生津止渴、清神利尿、止咳祛痰、消炎解毒等诸多功效。原文是散文,不是知识性的科普文，对于茶叶的诸多功效，并不需要详述，只有两处简略提及，如例[2]和例[3]所示。

> [2] 喝茶要大口，大口才过瘾，喝茶者所求的是茶叶的实用功能，比如其"<u>生津止渴</u>""<u>养生保健</u>"之功。
>
> People ... drink tea for its practical function of *quenching thirst* or *promoting health*. For such a purpose, tea drinking can only be satiating when the liquor is quaffed down.

> [3] ……我们那里从来就不成茶树，大多没见过茶叶，听说<u>药铺里</u>有，是专给人治病用的。
>
> ... that my native land was never suitable for tea tree growth, and that local people had no access to tea leaves elsewhere except in *pharmacies of Chinese herbal medicine*, where tea leaves were available only for medical treatments.

例[2]提到了一般大众熟悉的茶叶所具有的"生津止渴"和"养生保健"的功能。在这两个四字词语中，前后两个双音节词语分别表达了方式和结果，"生津"的结果是"止渴"，"养生"的结果是"保健"。为了表达简洁起见，省去了方式信息，将"生津止渴"译为 quenching thirst，将"养生保健"译为 promoting health，仅使结果信息浮出足矣。

尽管茶叶具有诸多功效，但在物资匮乏的年代，茶叶在作者故乡难觅踪迹，仅见于药铺。例[3]中的"药铺"特指卖中药的商店。英语中卖药的商店用 drugstore, pharmacy 等词汇来指称，因中国的"药铺"卖的是中药，在指称意义上和 drugstore, pharmacy 等并不对称，添加 of Chinese herbal medicine 这个修饰语是必要的，否则便无法表达"药铺"的确切所指。

第三，茶的境界。

喝茶不仅能让人身心舒畅，还可陶冶性情，提升品位。在中国文化中，茶不仅仅是一种"生津止渴""养生保健"的饮品，更代表了一种精神上的追求。因此，根据不同的目的，原文将同一种行为区分为"喝茶"和"品茶"，并认为二者属于不同的境界和层次。例如：

> [4] 显然，"喝茶"属于物质层面，"品茶"属于精神层面。或者说，"喝茶"<u>重在解渴</u>，"品茶"旨在怡情，而我在以往最多只能算是"喝茶"者，甚至连"喝茶"者也算不上，只能算作"喝水"的吧。
>
> Obviously, tea drinking *nurtures the body* and tea sipping *the mind*. Or in other words, the former *serves for physical content* and

the latter *for mental delight*. In terms of the level that tea enjoyers get to, I could be ranked at the most as a "tea" drinker previously, or even as less of a "tea" drinker than a water drinker.

例[4]中的两个"在"字结构是对两个"层面"结构的补充说明,四个结构两两相对,语义上工整对仗。译文没有拘泥于原文的形式,而是在理解原文意义的基础上,将两个"层面"结构表达为 nurtures the body 和 the mind,其中 body 和 mind 构成对立关系,而两个"在"字结构则表达为 serves for physical content 和 for mental delight,以使 physical 和 mental 对立,content 和 delight 近义,工整对仗。总体上,例[4]的译文在阅读效果上接近了原文。

二、动态信息及其翻译

第一,"喝茶""品茶"。

茶如何饮,大有讲究,这是茶道,"喝"和"品"就表明了区别。"喝"指大口饮,重在解渴;"品"指小口饮,重在品味。在英语中,与"喝"和"品"基本对应的是 drink 和 sip。对于 drink 和 sip 的释义,各大英语词典基本大同小异,其中最能体现这两个英语词之间区别的是 *Longman Dictionary of American English*(4th edition)的解释。该词典将 drink 解释为 to pour a liquid into your mouth and swallow it,将 sip 解释为 to drink something slowly, swallowing only small amounts。在 drink 的释义中,pour 说明了饮量大、饮速快,而在 sip 的释义中,slowly 和 small amounts 则说明了饮量小、饮速慢。严格地说,sip 仅仅表示"小口慢慢喝"的意思,词义本身并不包含"品味",但和 tea, wine, alcohol 等实体名词搭配时,sip 就获得了"品味""享受"的意义,因为这些词所指称的实体本身具有内涵,可供人的感觉官能辨别色香味等。若和 water 搭配,sip 就无法获得"品味"的意义,因为 water 无色无味,像 They sat sipping water the whole afternoon. 这样的句子听上去很不自然;若将句中的 water 替换为 tea, wine, alcohol 等词,句子的语义才符合逻辑事理。根据黄汝干(2010: 38)的考证,在英语国家语料库(British National Corpus)和美国当代英语语料库(Corpus of Contemporary American English)中,sip 和 tea 的搭配是比较常见的用法,可用来表示汉语"品茶"的意思,而一般认为表示"品味"的英语词 savor,与 tea 的搭配反而罕见。因此,"喝茶"可译为 drink tea,"品茶"可译为 sip tea。原文中凡是提到"喝茶"的情形,我们都译为 drink tea 或 tea drinking;凡是提到"品茶"的情形,我们都译为

sip tea 或 tea sipping。仅举一例：

　　［5］不管口头上邀人"喝茶"抑或"品茶"，本质上并没有什么不同，都是把茶做媒介而交友或谈事罢了。

　　　　When one invites people to tea, it basically makes no much difference whether he phrases it as "*to tea drinking*" or "*to tea sipping*", for tea only serves on such an occasion as a vehicle for social interaction.

既然"品茶"是一种慢慢享受的过程，那么"品茶"分步骤就是很自然的事了，原文提到了品茶的几个步骤，如例［6］所示。

　　［6］品茶有几个步骤："尝茶""闻香""观汤""品味"，对于我，能经常达到"观汤"和"品味"就算不错了。

　　　　There are steps to follow in tea sipping: *taking sips*, *sensing the aroma*, *observing the color* and *tasting the flavor*. As for me, I would be more than happy if I could go as far as the final two steps in most cases.

"品"和"尝"常用作一个双音词"品尝"，表达一个单纯的意义，即"仔细地辨别"，但分别使用时，"尝"意为"少量吃一点，以辨别"，是"品"的基础，而"品"则侧重"仔细辨别"，是"尝"的提升。在例［6］中，"尝茶"即"喝一点茶"，而"品味"不是一个双音节动词，而是一个动宾词组，意为"仔细辨别茶的味道"。在孤立的语境中，"尝茶"译为 taste tea 未尝不可，但因此处表现为品茶过程中的第一个步骤，和下文的"品味"这个步骤有一定的区别意义，故将"尝茶"译为 taking sips，将"品味"译为 tasting the flavor，以体现作者的着意用笔之处。

　　第二，"喝茶""喝茶叶茶""喝白茶"。

　　原文介绍了中原农村的茶文化。在当代的不同历史时期，"茶"在中原农村具有不同的内涵。农村人说的"喝茶"和城里人说的"喝茶"在概念上是不同的，前者只是"喝水"的意思。其实，在其他方言（例如吴方言）中，也有用"茶"来指称"白开水"的，有"吃茶""茶淘饭"等说法，"吃茶"即"喝白开水"，"茶淘饭"即"白开水泡饭"。为了进行有效的区分，原文中"喝茶""喝茶叶茶""喝白茶"等，一概按照字面的意义进行翻译。例如：

　　［7］城里人说的"喝茶"和农村人说的"喝茶"是不同的，农村人说的"喝茶"即城里人说的"喝水"，喝的是白开水，而"喝水"在农村又具体化为"喝凉水""喝井水"等不同的说法。

　　　　To rural people "*drinking tea*", which was not the same as *that* referred to by urban people, simply meant *drinking water*, i. e. drinking plain boiled water. And in rural areas "*drinking water*" was further specified into "*drinking cold water*", "*drinking well water*", etc.

[8] 现在有了茶叶,也就有了"<u>喝茶叶茶</u>"和"<u>喝白茶</u>"(喝白开水)的区别了。

When tea leaves were brought to the market in my native place, a new distinction was made between "*drinking tea with tea leaves in it*" and "*drinking tea white*", the latter actually meaning "*drinking water without any tea leaves brewed in it*".

例[7]提到的"喝茶""喝水"等都按照原文的表述进行了直译,原文逻辑关系清楚,所以直译不会产生理解的障碍。译文只是在表达习惯方面做了微调,原文多次重复"喝茶",而对应的 drinking tea 只出现了一次,其余的用关系代词 which 和指示照应词 that 来替换。

例[8]的"喝茶叶茶"直译为 drink tea with tea leaves in it,增加的 with tea leaves in it 附和了原文的意义,起对照和强调的作用,否则便有画蛇添足之嫌。例[8]"喝白茶"中的"白茶",不是指茶叶类别的"白茶",而是"白开水"的意思。作为茶叶种类或名称的白茶是 white tea,假如将这句中的"喝白茶"译为 drink white tea,是不恰当的。而将例[8]的"喝白茶"译为 drink tea without any tea leaves in it,虽然做到了表意精确,但失去了"白"的意象。鉴于英语中的 drink coffee black,指喝不加牛奶、糖等辅料的清咖啡,而喝不添加辅料的茶,则叫作 drink tea black,比照这个结构,我们将例[8]中的"喝白茶"变通处理为 drinking tea white。对于这个表述,译文的下文给出了解释性的成分 drinking water without any tea leaves brewed in it,因此,译语读者是完全可以理解其意的。

三、余 说

传播有效性的基础是翻译的有效性,或者可以说就是理解需要到位,表达需要准确,是习近平"阐释好中国特色"的"阐释好"和"讲好中国故事"中"讲好"的有关内容。所以,这里说的传播效果,是从翻译内部或者说是从翻译过程看问题的,并不是真正地从社会的角度讨论茶文化传播的文章,因此,有关传播的外围因素(如广告、销路、价格、市场等),一概从略。

附 录 I

> "第二十七届韩素音青年翻译奖"竞赛汉译英参考译文

To Preserve Ancient Villages Is to Preserve Cultural Roots

Traditional villages are those boasting both tangible and intangible heritages of historical, cultural, social, scientific, artistic or economic value. Rapid urbanization in recent years has, however, been relentlessly chipping away at or even threatens to obliterate much of traditional culture represented by such villages. Protective measures must be taken to preserve and restore historical structures in these villages together with their traditional streets, lanes and surroundings to prevent them from being deserted.

Ancient villages, a unique expression of traditional culture, are chronicles of local economic development and folk customs. They are associated with many essential aspects of traditional culture, such as the Chinese kinship system, communal life, ethics, ancestral worship, rules and institutions, *fengshui*, architecture and art, and regional characteristics.

They are also products of the scholar-farmer lifestyle and an agrarian economy. With the surge in urbanization, they are inevitably vulnerable to profiteering. Rather than attempting to restore an old order, much less to advocate the patriarchal system, preservation efforts are aimed at promoting understanding and cherishing our time-honored civilization, and this is an obligation we should all commit ourselves to fulfilling.

Instead of comprising merely old buildings, ancient villages bear the weight of history, and stand defiant as witnesses to the vicissitudes of times.

Weathering countless blistering summers and bitter winters and punishing storms and blizzards, they remain an inextinguishable source of vitality, and with their tattered frames provide shelter as well as emotional support for generations upon generations.

What we do about ancient villages mirrors our attitude towards culture, especially against the backdrop of today's urbanization process. Most people may not experience a sense of loss at the transformation or disappearance of an ancient village. But losing one such village would mean erasing a cultural footprint from the landscape of history, and disengaging us from an intimate feel of what has been passed along by history. A distinct danger would thus emerge that we may be further distancing ourselves from our own past. And any loss of our cultural attachment to an ancient village would create one more obstacle to the continuation of our cultural traditions.

To tell whether a place is fertile culturally, we should not only learn about its impressive cultural relics, but also walk into its ancient buildings to see their lofty halls, delicate carvings, exquisite building materials and superb classical craftsmanship … When it comes to rebuilding or bulldozing ancient villages, we, too, must think twice.

（集体讨论，杨成虎、陈文安执笔）

附　录　Ⅱ

My Life's Sentences 参考译文

我生命里的美句

上大学时,我常常画下那些让我为之震撼、为之深思的句子,但不一定是教授们指出来,或者会出现在考试中让我们进一步阐释的句子。我注意到,这些句子集简洁、韵味、美感和魅力于一体。想来真是不可思议,就有那么一些词,巧妙地摆在一起,足以令时光停滞。变出个地名、变出个人名、变出个情境,真实而细腻。它们对我们影响之深、改变之大,与现实中人和物所起的作用无异。

我记得读过乔伊斯写的一个句子,就在短篇小说《阿拉比》(Araby)的开头附近:"寒风咬,玩兴浓,玩到身上红彤彤。"我忘不掉,句子之完美,已臻极致。拿捏仔细、顺手溜出、直白质朴、卓尔不群,一股脑,这些感觉就都来了;充满动感,富于想象,凝聚为可感可知的氛围,意义闪着异彩,感觉真实自然。

复杂的故事或小说,主体宏大,情节众多,读来感觉似难连到一起。再读时会发现,某些句子就像老熟人向我热情打着招呼。我把它们认了出来,它们说我旧地重游。在我们的一生中,不同时期,会遇到不同的书籍,欣赏、理解各不相同。但语言是永恒的,美句就像夜空里的星星、像小道上的路标,引导我们前行。

不管是不是真正进入阅读,美句都值得反复咀嚼。再怎么吸引人的故事,若用的句子不能让我产生共鸣或者令我反感,就会让我麻木。小说主要的任务是传递信息、制造悬念、刻画人物,并使他们开口讲话。但只有某些句子会呼吸、会变化,就像泥土里的生命。一本书的第一句话写好了,就是向读者伸出的友好之手、敞开的温暖怀抱,无关风格和个性,可以正式,可以随意,高矮胖瘦,无所不能;或遵从规则,或打破常规，但一定要带着电，摄人魂魄，闪光发热。

　　了解并学会用外语阅读，加强了我对句子的亲近度，关系也由此变得复杂起来。最近一个时期，我主要阅读的是意大利语，并以别样的方式体验意大利语写就的小说和故事。我一句也不敢瞎猜，敏感有加，为了多一分了解，我更加用功。我驻足查询，对我在学习的句法结构也困惑不已，每个句子都生出了个翻译版孪生兄弟。当第二语言这一过滤器消失时，我和这些句子的联系虽然直接，却比我读英语时感觉更纯，有时更加亲近了。

　　把经历变成语法联结的一组词，是本能的冲动，是我生命中持续不竭的动力之源，是呼是应的习惯使然。多数的日子是从敲进日记里的句子开始的，外人不曾见过，因此，也就多了一分自由，多了一分不想写那些绞尽脑汁东西的自由。下笔处，多无惊人之语，是练手、练脑而已。在我困苦、忧伤、语塞的日子里，我习惯性地造些句子，珍藏起来，便成了让我重新凝神聚气唯一可做之事。

　　造个句子，就像宝丽莱快照：按下快门，观察成像。动笔成句，则是集记录和冲洗于一体，并非所有的句子其归宿都在小说或故事里，但小说和故事除了句子外，别无所有。句子是泥浆，是砖块，是燃料，是引擎，是机体的细胞，是衣服的针脚，它同时具备独居性和群体性的两面性。句子定调、定节奏，排着队，记录着行进的轨迹。

　　我的任务就是一句一句地积累美句。经过了第一个时期的耐心、浮躁、圈选、装订之后，句子就自然而然地涌进我的脑海里。也不知是谁将句子诵读出声，我迷迷糊糊要入睡时便学会了倾听。就是我读的，我心里有数，虽然声音的源头让人觉着清醒独立、深不可测，特别在开始那会儿。打开灯，一两个句子就会快速、潦草地画到纸片上，早上起床拿到楼上，放在本子里。凝视窗外时心里听着句子，切菜时心里听着句子，在地铁的站台上候车时心里还听着句子，这些句子就是智力拼图玩具上的零件，递到我手上，却不按什么顺序，也没有明显的逻辑。凭我的直觉，它们就是整个东西的一分子。

　　从长远看，我以这种随意的方式收集、记录的每个句子都要分类、挑拣、组织、改变，很多还要删掉。我做的所有修正——该过程动手快，且加进了自己的思想——发生于句子层面。对句子的精雕细琢，会让刻画的人物呼之欲出、让描绘的情节展露无遗。执迷于此，或者说急于对收集的句子加工整理，是先树木后森林之为，可也实在找不到构想森林更好的办法了。

　　书或故事快要完稿时，我对每个句子都有一股强烈的、着魔般的敏感力,好句子融入了血液,似乎有那么一瞬将其取而代之。到了该校对的时候,我与句子独处一室,看看这句,挑挑那句,颠来倒去。把这个句子判那儿,把那个句子判这儿。如此挑剔,难免导致盲目。有的时候,不免恐惧,句子竟不再传意。好不容易脱稿了,我却怅然若失,失去的是那些曾经在我生命中往复循环的美句,萎缩的是曾经维系枝繁叶茂的庞大根系。

即使印在纸上,装订成册,句子还是漂泊不定之物。再过多少年,我总能伸手抚平一丝乱发,而有的时候,我需要走得远远地,相信那些句子能够独自行事。我兀自回头,想着自己是不是还有可能将句子造得更好一些。我不想读自己写的书,若出于必须,便以陌生客近而审视,骗自己:那些句子可是别人写下的。

附　录　Ⅲ

试译原创散文

大美新疆

  之所以用"大美新疆"这样的文字做题目，首先是因为在新疆到处能见到这样的标语，建筑物的墙面上和宣传栏里都不乏这样的字眼，也有饭馆和旅行社以此命名的，更有导游手里晃着的"大美新疆"三角小旗，构成了一条条蜿蜒流动的风景。我们就跟随着这么一个"大美新疆"散客团，先上伟岸天山，再下秀美喀纳斯。用"大美新疆"做题目，还因为实在难以找到比它更加切题的表达了。

  "大美"本来是一个形容词，大约等于英语的 spectacular，但汉字的优势在于，几个汉字构成的一个词，可以拆分为一个一个的汉字，而意义又各自独立。"大美"拆分后，一个是"大"字，一个是"美"字，而"大"和"美"则构成了个性新疆的两大核心。

  要说新疆之大，是尽人皆知的事，它远在中国的西北边陲，与俄罗斯、哈萨克斯坦、吉尔吉斯斯坦、塔吉克斯坦、巴基斯坦、蒙古、印度、阿富汗等八国接壤；要说新疆之美，首先映入眼帘的是磅礴大气，比如广阔无垠的戈壁沙滩和崇高的天山之巅。磅礴之美，能带来排山倒海般的视觉冲击，同时又裹挟着娇小和秀丽。"大"字和"美"字构成了一对矛盾，要欣赏新疆的美景，就要首先过了"大"字关。"赏大美新疆者，必先劳其筋骨。"不攒足足够的耐力，又何以至远呢！

  新疆之大，有过"走三天路看一天景"之说。这个说法虽然有些夸张，但其大自不用说。就说去喀纳斯吧，我们首先要坐上一夜的火车到达北屯市，然后再转旅游大巴，继续随后大约七个小时的路程。到了喀纳斯山门里，还要坐个把小时的区间车，才能到达喀纳斯湖的中心风景区。

"到喀纳斯,在里面起码要玩上三天。"

这是在新疆乌鲁木齐时,出租汽车司机给我们打的"预防针"。我们早有了这样的心理预期,不仅在路上,就是在景区也要有足够的耐力。新疆的"大"和"美"是紧密联系在一起的。所谓路途耗时多,当然是对于中心风景区而言的。事实上,路上的风景又何尝不是风景呢?人景、物景,各显本色。旅游嘛,领略的就是与众不同的个性文化,经历的就是不曾有过的各种体验。

新疆的旅游旺季在7、8、9三个月,火车为了迎合这种需要,夕发朝至。但见火车站人山人海,人声鼎沸,到处拥挤着观光的人群。火车上写着"高铁",实际是普通的火车,据说真正的高铁正在建设之中。去景区的路途虽然遥远,但沿途风光足具个性。比如道路两边的地貌,左边数百公里秃头般点缀着时断时续的小草,蓬头垢面;右边数百公里沿着一条平缓的河流呈现为一条灌木丛的长带,昂然碧绿。这是中国唯一注入北冰洋的河流——额尔齐斯河,源于中国,流经哈萨克斯坦和俄罗斯。它没有高高的河岸,溜着地,平缓滑动,偶尔还有灌木长在河道里;它不像天山的雪水,一路击打着嶙峋怪石,从山顶到山脚,咆哮狂奔。真想下车到河水里嬉戏一把,在碧波荡漾里享受那份安逸。

汽车在不是高速公路的公路上高速飞驰。长途颠簸,打盹是难免的;打盹的时候,耳畔还不时响起周围游客用手机拍照路边风景的咔嚓声。抬眼处,成片的风车、向日葵、群马、零星的骆驼、满山坡的牛羊、孤零零的毡房,还有远山和印在山头的成团白云,慢镜头般缓缓向身后飘逝。新疆美景,无须我长篇累牍,网上早已充斥着赞美的文字。

谈旅游,除了谈风景外,没有不谈饮食的。新疆是众多少数民族的聚居地,若喜爱少数民族的美食,保证不会让你失望。

初尝奶茶,竟然没什么怪味;喜欢羊肉,然浓重的膻气把我逼得不再贪婪;馕现焦黄,若不喜油大,可别买带"馅儿"的,入口才知是油脂。串羊肉串很是讲究,几块瘦肉,总要两块肥肉相伴,而肥肉必须自尾巴来。

新疆日照时间长,瓜果就格外的甜。尝一口大西瓜,就如同雪糕掉进肚子里,甜彻肺腑;看一眼大葡萄,冰雪晶莹,冒着诱人的甜气。买一箱甜瓜,快递给父母。"这可是正宗的新疆甜瓜。"我在电话里向父母传递着兴奋。

登天山望远,获得的是广角风景的震撼;近身观湖水,传说中的喀纳斯"湖怪"能否再掀波澜?新疆美食,怎可能尝得遍!

捡 白 果

　　初冬时节的长江流域，虽然不像北方万木凋零，但也很难再见到前些天还让游人趋之若潮的银杏叶金黄铺地的胜景。金黄的叶片，让人间平添了不少欢快的气氛，但银杏叶毕竟难耐初冬的寒气，一朝风起，明黄不再，剩下几片，若枯叶蝶，在枝头随风抖动。此情此景，颇有"夕阳无限好，只是近黄昏"之感。校园里栽着一些银杏树，叶黄的时候，格外的显眼。随着冬天的临近，银杏叶逐渐淡出了人们的视野。

　　初冬寒意料峭，但在12月初这几日，天气却出奇地晴好，而且暖意融融。难得雾霾被吹到了别处，轮到我们享受这久别的艳阳了。也就是在这样的一个日子，我的研究生来找我谈论文写作，不待谈话结束，我便催她去陪我"踏春"，在遍地泛黄、地毯般的草地上搜寻着万物复苏、大地回春时才可能有的景象。

　　校园一隅，有片小树林，平时人迹罕至。此时钻进去，或有洞天。

　　"老师，你看这是什么果子？"果然，通幽处，就有了发现。

　　我循声望去，发现有杏黄色的果子，杏子一般大小，可不是一枚，而是一片一片地散落在茂盛的草地之上。我惊喜异常，因为在我的理念中，校园里就该都种上果树，既能看，也能吃，使观赏价值和应用价值兼而有之。

　　我举头望树枝，深谙尚有残叶悬挂枝头，按我这个"农村人"的见识，定能分辨出个大概。是银杏树！叶子是扇状的，虽然呈现的是黄褐色，但能想象水分饱满时的靓丽。再搜寻地面，东一片，西一片，虽然干瘪，但形状还算完好。这些果子定是银杏果，也就是俗称的"白果"啦。

　　杏子一般大小的"白果"，就应该是白色的，所以学名"银杏"。但"白果"是内核部分的硬壳所呈现的颜色，外面还有一层果肉，这层果肉是不能食用的。也就是说，白果是由外层不能食用的果肉、中层的硬壳和里层可食用的果肉三层构成的。或者说，可食用果肉的外面，有着软、硬两层保护。

　　白果有很高的药用价值，有祛痰、止咳、润肺、定喘等功效。网上说，它在宋代被列为皇家贡品。在日本，人们有每日食用白果的习惯。白果也是西方人圣诞节上的必备果品。遇到了这么好的东西，哪有不捡的道理！可要捡白果，首先就遇到了盛放的难题，我们可不是有备而来的。最好有个塑料袋。我把这个念头一告诉学生，学生便笑答："哪会这么巧呢!"

我知道有人有随手丢弃废品的习惯,塑料袋是最常见的。想到这里,我们就去四周搜寻。果然不负我望,就有那么一只塑料袋,在不远处的一棵小树的根部绊着。捡起一看,还相当完好,而且足够大,装上个八九公斤也不成问题。万事俱备,说捡就捡。

果子不算太小,好捡。弯腰捡,感觉还有捡完的可能,毕竟树不算大,料想果子不会很多。但蹲下捡,扒开草丛一看,才发现还有很多藏在深处。怎么越捡越多呢?不一会儿,塑料袋子就满了。不捡了,我们抬着往回走,并特意留影纪念。这可是一份意想不到的收获。白果虽然便宜,只有几元钱一斤,但经过自己劳动捡来的天然之物,成就感可不一般。

话虽如此,可要把外层的果肉去掉,是个技术活。外层的果肉微臭,有腐蚀性,听说需要戴上橡皮手套。我学着做,好不容易剥去一些,发现有些果子太小,也不想耗费过多的时间,转念又扔掉了不少。

捡拾白果这件小事,想来有些奇妙。主观上想散步,却在客观上收获了白果;主观上想找个盛放的塑料袋,客观上就真的没负我望,而且足够大;主观上认为捡拾的白果是一份收获,却因为难拾掇,又浪费多多。人生就有很多的偶然,有的根本不在计划中。而在计划中的,也未必能收获主观上想要的结果,也许原本都是冥冥中注定了的。不过,收获了这篇短文,也就是收获了一份抹不掉的人生记忆了。

参考文献

[1] Collins COBUILD essential English dictionary[M]. 北京：中国对外翻译出版公司,1989.

[2] Longman dictionary of American English[M]. 4th ed. Essex: Pearson Education Limited, 2008/2009.

[3] NEWMARK P. A textbook of translation[M]. London: Prentice Hall International Limited, 1988.

[4] PARRY A E. Interventions into modernist cultures: poetry from beyond the empty screen[M]. Durham, NC: Duke University Press, 2007.

[5] The American heritage dictionary of the English language[M]. 3rd ed. Boston: Houghton Mifflin Company, 1992.

[6] WILSON K C, CLIFFORD M N. Tea: cultivation to consumption[C]. London: Chapman & Hall, 1992.

[7] 巴金. 一点感想[J]. 翻译通讯,1951(5): 5-6.

[8] 曹明伦. 翻译中的借情写景和意象转换[J]. 中国翻译,2002(5): 92-93.

[9] 曹明伦. 散文体译文的音韵节奏[J]. 中国翻译,2004,25(4): 89-90.

[10] 陈昌来. 现代汉语句子[M]. 上海：华东师范大学出版社,2000.

[11] 陈君朴. 汉英对照唐诗绝句150首[M]. 上海：上海大学出版社,2005.

[12] 党争胜. 文学翻译鉴赏导论[M]. 北京：外语教学与研究出版社,2008.

[13] 丁帆. 中国乡土小说史[M]. 北京：北京大学出版社,2007.

[14] 段连城. 呼吁：请译界同仁都来关心对外宣传[C]//《中国翻译》编辑部. 中译英技巧文集. 北京：中国对外翻译出版公司,1992: 19-37.

[15] 范开泰,张亚军. 现代汉语语法分析[M]. 上海：华东师范大

学出版社,2000.

[16] 范仲英.实用翻译教程[M].北京：外语教学与研究出版社,1997.

[17] 高健.近年来林语堂作品重刊本中的编选、文本及其他问题[J].山西大学学报,1994(4)：42－50.

[18] 顾明栋.论理想译者的多重身份：以庞德的翻译实践为例[J].翻译论坛,2016(1)：1－7.

[19] 郭著章,江安,鲁文忠.唐诗精品百首英译[M].修订版.武汉：武汉大学出版社,2010.

[20] 黄伯荣,廖序东.现代汉语：下册[M].3版.北京：高等教育出版社,2002.

[21] 黄汝干.中国茶文化对外交流与翻译人才的培养[J].农业考古,2010(2)：37－39,44.

[22] 黄忠廉,等.翻译方法论[M].北京：中国社会科学出版社,2009.

[23] 季羡林.《成语源流大辞典》序[J].中国语文,2003(5)：469－471.

[24] 贾卫国.英汉对照描写辞典[M].上海：上海交通大学出版社,2000.

[25] 焦鹏帅.一部全面思考翻译核心话题的力作：苏珊·巴斯内特著《翻译思考录》评介[J].外语与翻译,2015(2)：88－92.

[26] 焦鹏帅,曹明伦.诗歌译者应善于捕捉原作者的情感[J].山东外语教学,2012(6)：3－7.

[27] 金隄.等效翻译探索[M].北京：中国对外翻译出版公司,1989.

[28] 金杰.从意象、物象看描写语言的翻译[J].外语教学,2005(1)：90－93.

[29] 连淑能.英汉对比研究[M].北京：高等教育出版社,1993.

[30] 刘丹青.汉语是一种动词型语言：试说动词型语言和名词型语言的类型差异[J].世界汉语教学,2010,24(1)：3－17.

[31] 刘宓庆.文体与翻译[M].北京：中国对外翻译出版公司,1998.

[32] 刘士聪.汉英·英汉美文翻译与鉴赏[M].南京：译林出版社,2002.

[33] 刘英凯.论中国译论的潜科学现状[J].外语与外语教学,

2002(1):49-53.

[34] 吕俊,侯向群.英汉翻译教程[M].上海:上海外语教育出版社,2001.

[35] 吕叔湘.吕叔湘语文论集[M].北京:商务印书馆,1983.

[36] 钱锺书.林纾的翻译[C]//罗新璋编.翻译论集.北京:商务印书馆,1984:696-725.

[37] 单德兴.翻译与脉络[M].北京:清华大学出版社,2007.

[38] 宋天锡.翻译新概念:英汉互译实用教程[M].4版.北京:国防工业出版社,2007.

[39] 唐一鹤.英译唐诗三百首[M].天津:天津人民出版社,2005.

[40] 王秉钦.20世纪中国翻译思想史[M].天津:南开大学出版社,2004.

[41] 王银泉."福娃"英译之争与文化负载词的汉英翻译策略[J].中国翻译,2006,27(3):74-76.

[42] 王治江.再现汉语抒情散文的诗情画意[J].外语与外语教学,2003(12):39-43.

[43] 肖维青.翻译批评模式研究[M].上海:上海外语教育出版社,2010.

[44] 谢真元.一生必读唐诗三百首鉴赏:汉英对照[M].北京:中国对外翻译出版公司,2006.

[45] 徐莉娜.英汉翻译原理[M].上海:上海外语教育出版社,2014.

[46] 许国璋. Culturally loaded words and English language teaching[J].现代外语,1980(4):19-25.

[47] 许钧.译事探索与译学思考[M].北京:外语教学与研究出版社,2002.

[48] 许钧,穆雷.翻译学概论[M].南京:译林出版社,2009.

[49] 许钧,周领顺.当前译学界应该关注的若干倾向[J].山东外语教学,2015,36(4):96-100.

[50] 许渊冲.新世纪的新译论[J].中国翻译,2000(3):2-6.

[51] 许渊冲.翻译的艺术[M].2版.北京:五洲传播出版社,2006.

[52] 杨自俭.关于重译《印度之行》的几个问题[J].外语与外语教学,2003(5):48-53.

[53] 叶子南.高级英汉翻译理论与实践[M].北京:清华大学出版

社,2001.

[54] 张爱玲. 散文卷四:1952年以后作品[M]. 哈尔滨:哈尔滨出版社,2003.

[55] 张保红. 文学翻译[M]. 北京:外语教学与研究出版社,2010.

[56] 张斌. 新编现代汉语[M]. 上海:复旦大学出版社,2002.

[57] 中国社会科学院语言研究所词典编辑室. 现代汉语词典[M]. 6版. 北京:商务印书馆,2012.

[58] 周领顺. 译者行为与"求真-务实"连续统评价模式:译者行为研究(其一)[J]. 外语教学,2010,31(1):93-97.

[59] 周领顺. "译内效果"和"译外效果":译文与译者行为的双向评价:译者行为研究(其六)[J]. 外语教学,2011,32(2):86-91.

[60] 周领顺. 散文英译过程[M]. 北京:国防工业出版社,2012.

[61] 周领顺. 译者行为批评:理论框架[M]. 北京:商务印书馆,2014a.

[62] 周领顺. 译者行为批评:路径探索[M]. 北京:商务印书馆,2014b.

[63] 周领顺. "作者译"与"译者译":为"自译"重新定性[J]. 解放军外国语学院学报,2016,39(6):102-107,159.

[64] 周领顺,强卉. "厚译"究竟有多厚?:西方翻译理论批评与反思之一[J]. 外语与外语教学,2016(6):103-112.

[65] 周领顺,周怡珂. 翻译识途:学·赏·用[M]. 北京:国防工业出版社,2014.

[66] 朱德熙. 语法讲义[M]. 北京:商务印书馆,1982.

后　记

本书所收录的散文均为笔者有感而发。因忘情于生活的点点滴滴，所以连绵不断；因陶醉于打造精品的过程，所以研之再三。"玩文字，玩生活"，构成了本书的主基调。

从初创到成品经过了这样一个过程：散文写好后投寄给报刊，发表后再译成英语。笔者是作者，除了反复斟酌原文外，还要经常和第二作者露丝·蒔（译者、译评者）就原文的翻译不断讨论和试笔，待达成一致意见后，再请美籍或英籍人士审阅并润饰。我们将部分原文和译文做成专题，并已有部分见刊。在此期间，笔者让本科生和研究生群体试译了全部散文，在翻译课堂上反复试用，直到他们的翻译实践能力和理论认识水平得到明显提高为止，而每篇原文和译文后的注释针对的就是学生中普遍存在和容易忽略的问题。

笔者是译者，却又不同于林语堂、张爱玲等带有双语创作性质的"自译者"。笔者以原文为出发点，最大限度地做到"求真"于原文，同时又"务实"于译文的读者。笔者主要从事翻译批评研究，构建了我国本土翻译理论之一的"译者行为批评"（Translator Behavior Criticism），出版了《译者行为批评：理论框架》《译者行为批评：路径探索》等理论专著。在进行理论研究的同时，也不偏废实践，出版了《翻译识途：学·赏·用》《散文英译过程》等书籍。只有将理论与实践相结合，才能做到译、评到位。

感谢曹明伦、杨平、苑爱玲、Fred Previc、Julia Benton、Michael Flegg、吴文智、美国北得州文友社（North Texas Chinese Literary Society）陈玉琳等师友，以及吴春容、唐红英等青年学者和众多学生提供的各种支持。每篇散文的写作都有"故事"，在此一并向提供素材的有关人士表示谢意。

最后，向付出辛勤劳动的苏州大学出版社有关人士表示衷心的感谢。

周领顺　谨识
2017 年 1 月